MW00573981

FTCE Social Science 6-12
Teacher Certification

By: Sharon Wynne, M.S.

XAMonline, INC.
Boston

XAMonline, Inc.
21 Orient Avenue
Melrose, MA 02176
Toll Free: 1-800-509-4128
Email: info@xamonline.com
Web: www.xamonline.com
Fax: 1-617-583-5552

Library of Congress Cataloging-in-Publication Data

Wynne, Sharon A.

Social Science 6-12: Teacher Certification / Sharon A. Wynne. ISBN 978-1-60787-381-5

1. Social Science 6-12.   2. Study guides.   3. FTCE
4. Teachers' Certification & Licensure.   5. Careers

Disclaimer:

The opinions expressed in this publication are the sole works of XAMonline and were created independently from the National Education Association, Educational Testing Service, or any State Department of Education, National Evaluation Systems, or other testing affiliates.

Between the time of publication and printing, state-specific standards as well as testing formats and website information may change that is not included in part or in whole within this product. Sample test questions are developed by XAMonline and reflect similar content as on real tests; however, they are not former tests. XAMonline assembles content that aligns with state standards but makes no claims nor guarantees teacher candidates a passing score. Numerical scores are determined by testing companies such as NES or ETS and then are compared with individual state standards. A passing score varies from state to state.

Printed in the United States of America   œ-1

FTCE: Social Science 6-12
ISBN: 978-1-60787-381-5

About the Subject Assessments

FTCE: Subject Assessment in the Social Science 6-12 examination

Purpose: The assessments are designed to test the knowledge and competencies of prospective secondary level teachers. The question bank from which the assessment is drawn is undergoing constant revision. As a result, your test may include questions that will not count towards your score.

Test Version: There are two versions of subject assessments for social science tests in Florida. Although both versions of the test emphasize conceptual comprehension, synthesis, and analysis of the principles of the social sciences, the major difference between versions lies in the *degree* to which the examinee's knowledge is tested.

Version 1: Social Science 6-12 This version requires a greater depth of comprehension in U.S. history, world history, economics, geography, political science, anthropology, and psychology. The social science 6-12 guide is based on a typical knowledge level of persons who have completed a *bachelor's degree program* in social science.

Taking the Correct Version of the Subject Assessment: While some states other than Florida offer just one test called a social science secondary test, Florida breaks out those topics into two tests. The 5-9 covers what one would take to become a middle school teacher, and the 6-12 covers what one who plans to teach at the high school level would take. However, as Florida's licensure requirements change, it's highly recommended that you consult your educational institution's teaching preparation counselor, or your state Board of Education's teacher licensure division to verify which version of the assessment you should take. Not mentioned is a History test. If you plan on applying for a position in another state as well as Florida, consider a History option. XAMonline.com website can inform you what you need to do to become certified in any particular state.

Time Allowance, Format, and Length: The time allowance and format for both versions are identical; you will have 2 hours to complete the test and the questions are presented in a 125-question, multiple-choice format. Florida does not test using construct essays or other essay formats.

Content Areas: Both versions of the subject assessments share a degree of commonality in that the test content categories are divided into six broad areas that roughly overlap between test versions. However, version 1 has a narrower focus on specific disciplines than does version 2.

Test Taxonomy: Both versions of the subject assessments are constructed on the comprehension, synthesis, and analysis levels of Bloom's Taxonomy. In many questions, the candidate must apply knowledge of more than one discipline in order to correctly answer the questions.

Additional Information about the FTCE Assessments: The FTCETM series subject assessments are developed by the *Florida Department of Education* of Tallahassee, FL. They provide additional information on the FTCE series assessments, including registration, preparation, and testing procedures, and study materials such as topical guides that are about 30 pages of information with approximately 25 additional sample questions.

Table of Contents

Great Study and Testing Tips!

What to study in order to prepare for the subject assessments is the focus of this study guide, but equally important is *how* you study.

You can increase your chances of truly mastering the information by taking some simple, but effective steps.

Study Tips:

1. **Some foods aid the learning process.** Foods such as milk, nuts, seeds, rice, and oats help your study efforts by releasing natural memory enhancers called CCKs (*cholecystokinin*) composed of *tryptopha*n, *choline*, and *phenylalanine*. All of these chemicals enhance the neurotransmitters associated with memory. Before studying, try a light, protein-rich meal of eggs, turkey, or fish. All of these foods release the memory-enhancing chemicals. The better the connections, the more you comprehend.

Likewise, before you take a test, stick to a light snack of energy-boosting and relaxing foods. A glass of milk, a piece of fruit, or some peanuts all release various memory-boosting chemicals and help you to relax and focus on the subject at hand.

2. **Learn to take great notes.** A by-product of our modern culture is that we have grown accustomed to getting our information in short doses (i.e. TV news sound-bytes or *USA Today*-style newspaper articles.)

Consequently, we've subconsciously trained ourselves to assimilate information better in neat little packages. If your notes are scrawled all over the paper, it fragments the flow of the information. Strive for clarity. Newspapers use a standard format to achieve clarity. Your notes can be much clearer through use of proper formatting. A very effective format is called the *Cornell Method*

Take a sheet of loose-leaf lined notebook paper and draw a line all the way down the paper about 2-1/2" from the left-hand edge. Draw another line across the width of the paper about 2" up from the bottom. Repeat this process on the reverse side of the page.

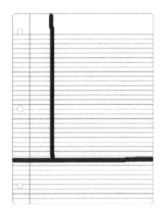
Look at the highly effective result. You have ample room for notes, a left-hand margin for special-emphasis items or to insert supplementary data from the textbook, a large area at the bottom for a brief summary, and a little rectangular space for just about anything you want.

3. __Get the concept then the details.__ Too often we focus on the details and don't gather an understanding of the concept. However, if you simply memorize only dates, places, or names, you may well miss the whole point of the subject.

A key way to understand things is to put them in your own words. If you are working from a textbook, automatically summarize each paragraph in your mind. If you are outlining text, don't simply copy the author's words.

Rephrase them in your own words. You remember your own thoughts and words much better than someone else's, and subconsciously tend to associate the important details to the core concepts.

4. __Ask Why?__ Pull apart written material paragraph by paragraph, and don't forget the captions under the illustrations.

Example: If the heading is "Stream Erosion," flip it around to read "Why do streams erode?" Then answer the question.

If you train your mind to think in a series of questions and answers, not only will you learn more, but it also helps to lessen the test anxiety because you are used to answering questions.

5. __Read for reinforcement and future needs.__ Even if you only have ten minutes, put your notes or a book in your hand. Your mind is similar to a computer; you have to input data in order to have it processed. *By reading, you are creating the neural connections for future retrieval.* The more times you read something, the more you reinforce the learning of ideas.

Even if you don't fully understand something on the first pass, *your mind stores much of the material for later recall.*

6. __Relax to learn; go into exile.__ Our bodies respond to an inner clock called biorhythms. Burning the midnight oil works well for some people but not for everyone.

If possible, set aside a particular place to study that is free of distractions. Shut off the television, cell phone and pager, and exile your friends and family during your study period.

If you really are bothered by silence, try background music. *Light classical music* at a low volume has been shown to aid in concentration.

Music that evokes pleasant emotions without lyrics is highly suggested. Try just about anything by Mozart. It relaxes you.

7. <u>**Use arrows not highlighters.**</u> At best, it's difficult to read a page full of yellow, pink, blue, and green streaks.

Try staring at a neon sign for a while, and you'll soon see how the horde of colors obscures the message.

A quick note, a brief dash of color, an underline, and an arrow pointing to a particular passage is much clearer than a horde of highlighted words.

8. <u>**Budget your study time.**</u> Although you shouldn't ignore any of the material, *allocate your available study time in the same ratio that topics may appear on the test.*

Testing Tips:

1. **Get smart; play dumb.** **Don't read anything into questions.** Don't make an assumption that the test writer is looking for something besides what is asked. Stick to the question as written, and don't read extra things into it.

2. **Read the question and all the choices *twice* before answering the question.** You may miss something by not carefully reading and then re-reading both the question and the answers.

If you really don't have a clue as to the right answer, leave it blank on the first time through. Go on to the other questions because they may provide a clue as to how to answer the skipped questions.

If later on, you still can't answer the skipped ones . . . ***Guess.***
The only penalty for guessing is that you *might* get it wrong. Only one thing is certain; if you don't put anything down, you *will* get it wrong!

3. **Turn the question into a statement.** Look at the way the questions are worded. The syntax of the question usually provides a clue. Does it seem more familiar as a statement rather than as a question? Does it sound strange?

By turning a question into a statement, you may be able to spot if an answer sounds right, and it may also trigger memories of material you have read.

4. **Look for hidden clues.** It's actually very difficult to compose multiple-choice questions without giving away part of the answer in the options presented.

In most multiple-choice questions you can often readily eliminate one or two of the potential answers. This leaves you with only two real possibilities, and automatically your odds go to 50-50 for very little work.

5. **Trust your instincts.** For every fact that you have read, you subconsciously retain something of that knowledge. On questions that you aren't really certain about, go with your basic instincts. **Your first impression on how to answer a question is usually correct.**

6. **Mark your answers directly on the test booklet.** Don't bother trying to fill in the optical scan sheet on the first pass through the test.

Just be very careful not to miss-mark your answers when you eventually transcribe them to the scan sheet.

7. **Watch the clock!** You have a set amount of time to answer the questions. Don't get bogged down trying to answer a single question at the expense of ten questions you can more readily answer.

Three full Practice Tests

Now with Adaptive Assessments!

Adaptive learning is an educational method which uses computers as interactive teaching devices. Computers adapt the presentation of educational material according to students' learning needs, as indicated by their responses to questions. The technology encompasses aspects derived from various fields of study including computer science, education, and psychology.

In Computer Adaptive Testing (CAT), the test subject is presented with questions that are selected based on their level of difficulty in relation to the presumed skill level of the subject. As the test proceeds, the computer adjusts the subject's score based on their answers, continuously fine-tuning the score by selecting questions from a narrower range of difficulty.

The results are available immediately, the amount of time students spend taking tests decreases, and the tests provided more reliable information about what students know—especially those at the very low and high ends of the spectrum. With Adaptive Assessments, the skills that need more study are immediately pinpointed and reported to the student.

Adaptive assessments provide a unique way to assess your preparation for high stakes exams. The questions are asked at the mid-level of difficulty and then, based on the response, the level of difficulty is either increased or decreased. Thus, the test adapts to the competency level of the learner. This is proven method which is also used by examinations such as SAT and GRE. The Adaptive Assessment Engine used for your online self-assessment is based on a robust adaptive assessment algorithm and has been validated by a large pool of test takers. Use this robust and precise assessment to prepare for your exams.

Our Adaptive Assessments can be accessed here:
xamonline.4dlspace.com/AAE
You will be presented with a short form to complete for your account
registration. You will need an active email address to register.

COMPETENCY 1.0   KNOWLEDGE OF GEOGRAPHY

Skill 1.1   Apply the six essential elements of geography.

GEOGRAPHY involves studying location and how living things and earth's features are distributed throughout the earth. It includes where animals, people, and plants live and the effects of their relationship with earth's physical features. Geographers also explore the locations of earth's features, how they got there, and why it is so important.

What geographers study can be broken down into six themes:

Location (including relative and absolute location) – A relative location refers to the surrounding geography, e.g., "on the banks of the Mississippi River." Absolute location refers to a specific point, such as 41 degrees North latitude, 90 degrees West longitude, or 123 Main Street.

Place - A place has both human and physical characteristics. Physical characteristics include features such as mountains, rivers, and deserts. Human characteristics are the features created by human interaction with the environment such as canals and roads.

Human-Environmental Interaction - The theme of human-environmental interaction has three main concepts: 1) humans adapt to the environment (wearing warm clothing in a cold climate, for instance); 2) humans modify the environment (planting trees to block a prevailing wind, for example); 3) and humans depend on the environment (for food, water and raw materials.

Movement - The theme of movement covers how humans interact with one another through trade, communications, emigration, and other forms of interaction.

Regions - A region is an area that has some kind of unifying characteristic, such as a common language or a common government. There are three main types of regions. 1) Formal regions are areas defined by actual political boundaries, such as a city, county, or state. 2) Functional regions are defined by a common function, such as the area covered by a telephone service. 2) Vernacular regions are less formally defined areas that are formed by people's perception, e.g., "the Middle East," or "the South."

And the uses of Geography.

- Geographical studies are divided into:

- Regional: Elements and characteristics of a place or region

- Topical: One earth feature or one human activity occurring throughout the entire world

- Physical: Earth's physical features, what creates and changes them, their relationships to each other as well as to human activities

- Human: Human activity patterns and how they relate to the environment including political, cultural, historical, urban, and social geographical fields of study.

Special research methods used by geographers include mapping, interviewing, field studies, mathematics, statistics, and scientific instruments.

Skill 1.2   Identify the ways natural processes and human-environment interactions shape the Earth's physical systems and features.

Physical Systems

Weather is the condition of the air which surrounds the day-to-day atmospheric conditions such as temperature, air pressure, wind, moisture or precipitation (which includes rain, snow, hail, or sleet).

Climate is average weather or daily weather conditions for a specific region or location over a long or extended period of time. Studying the climate of an area includes information gathered on the area's monthly and yearly temperatures and its monthly and yearly amounts of precipitation. In addition, a characteristic of an area's climate is the length of its growing season. Four reasons for the different climate regions on the earth are differences in:

1. Latitude
2. Amount of moisture
3. Temperatures in land and water
4. Land surface.

There are many different climates throughout the earth. It is most unusual for a country to contain just one kind of climate. Regions of climates are divided according to latitudes:

- Low latitudes: 30 degrees north and south of the equator
- Middle latitudes: 30-60 degrees north and south of the
- High latitudes: 60 degrees to the North and South Poles

The low latitudes are comprised of the rainforest, savanna, and desert climates. The tropical rainforest climate is found in equatorial lowlands and is hot and wet. There is sun, extreme heat, and rain—every day. Although daily temperatures rarely rise above 90 degrees F, the daily humidity is always high, leaving everything sticky and damp. North and south of the tropical rainforests are the tropical grasslands called "savannas"—the "lands of two seasons"—a winter dry season and a summer wet season. Further north and south of the tropical grasslands or savannas are the deserts. These areas are the hottest and driest parts of the earth receiving less than 10 inches of rain a year. These areas have extreme temperatures between night and day. After the sun sets, the land cools quickly dropping the temperature more than 50 degrees Fahrenheit.

The middle latitudes contain the Mediterranean, humid-subtropical, humid-continental, marine, steppe, and desert climates. Lands containing the Mediterranean climate are considered "sunny" lands and are found in six areas of the world: lands bordering the Mediterranean Sea, a small portion of southwestern Africa, areas in southern and southwestern Australia, a small part of the Ukraine near the Black Sea, central Chile, and Southern California. Summers are hot and dry with mild winters. The growing season usually lasts all year, and the rainfalls are during the winter months. Mediterranean climates are located between 30 and 40 degrees North and South latitude, and the land is on the western coasts.

The humid subtropical climate is found north and south of the tropics and is moist indeed. The areas having this type of climate are found on the eastern side of their continents and include Japan, mainland China, Australia, Africa, South America, and the United States—the southeastern coasts of these areas. An interesting feature of their locations is that warm ocean currents are found there. The winds that blow across these currents bring in warm moist air all year round. Long, warm summers; short, mild winters; and a long growing season allow for different crops to be grown several times a year. All contribute to the productivity of this climate, which supports more people than any of the other climates.

The marine climate is found in Western Europe, the British Isles, the U.S. Pacific Northwest, the western coast of Canada and southern Chile, along with southern New Zealand and southeastern Australia. A common characteristic of these lands is that they are near water or surrounded by it. The ocean winds are wet and warm bringing a mild rainy climate to these areas. In the summer, the daily temperatures average at or below 70 degrees F. During the winter, because of the warming effect of the ocean waters, the temperatures rarely fall below freezing.

In northern and central United States, northern China, south central and southeastern Canada, and the western and southeastern parts of the former Soviet Union is found the "climate of four seasons," the humid continental climate–spring, summer, fall, and winter. Cold winters, hot summers, and enough rainfall to grow a variety of crops are the major characteristics of this climate. In areas where the humid continental climate is found are some of the world's best farmlands (as well as important activities such as trading and mining). Differences in temperatures throughout the year are determined by the distance a place is from the coast.

The steppe or prairie climate is located in the interiors of the large continents like Asia and North America. These dry flatlands are far from ocean breezes and are called prairies or the Great Plains in Canada and the United States and steppes in Asia and in Russia. Although the summers are hot and the winters are cold as in the humid continental climate, the big difference is rainfall. In the steppe climate, rainfall is light and uncertain–10 to 20 inches a year, mainly in spring and summer, is considered normal. Where rain is more plentiful, grass grows; in areas of less rain, the steppes or prairies gradually become deserts. These are found in the Gobi Desert of Asia, in central and Western Australia, and in the southwestern United States, and there are smaller deserts in Pakistan and in Argentina and Africa south of the Equator.

The two major climates found in the high latitudes are "tundra" and "taiga." The word "tundra"– meaning "marshy plain"–is a Russian word and aptly describes the climatic conditions in the northern areas of Russia, Europe, and Canada. Winters are extremely cold and long. The ground is frozen most of the year, and it becomes mushy during the short summer months. Surprisingly, less snow falls in the area of the tundra than in the eastern part of the United States. However, due to the harshness of the extreme cold, very few people live there, and no crops can be raised. Despite having a small human population, many plants and animals are found there.

The "taiga" is the northern forest region and is located south of the tundra. In fact, the Russian word "taiga" means 'forest." The world's largest forestlands are found here along with vast mineral wealth and furbearing animals. The climate is so extreme that very few people live here, not being able to raise crops due to the extremely short growing season. The winter temperatures are colder and the summer temperatures hotter than those in the tundra because the taiga climate region is farther from the waters of the Arctic Ocean. The taiga is found in the northern parts of Russia, Sweden, Norway, Finland, Canada, and Alaska with most of the lands covered with marshes and swamps.

In certain areas of the earth there exists a type of climate unique to areas with high mountains, usually different from their surroundings. This type of climate is called a "vertical climate" because the temperatures, crops, vegetation, and human activities change and become different as one ascends the different levels of elevation. At the foot of the mountain, a hot and rainy climate is found with the cultivation of many lowland crops. As one climbs higher, the air becomes cooler, the climate changes sharply, and different economic activities change, such as grazing sheep and growing corn. At the top of many mountains, snow may be found year-round.

Human Systems

Competition for control of areas of the earth's surface is a common trait of human interaction throughout history. This competition has resulted in both destructive conflict and productive cooperation. Societies and groups have sought control of regions of the earth's surface for a variety of reasons including religion, economics, politics and administration. Numerous wars have been fought over the centuries for the control of territory for each of these reasons.

At the same time, groups and societies, have peacefully worked together to establish boundaries around regions or territories that served specific purposes in order to sustain the activities that support life and social organization.

Individuals and societies have divided the earth's surface through conflict for a number of reasons:

- Domination of peoples or societies (e.g., colonialism)
- Control of valuable resources (e.g., oil)
- Control of strategic routes (e.g., the Panama Canal)

Conflicts can be spurred by religion, political ideology, national origin, language, and race. Conflicts can result from disagreement over how land, ocean, or natural resources will be developed, shared, and used. Conflicts have resulted from trade, migration, and settlement rights. Conflicts can occur between small groups of people, between cities, between nations, between religious groups, and between multi-national alliances.

Today, the world is primarily divided by political/administrative interests into state sovereignties. A particular region is recognized to be controlled by a particular government, including its territory, population, and natural resources. The only areas of the earth's surface that today are not defined by state or national sovereignty is Antarctica and portions of the world's water bodies.

Alliances are developed among nations based on political philosophy, economic concerns, cultural similarities, religious interests, and/or for military defense. Some of the most notable alliances today are:

- United Nations
- North Atlantic Treaty Organization (NATO)
- Caribbean Community
- Common Market
- Council of Arab Economic Unity
- European Union

Large companies and multi-national corporations also compete for control of natural resources for manufacturing, development, and distribution.

Throughout human history, there have been conflicts on virtually every scale over the right to divide the Earth according to differing perceptions, needs, and values. These conflicts have included tribal conflicts, urban riots, civil wars, regional wars, and world wars. While these conflicts have traditionally centered on control of land surfaces, new disputes are beginning to arise over the resources of the oceans and space.

On smaller scales, conflicts have created divisions between rival gangs, use zones in cities, water supplies, school districts, and economic divisions including franchise areas and trade zones.

The Agricultural Revolution, initiated by the invention of the plow, led to a complete transformation of human society by making large-scale, agricultural production possible and facilitating the development of agrarian societies. During the period during which the plow was invented, the wheel, numbers, and writing were also invented. Coinciding with the shift from hunting wild game to the domestication of animals, this period was one of dramatic social and economic change.

In the beginning of the transition to agriculture, the tools that were used for hunting and gathering were adequate to the tasks of agriculture. The initial challenge was in adapting to a new way of life. Once that challenge was met, attention turned to the development of more advanced tools and sources of energy. Six thousand years ago, the first plow was invented in Mesopotamia. This plow was pulled by animals. Agriculture was now possible on a much larger scale. Soon tools were developed that made such basic tasks as gathering seeds, planting, and cutting grain faster and easier.

It also became necessary to maintain social and political stability to ensure that planting and harvesting times were not interrupted by internal discord or a war with a neighboring community. It also became necessary to develop ways to store the crop, protect it from thieves, and shield it from destruction by the elements and animals.

The ability to produce surplus crops created the opportunity to trade or barter with other communities in exchange for desired goods. Traders and trade routes began to develop between villages and cities. The domestication of animals expanded the range of trade and facilitated an exchange of ideas and knowledge.

Numerous changes in lifestyle and thinking accompanied the development of stable agricultural communities. Rather than gathering a wide variety of plants as hunter-gatherers did, agricultural communities became dependent on a limited number of plants and crops that were harvested. Subsistence became vulnerable to the weather and dependent upon planting and harvesting times. Agriculture also required a great deal of physical labor and the development of a sense of discipline. The communities became sedentary or stable in terms of location, which made the construction of dwellings appropriate. These tended to be built relatively close together, creating villages or towns. Stable communities also freed people from the need to carry everything with them as they moved from hunting ground to hunting ground. This facilitated the invention of larger, more complex tools. As new tools were developed, it began to make sense to have some specialization within the society. Skills began to have greater value, and people began to work on behalf of the community, which utilized their particular skills and abilities. Settled community life also gave rise to the notion of wealth because it was now possible to keep possessions.

Skill 1.3   Identify the ways natural processes and human-environment interactions shape cultural features (e.g., communities, language, technology, political, and economic institutions).

Physical locations of the earth's surface features include the four major hemispheres and the parts of the earth's continents in them. Political locations are the political divisions, if any, within each continent. Both physical and political locations are precisely determined in two ways: (1) Surveying is done to determine boundary lines and distance from other features. (2) Exact locations are precisely determined by imaginary lines of latitude (parallels) and longitude (meridians). The intersection of these lines at right angles forms a grid, making it impossible to pinpoint an exact location of any place using any two grip coordinates.

The Eastern Hemisphere, located between the North and South Poles and between the Prime Meridian (0 degrees longitude) east to the International Date Line at 180 degrees longitude, consists of most of Europe, all of Australia, most of Africa, and all of Asia, except for a tiny piece of the easternmost part of Russia that extends east of 180 degrees longitude.

The Western Hemisphere, located between the North and South Poles and between the Prime Meridian (0 degrees longitude) west to the International Date Line at 180 degrees longitude, consists of all of North and South America, a tiny part of the easternmost part of Russia that extends east of 180 degrees longitude, and a part of Europe that extends west of the Prime Meridian (0 degrees longitude).

The Northern Hemisphere, located between the North Pole and the Equator, contains all of the continents of Europe and North America and parts of South America, Africa, and most of Asia.

The Southern Hemisphere, located between the South Pole and the Equator, contains all of Australia, a small part of Asia, about one-third of Africa, most of South America, and all of Antarctica.

Of the seven continents, only one contains just one entire country and is the only island continent, Australia. Its political divisions consist of six states and one territory: Western Australia, South Australia, Tasmania, Victoria, New South Wales, Queensland, and Northern Territory.

Africa is made up of 54 separate countries, the major ones being Egypt, Nigeria, South Africa, Zaire, Kenya, Algeria, Morocco, and the large island of Madagascar.

Asia consists of 49 separate countries, some of which include China, Japan, India, Turkey, Israel, Iraq, Iran, Indonesia, Jordan, Vietnam, Thailand, and the Philippines.

Europe's 43 separate nations include France, Russia, Malta, Denmark, Hungary, Greece, Bosnia, and Herzegovina.

North America consists of Canada, the United States of America, the island nations of the West Indies, and the "land bridge" of Middle America, including Cuba, Jamaica, Mexico, and Panama.

Thirteen separate nations together occupy the continent of South America, among them Brazil, Paraguay, Ecuador, and Suriname.

The continent of Antarctica has no political boundaries or divisions but has a number of science and research stations managed by nations such as Russia, Japan, France, Australia, and India.

The earth's surface is made up of 70% water and 30% land. Physical features of the land surface include mountains, hills, plateaus, valleys, and plains. Other minor landforms include deserts, deltas, canyons, mesas, basins, foothills, marshes and swamps. Earth's water features include oceans, seas, lakes, rivers, and canals.

Mountains are landforms with rather steep slopes at least 2,000 feet above sea level. Mountains are found in groups called mountain chains or mountain ranges. At least one range can be found on six of the earth's seven continents. North America has the Appalachian and Rocky Mountains; South America the Andes; Asia the Himalayas; Australia the Great Dividing Range; Europe the Alps; and Africa the Atlas, Ahaggar, and Drakensburg Mountains. Mountains are commonly formed by volcanic activity, or when land is thrust upward when two tectonic plates collide.

Hills are elevated landforms rising to an elevation of about 500 to 2000 feet. They are found everywhere on earth including Antarctica where they are covered by ice.

Plateaus are elevated landforms usually level on top. Depending on location, they range from being an area that is very cold to one that is cool and healthful. Some plateaus are dry because they are surrounded by mountains that keep out any moisture. An example is the Kenya Plateau in East Africa, which is very cool. The plateau extending north from the Himalayas is extremely dry while those in Antarctica and Greenland are covered with ice and snow. Plateaus can be formed by underground volcanic activity, erosion, or colliding tectonic plates.

Plains are described as areas of flat or slightly rolling land, usually lower than the landforms next to them. Sometimes called lowlands (and sometimes located along seacoasts), they support the majority of the world's people. Some are found inland, and many have been formed by large rivers. This results in extremely fertile soil for successful cultivation of crops and results in numerous and large settlements of people. In North America, the vast plains extend from the Gulf of Mexico north to the Arctic Ocean and between the Appalachian and Rocky Mountains. In Europe, rich plains extend east from Great Britain into central Europe and on into the Siberian region of Russia. Plains in river valleys are found in China (the Yangtze River valley), India (the Ganges River valley), and Southeast Asia (the Mekong River valley).

Valleys are land areas that are found between hills and mountains. Some have gentle slopes containing trees and plants; others have very steep walls and are referred to as canyons. One famous example is Arizona's Grand Canyon of the Colorado River, which was formed by erosion.

Deserts are large dry areas of land receiving ten inches or less of rainfall each year. Among the better known deserts are Africa's large Sahara Desert, the Arabian Desert on the Arabian Peninsula, and the desert Outback covering roughly one third of Australia. Deserts are found mainly in the tropical latitudes, and are formed when surrounding features such as mountain ranges extract most of the moisture from the prevailing winds

Deltas are areas of lowlands formed by soil and sediment deposited at the mouths of rivers. The soil is generally very fertile, and most fertile river deltas are important crop-growing areas. One well-known example is the delta of Egypt's Nile River, known for its production of cotton.

Mesas are the flat tops of hills or mountains usually with steep sides. Mesas are similar to plateaus, but smaller.

Basins are considered to be low areas drained by rivers or low spots in mountains.

Foothills are generally considered a low series of hills found between a plain and a mountain range.

Marshes and swamps are wet lowlands providing growth of such plants as rushes and reeds.

Oceans are the largest bodies of water on the planet. The four oceans of the earth are the Atlantic Ocean, one-half the size of the Pacific and separating North and South America from Africa and Europe; the Pacific Ocean, covering almost one-third of the entire surface of the earth and separating North and South America from Asia and Australia; the Indian Ocean, touching Africa, Asia, and Australia; and the ice-filled Arctic Ocean, extending from North America and Europe to the North Pole. The waters of the Atlantic, Pacific, and Indian Oceans also touch the shores of Antarctica.

Seas are smaller than the Atlantic or Pacific oceans and are partially surrounded by land. Some examples include the Mediterranean Sea found between Europe, Asia, and Africa; and the Caribbean Sea, touching the West Indies, South and Central America.

A lake is a body of standing water surrounded by land. The Great Lakes in North America are a good example. The deepest lake in the world is Lake Baikal in Siberia which contains as much water as all the Great Lakes put together.

Rivers, considered a nation's lifeblood, begin as very small streams, formed by melting snow and rainfall, flowing from higher to lower land, emptying into a larger body of water, usually a sea or an ocean. Examples of important rivers for the people and countries affected by and/or dependent on them include the Nile, Niger, and Zaire Rivers of Africa; the Rhine, Danube, and Thames Rivers of Europe; the Yangtze, Ganges, Mekong, Hwang He, and Irrawaddy Rivers of Asia; the Murray-Darling in Australia; and the Orinoco in South America. River systems are made up of large rivers and numerous smaller rivers or tributaries flowing into them. Examples include the vast Amazon Rivers system in South America and the Mississippi River system in the United States.

Canals are man-made water passages constructed to connect two larger bodies of water. Famous examples include the Panama Canal across Panama's isthmus connecting the Atlantic and Pacific Oceans and the Suez Canal in the Middle East between Africa and the Arabian peninsulas connecting the Red and Mediterranean Seas.

Social scientists use the term culture to describe the way of life of a group of people. This would include not only art, music, and literature but also beliefs, customs, languages, traditions, inventions—in short, any way of life whether complex or simple. The term geography is defined as the study of earth's features and living things as to their location, relationship with each other, how they came to be there, and why so important.

Physical geography is concerned with the locations of such earth features as climate, water, and land and how these relate to and affect each other and human activities; and what forces shaped and changed them. All three of these earth features affect the lives of all humans having a direct influence on what is made and produced, where it occurs, how it occurs, and what makes it possible. The combination of the different climate conditions and types of landforms and other surface features work together all around the earth to give the many varied cultures their unique characteristics and distinctions.

Cultural geography studies the location, characteristics, and influence of the physical environment on different cultures around the earth. Also included in these studies are comparisons and influences of the many varied cultures. Ease of travel and up-to-the-minute, state-of-the-art communication techniques ease the difficulties of understanding cultural differences making it easier to come in contact with them.

Skill 1.4   **Analyze geographic information from maps, charts, and graphs.**

We use illustrations of various sorts because it is often easier to demonstrate a given idea visually instead of orally. Sometimes it is even easier to do so with an illustration than a description. This is especially true in the areas of education and research because humans are visually stimulated. Any idea presented visually in some manner is always easier to understand and to comprehend than simply getting an idea across verbally, by hearing it or reading it. Throughout this document, there are several illustrations that have been presented to explain an idea in a more precise way. Sometimes these will demonstrate some of the types of illustrations available for use in the arena of political science. Among the more common illustrations used in geography and other disciplines are various types of maps, graphs, and charts.

Although maps have advantages over globes and photographs, they do have a major disadvantage: Most maps are flat and the Earth is a sphere. It is impossible to reproduce exactly on a flat surface a spherical object. In order to put the earth's features onto a map, the features must be stretched in some way. This stretching is called distortion. Distortion does not mean that maps are wrong. It simply means that they are not perfect representations of the Earth or its parts. Cartographers, or mapmakers, understand the problems of distortion. They try to design maps so that there is as little distortion as possible.

The process of putting the features of the Earth onto a flat surface is called projection. All maps are really map projections. Each of the different types deals in a different way with the problem of distortion. Map projections are made in a number of ways. Some are done using complicated mathematics. However, the basic ideas behind map projections can be understood by looking at the three most common types:

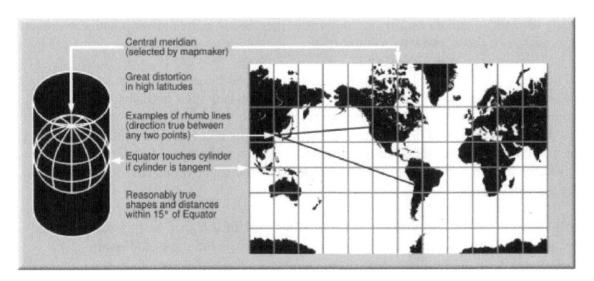

(1) Cylindrical Projections - These are done by taking a cylinder of paper and wrapping it around a globe. A light is used to project the globe's features onto the paper. Distortion is least where the paper touches the globe. For example, suppose that the paper was wrapped so that it touched the globe at the equator. The map from this projection would have just a little distortion near the

equator. However, in moving north or south of the equator, the distortion would increase as you moved further away from the equator. The best known and most widely used cylindrical projection is the Mercator Projection. It was first developed in 1569 by Gerardus Mercator, a Flemish mapmaker.

(2) Conical Projections - The name for these maps comes from the projection being made onto a cone of paper. The cone is made so that it touches a globe at the base of the cone only. It can also be made so that it cuts through part of the globe in two different places. Again, there is the least distortion where the paper touches the globe. If the cone touches at two different points, there is some distortion at both of them. Conical projections are most often used to map areas in the middle latitudes. Maps of the United States are most often conical projections. This is because most of the country lies within these latitudes.

(3) Flat-Plane Projections - These are made with a flat piece of paper that touches the globe at one point only. Areas near this point show little distortion. Flat-plane projections are often used to show the areas of the north and south poles. One such flat projection is called a Gnomonic Projection. On this kind of map, all meridians appear as straight lines, Gnomonic projections are useful because any straight line drawn between points on it forms a Great-Circle Route.

Great-Circle Routes can best be described by thinking of a globe and how when using the globe, the shortest route between two points on it can be found by simply stretching a string from one point to the other. However, if the string was extended in reality so that it took into effect the globe's curvature, it would then make a great-circle. A great-circle is any circle that cuts a sphere, such as the globe, into two equal parts. Because of distortion, most maps do not show great-circle routes as straight lines, Gnomonic projections, however, do show the shortest distance between the two places as a straight line, and because of this, they are valuable for navigation. They are called Great-Circle Sailing Maps.

To properly analyze a given map one must be familiar with the various parts and symbols that most modern maps use. For the most part, this is standardized, with different maps using similar parts and symbols. These include:

The Title - All maps should have a title, just like all books should. The title tells you what information is to be found on the map.

The Legend - Most maps have a legend. A legend tells the reader about the various symbols that are used on that particular map and what the symbols represent (also called a map key).

The Grid - A grid is a series of lines that are used to find exact places and locations on the map. There are several different kinds of grid systems in use; however, most maps do use the longitude and latitude system, known as the

Geographic Grid System.

Directions - Most maps have some directional system to show which way the map is being presented. Often on a map, a small compass will be present, with arrows showing the four basic directions of north, south, east, and west.

The Scale - This is used to show the relationship between a unit of measurement on the map versus the real world measure on the Earth. Maps are drawn to many different scales. Some maps show a lot of detail for a small area. Others show a greater span of distance. One should always be aware of what scale is being used. For instance, the scale might be: 1 inch = 10 miles for a small area, or for a map showing the whole world, it might have a scale of 1 inch = 1,000 miles. The point is that one must look at the map key in order to see what units of measurements the map is using.

Maps have four main properties. They are 1) the size of the areas shown on the map; 2) the shapes of the areas; 3) consistent scales; and 4) straight line directions. A map can be drawn so that it is correct in one or more of these properties. No map can be correct in all of them.

Equal areas - One property that maps can have is that of equal areas, In an equal area map, the meridians and parallels are drawn so that the areas shown have the same proportions as they do on the Earth. For example, Greenland is about 118th the size of South America. Thus it will be show as 118th the size on an equal area map. The Mercator projection is an example of a map that does not have equal areas. In it, Greenland appears to be about the same size of South America. This is because the distortion becomes large at the poles, and Greenland lies near the North Pole.

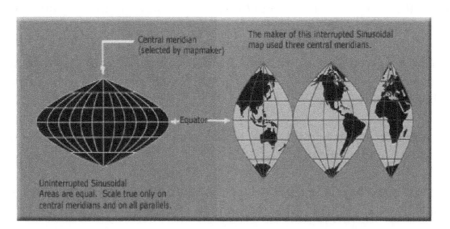

Conformality - A second map property is conformality, or correct shapes. There are no maps which can show very large areas of the earth in their exact shapes. Only globes can really do that, however Conformal Maps are as close as possible to true shapes. The United States is often shown by a Lambert Conformal Conic Projection Map.

Consistent Scales - Many maps attempt to use the same scale on all parts of the map. Generally, this is easier when maps show a relatively small part of the earth's surface. For example, a map of Florida might be a Consistent Scale Map. Generally maps showing large areas are not consistent-scale maps. This is so because of distortion. Often such maps will have two scales noted in the key. One scale, for example, might be accurate to measure distances between points along the Equator. Another might be then used to measure distances between the North Pole and the South Pole.

Maps showing physical features often try to show information about the elevation or relief of the land. Elevation is the distance above or below the sea level. The elevation is usually shown with colors. For instance, all areas on a map which are at a certain level will be shown in the same color.

Relief Maps - Show the shape of the land surface as flat, rugged, or steep. Relief maps usually give more detail than simply showing the overall elevation of the land's surface. Relief is also sometimes shown with colors, but another way to show relief is by using contour lines. These lines connect all points of a land surface which are the same height surrounding the particular area of land.

Thematic Maps - These are used to show more specific information, often on a single theme, or topic. Thematic maps show the distribution or amount over a certain given area of things such as population density, climate, economic information, or cultural or political information.

Political science would be almost impossible without maps. Information can be gained looking at a map that might take hundreds of words to explain otherwise. Maps reflect the great variety of knowledge covered by political science. To show such a variety of information, maps are made in many different ways. Because of this variety, maps must be understood in order to make the best sense of them. Once they are understood, maps provide a solid foundation for political science studies.

To apply information obtained from graphs one must understand the two major reasons why graphs are used:

1. To present a model or theory visually in order to show how two or more variables interrelate.

2. To present real world data visually in order to show how two or more variables interrelate.

Most often used are those known as bar graphs and line graphs. (Charts are often used for similar reasons and are explained in the next section.)

Graphs are most useful when one wishes to demonstrate the sequential increase, or decrease of a variable or to show specific correlations between two or more variables in a given circumstance.

Most common is the bar graph, because it has a way of visually showing the difference in a given set of variables. However, it is limited in that it can not really show the actual proportional increase or decrease of each given variable to each other. (In order to show a decrease, a bar graph must show the "bar" under the starting line, thus removing the ability to really show how the various different variables would relate to each other.)

Thus in order to accomplish this one must use a line graph. Line graphs can be of two types a linear or non-linear graph. A linear line graph uses a series of straight lines a non-linear line graph uses a curved line. Though the lines can be either straight or curved, all of the lines are called curves.

A line graph uses a number line or axis. The numbers are generally placed in order, equal distances from one another. The number line is used to represent a number, degree, or some such other variable at an appropriate point on the line. Two lines are used, intersecting at a specific point. They are referred to as the X-axis and the Y-axis. The Y-axis is a vertical line; the X-axis is a horizontal line. Together they form a coordinate system. The difference between a point on the line of the X-axis and the Y-axis is called the slope of the line, or the change in the value on the vertical axis divided by the change in the value on the horizontal axis. The Y-axis number is called the rise and the X-axis number is called the run, thus the equation for slope is:

SLOPE =   RISE - Change in value on the vertical axis
          RUN - Change in value on the horizontal axis

The slope tells the amount of increase or decrease of a given specific variable. When using two or more variables, one can plot the amount of difference between them in any given situation. This makes presenting information on a line graph more involved. It also makes it more informative and accurate than a simple bar graph. Knowledge of the term "slope" and understanding what it is and how it is measured helps us to describe verbally the pictures we are seeing visually. For example, if a curve is said to have a slope of "zero," you should picture a flat line. If a curve has a slope of "one," you should picture a rising line that makes a 45-degree angle with the horizontal and vertical axis lines.

The preceding examples are of linear (straight line) curves. With non-linear curves (the ones that really do curve), the slope of the curve is constantly changing, so as a result, we must then understand that the slope of the nonlinear curved line will be at a specific point. How is this done? The slope of a non-linear curve is determined by the slope of a straight line that intersects the curve at that specific point.

In all graphs, an upward sloping line represents a direct relationship between the two variables. A downward slope represents an inverse relationship between the two variables. In reading any graph, one must always be very careful to understand what is being measured, what can be deduced, and what cannot be deduced from the given graph.

To use charts correctly, one should remember the reasons one uses graphs. The general ideas are similar. It is usually a question as to whether a graph or chart is more capable of adequately portraying the information one wants to illustrate. It is easy to see the difference between them and realize that in many ways graphs and charts are interrelated.

One of the most common types, because it is easiest to read and understand even for the layperson, is the pie-chart.

Pie-charts are used often, especially to illustrate the differences in percentages among various items or to demonstrate the divisions of a whole.

Realistically, a chart can be made out of almost any multiple set of variables. Remember to properly show the differences between them and what you are trying to prove and keep it clear enough to read and understand with a minimum of effort. The usefulness of a chart is wasted if too much time is taken in order to understand it. Charts are always used to simplify an idea, never to complicate it.

In geography and related fields, all type of illustrations, maps, graphs and charts are useful tools for both education and research. As such, they are quite often used to better demonstrate an idea rather than simply stating it because some problems and situations are easier to understand visually than verbally. The illustrations are also excellent for showing relationships between any given set of variables or circumstances. However, one must always remember that though a picture may "be worth a thousand words," it still can't say everything so one should always be aware of the limits of any diagrammatic model. In other words: "Seeing is not always believing."

COMPETENCY 2.0   KNOWLEDGE OF ECONOMICS

Skill 2.1   Analyze how scarcity and opportunity cost influence choices about how to allocate resources.

Free enterprise, individual entrepreneurship, competitive markets, and consumer sovereignty are all parts of a market economy. Individuals have the right to make their own decisions as to what they want to do as a career. The financial incentives are there for individuals who are willing to take the risk. A successful venture earns profit. It is these financial incentives that serve to motivate inventors and small businesses. The same is true for big businesses. They are free to determine what production technique to use and what output to produce within the confines of the legal system. They can make investments based on their own decisions. Competitive markets, relatively free from government interference, are also a manifestation of the freedom that the U.S. economic system is based on. These markets function on the basis of supply and demand to determine output mix and resource allocation. Since consumers buy the goods and services that give them satisfaction, this means that, for the most part, they don't buy the goods and services that they either don't want or that don't give them satisfaction.

Consumers are, in effect, voting for the goods and services that they want with their dollars or what is called "dollar voting." Consumers signal firms as to how they want society's scarce resources used with their dollar votes. A good that society wants acquires enough dollar votes for the producer to experience profits–a situation where the firm's revenues exceed the firm's costs. The existence of profits indicate to the firm that it is producing the goods and services that consumers want and that society's scarce resources are being used in accordance with consumer preferences. When a firm does not have a profitable product, it is because that product is not tabulating enough dollar votes of consumers. Consumers don't want the good or service and they don't want society's scarce resources being used in its production.

This process where consumers vote with their dollars is called consumer sovereignty. Consumers are directing the allocation of scarce resources in the economy with the dollar spending. Firms, who are in business to earn profit, then hire resources or inputs in accordance with consumer preferences. This is the way in which resources are allocated in a market economy. This is the manner in which society achieves the output mix that it desires.

The fact that resources are scarce is the basis for the existence of economics. Economics is defined as a study of how scarce resources are allocated to satisfy unlimited wants. Resources refer to the four factors of production: labor, land and entrepreneurship. The fact that the supply of these resources is finite means that society cannot have as much of everything that it wants. There is a constraint on production and consumption and on the kinds of goods and services that can be produced and consumed. Scarcity means that choices have to be made. If society decides to produce more of one good, this means that there are fewer resources available for the production of other goods.

Assume a society can produce two goods, good A and good B. The society uses resources in the production of each good. If producing one unit of good A results in an amount of resources used to produce three units of good B then producing one more unit of good A results in a decrease in

3 units of good B. In effect, one unit of good A "costs" three units of good B. This cost is referred to as opportunity cost. Opportunity cost is the value of the sacrificed alternative, the value of what had to be given up in order to have the output of good A. Opportunity cost does not just refer to production. Your opportunity cost of studying with this guide is the value of what you are not doing because you are studying, whether it is watching TV, spending time with family, working, or whatever. Every choice has an opportunity cost.

Skill 2.2   Identify how economic systems (e.g., market, command, traditional) answer the three basic economic questions.

Economic systems refer to the arrangements a society has devised to answer what are known as the Three Questions: 1) What goods to produce; 2) how to produce the goods; and 3) for whom are the goods being produced. Different economic systems answer these questions in different ways. These are the different "isms" that define the method of resource and output allocation. A market economy answers these questions in terms of demand and supply and the use of markets.

Consumers vote for the products they want with their dollar spending. Goods acquiring enough dollar votes are profitable, signaling to the producers that society wants their scarce resources used in this way. This is how the "What" question is answered. The producer then hires inputs in accordance with the goods consumers want, looking for the most efficient or lowest cost method of production. The lower the firm's costs for any given level of revenue, the higher the firm's profits. This is the way in which the "How" question is answered in a market economy. The "For Whom" question is answered in the marketplace by the determination of the equilibrium price. Price serves to ration the good to those who can and will transact at the market price- those who cannot or will not are excluded from the market. This mechanism results in market efficiency or obtaining the most output from the available inputs that are consistent with the preferences of consumers. Society's scarce resources are being used the way society wants them to be used.

Another term of importance is comparative advantage. This term refers to international trade and states that a nation should specialize in the production of the good which it can produce at a relatively lower opportunity cost than the other nation and trade for goods that it can't produce as cheaply. Trade on this basis results in higher levels of output, income, and employment for the trading nations. This is the reasoning behind free trade agreements such as NAFTA.

The opposite of the market economy is called the centrally planned economy. This used to be called Communism, even though the term in not correct in a strict Marxian sense. In a planned economy, the means of production are publicly owned with little if any private ownership. Instead of the Three Questions being solved by markets, a planning authority makes the decisions in place of markets. The planning authority decides what will be produced and how. Since most planned economies directed resources into the production of capital and military goods, there was little remaining for consumer goods, and the result was chronic shortages. Price functioned as an accounting measure and did not reflect scarcity. The former Soviet Union and most of the Eastern Bloc countries were planned economies of this sort.

In between the two extremes is market socialism. This is a mixed economic system that uses both markets and planning. Planning is usually used to direct resources at the upper levels of the economy, with markets being used to determine prices of consumer goods and wages. This kind of economic system answers the three questions with planning and markets. The former Yugoslavia was a market socialist economy.

The social structure of a society is definitely affected by the type of economic system. A traditional economy is based on tradition and is not receptive to change. The social structure is the same as it was generations ago. Incentives are there to improve or get ahead because of tradition. There is not much of a tax base to raise revenues and implement social welfare programs.

A planned economy with government ownership of the means of production was supposed to be a classless society, but the upper levels of government and the military were a notch above the population. Individual and entrepreneurial incentives were lacking since there was no private ownership of business or possibility of profit. In a mixed economy and in a market economy, the individual is allowed the financial rewards for his entrepreneurial ventures. More people are willing to take the risk for the chance of succeeding. Therefore, the resulting social structure is a spectrum from very poor to very rich.

You can put each nation of the world on a continuum in terms of these characteristics and rank them from most capitalistic to the most planned. The United States would probably rank as the most capitalistic and North Korea would probably rank as the most planned, but this doesn't mean that the United States doesn't engage in planning or that economies like mainland China don't use markets.

Skill 2.3   **Analyze the interaction of supply and demand in determining production, distribution, and consumption.**

Economics is divided into two broad categories: macroeconomics and microeconomics. Macroeconomics is a study of the aggregates that comprise the economy on the national level: output, consumption, investment, government spending, and net exports. Microeconomics is a study of the economy at the industry or firm level. Microeconomics is concerned with consumer behavior, output and input markets, and the distribution of income.

A firm's production decisions are based on its costs. Every product is produced using inputs or resources. These are called factors of production, and there are four that are used in the production of every good and service: labor, land, capital, and entrepreneurship. The firm hires these factors in the input or resource market. The production process refers to the method in which resources are combined to produce a good or service. The costs for fixed factors of production, such as land, plant, and equipment, are called fixed costs. The costs for variable factors, such as labor, are called variable costs. Costs of production, then, are the total of fixed and variable costs.

Each factor of production earns its factor income in the resource market. Labor earns wages, capital earns interest, land earns rent, and the entrepreneur earns profit. The size of the factor income depends on the scarcity of the factor and the significance of its contribution to the production process. A market economy does not result in the equality of income. Each factor earns an income based on its contribution.

Firms sell their outputs in different output market structures. There are four kinds of market structures in the output market: perfect competition, monopoly, monopolistic competition, and oligopoly.

For the most part, perfect competition is a theoretical extreme, most closely approximated by agriculture. The numerous firms sell a product identical to that sold by all other firms in the industry and have no control over the price. The price is a given to the firm. Buyers and sellers have full market information, and there are no barriers to entry. A barrier to entry is anything that makes it difficult for firms to enter or leave the industry.

The opposite of a perfectly competitive firm is a monopolist. Monopoly is a market structure in which there is only one seller who can control his price. The firm is equal to the industry. A monopolist becomes a monopolist and remains a monopolist because of barriers to entry, which are very high. These barriers to entry include a very high fixed cost structure, which functions to keep new firms from entering the industry. Monopoly is illegal in the U.S. economy.

Between the two extremes are the two market structures that all U.S. firms fall into. Oligopoly is a market structure in which there are a few sellers of products that may be either homogeneous (steel), or heterogeneous (automobiles). There are high barriers to entry, which is why there are only a few firms in each industry.

Monopolistic competition is the situation you see in shopping centers. There are numerous firms, each selling products that are similar but not identical, such as brand name shoes or clothing. Barriers to entry are not as high as in an oligopoly which is why there are more firms.

Demand is based on consumer preferences. Satisfaction refers to the quantities of a good or service that buyers are willing and able to buy at different prices during a given period of time. Supply is based on costs of production and refers to the quantities that sellers are willing and able to sell at different prices during a given period of time. The determination of market equilibrium price is when the decisions of buyers coincide with the decisions of sellers.

Demand curves and supply curves have different shapes. We can define the term elasticity to be a measure of the responsiveness of quantity to changes in price. If quantity is very responsive to changes in price, then demand is said to be elastic; if quantity is not very responsive to changes in price, then demand is inelastic.

Skill 2.4   Analyze how macroeconomic factors (e.g., national income, employment, price stability) influence the performance of economic systems.

Macroeconomics refers to the functioning of the economy on the national level and the functioning of the aggregate units that comprise the national economy. Macroeconomics is concerned with a study of the economy's overall economic performance or what is called the Gross Domestic Product (GDP). The GDP is a measure of the economy's output during a specified time period. Tabulating the economy's output can be measured in two ways, both of which give the same result: the expenditures approach and the incomes approach. What is spent on the national output by each sector of the economy is equal to what is earned producing the national output by each of the factors of production.

The macroeconomy consists of four broad sectors: consumers, businesses, government, and the foreign sector. In the expenditures approach, GDP is determined by the amount of spending in each sector. GDP is equal to the consumption expenditures of consumers plus the investment expenditures of businesses plus spending of all three levels of government plus the net export spending in the foreign sector.

$$GDP = C + I + G + (X-M)$$

What is spent buying the national output has to equal what is earned in producing the national output.

- Labor earns wages, which is called Compensation of Employees
- Land earns Rental Income
- Capital earns Interest Income (Since entrepreneurial ability can be in the form of individual effort or corporations, there are two different categories here.)

The return to the individual entrepreneur is called Proprietor's Income. The return to the corporation is called Corporate Profit. Corporations do three things with their profits: pay the corporate profits tax; pay dividends; and keep the rest as retained earnings. These are the three components of corporate profits. To complete the tabulation of GDP from the incomes approach, we have to adjust for two non-income charges. First are Indirect Business Taxes, such as property taxes and sales taxes. Second is depreciation (the amount of capital assets that are worn out producing the current term's output). Both of these are subtracted.

When the economy is functioning smoothly, the amount of national output produced (aggregate supply) is just equal to the amount of national output purchased (aggregate demand). Then we have an economy in a period of prosperity without economic instability.

But market economies experience the fluctuations of the business cycle, the ups and downs in the level of economic activity. There are four phases: boom (period of prosperity), recession (a period of declining GDP and rising unemployment), trough (the low point of the recession), and recovery (a period of lessening unemployment and rising prices). There are no rules pertaining to the duration or severity of any of the phases. The phases result in periods of unemployment and periods of inflation. Inflation results from too much spending in the economy. Buyers want to buy more than sellers can produce and bid up prices for the available output. Unemployment occurs when there is not enough spending in the economy. Sellers have produced more output than buyers are buying, and the result is a surplus situation. Firms faced with surplus merchandise lower their production levels and lay off workers, which leads to unemployment. These situations can require government policy actions.

GDP, computed either by the expenditures approach or the incomes approach, is a measure of the overall performance of the national economy. From GDP, government policymakers can determine what is happening in the economy and where the problem areas are. The GDP is a way of measuring economic growth. Then the policymakers can devise policies to help those problem areas.

The overall macroeconomic instability problems of inflation and unemployment are, for the most part, caused by the inequality of aggregate demand and aggregate supply. An economy that is growing too rapidly and has too high a level of spending has inflation—a period of rises in the price level. Inflation results in a dollar with less purchasing power and represents a situation where the appropriate governmental action is to slow down the economy. The government will implement policies that results in less spending in the economy to end the inflation. When there isn't enough spending in the economy, producers who have surplus merchandise, lower production levels and lay off workers. The appropriate action for government is to stimulate the economy and to take actions that result in higher levels of spending. The increase in demand leads to higher levels of employment.

Government can implement contractionary policies for inflation or expansionary policies for unemployment in two ways. Fiscal policy refers to changes in the level of government spending and/or taxes. Expansionary fiscal policy consists of rising government spending and/or lowering taxes to increase spending in the economy, thus eliminating unemployment. Contractionary policies to stop inflation consist of a decrease in government spending and/or an increase in taxes, both of which lower the levels of spending in the economy. Fiscal policy requires legislative action, and laws have to be enacted.

The other policy tool open to the government is monetary policy. Monetary policy is implemented by the Federal Reserve System (Fed) through changing the level of money in the banking system. Simply put, banks earn income by making loans. People and businesses borrow from banks and spend the borrowed funds. If the Fed changes the amount of funds that banks have available to loan out, the Fed changes the level of spending in the economy. There are three ways that the Fed can do this. First of all, banks cannot loan out all of their deposits. They are required to hold a certain percentage as reserves. The percentage is called the reserve ratio. Raising the reserve ratio leaves banks with fewer reserves to loan out, and it is, therefore, an aspect of contractionary monetary policy (used during recessions). Lowering the reserve ratio increases lending ability and spending and is thus an aspect of expansionary monetary policy.

A second mechanism for implementing monetary policy is called the Discount Rate, which is the rate of interest charged by the Fed to banks that borrow from it. Lowering the Discount Rate encourages banks to borrow and make loans, thus leading to higher levels of spending. This is a form of expansionary monetary policy. Contractionary monetary policy would be indicated by an increase in the Discount Rate.

The third means of influencing the money supply is through Open Market Operations. This is when the Fed buys or sells bonds in the open market. When the Fed buys bonds from the public or banks, the Fed pays with dollars that are put into circulation. Thus, the Fed buying bonds represents a form of expansionary monetary policy as there are more dollars in the system for loans and spending. The Fed selling bonds is a form of contractionary monetary policy.

Since today's financial markets are international, banks can borrow and lend in foreign markets. They aren't constrained by the domestic market. Financial capital goes where it earns the highest rate of return, regardless of national boundaries. This means that if the Fed is trying to implement contractionary monetary policy, banks and businesses can just borrow in international markets and get around the Fed's contractionary policies, at least in the short-run.

Skill 2.5 **Analyze the roles of government, central banking systems, and specialized institutions (e.g., corporations, labor unions, banks, stock markets) in market and command economies.**

The roles of political and personal liberty differ greatly depending on the economic regime. The cause of the difference is the role of incentives. A market economy functions on the basis of the financial incentive. Firms use society's scarce resources to produce the goods that consumers want. Firms know they have a good that society wants when they earn profit. Firms have a good that consumers don't want when they consistently incur losses. Firms with consistent losses eventually go out of business, and those resources shift into other industries, producing goods that consumers do want. Consumers are, in effect, voting for the goods and services they want and don't want, with their dollars.

Technological progress is advanced because of financial incentives, whether personal or corporate. Firms invest in research and development activities to find newer and more efficient technologies that result in greater output at lower prices. Individuals risk their own time and money on inventions because of potential financial rewards. They live in the structure of a market economy that allows them the liberty of choosing what to do with their own resources within the confines of the law. Students study whatever it is that they want to major in. There are more scholarships available for certain needed occupations, but the student can still obtain an education if s/he doesn't want to be in one of those needed areas.

In a planned economy, particularly one based on public ownership of the means of production, a planning entity substitutes for the market, in varying degrees from partial to total. Instead of consumers voting with their dollars, they have a bureaucratic entity trying to substitute for the functions of supply and demand in making production decisions. This is why planned economies are often plagued by a misallocation of resources that result in shortages and surpluses. In most cases, the incentive for technological progress and innovation is absent because of the lack of financial rewards. There is no financial incentive for the inventor. There is no financial incentive for the firm to engage in research and development activities, even if they have the authorization to do so. What's in it for them? Many planned economies have less personal and political freedom than do market economies. The economy needs resources for a particular area. The labor force is directed into that area by assignment for the most part, not by financial incentives. More engineers are attracted, not by higher salaries and more perks for engineers, but by assigning people to be engineers. Their schooling isn't financed if they don't study the required disciplines.

It is obvious why there is a differing degree of political freedom in each of the above paradigms. The lack of freedom of choice in a planned economy carries over to the political area. Most planned economies are usually headed by dictators whereas market economies have elected officials. A populace does not vote for and elect those officials who suppress them. So, for the most part, a market economy allows for more political and personal freedoms than a planned economy does.

A central bank in a market economy is responsible for price stability and stabilization of the economy. Its purpose is also to prevent the commercial banking system from failing and to control inflation. In a market economy, the central bank functions best when it is not influenced by political concerns and when it remains independent from the government's fiscal policy. The Federal Reserve is the central bank of the United States.

Specialized institutions such as corporations, labor unions, banks, and stock markets also have a role in government. In a command economy, such as Socialism, the government has varying degrees of controls over the economy. Corporations are business entities that exist because of state law. The biggest advantage of a corporation for its shareholders is limited liability. In a free market economy, corporations are independent and assume the risk of their behavior. In a command economy, the government directs various aspects of production, such as capacity, courses of action, and volume.

Labor unions negotiate with businesses on behalf of their members. Unions can be trade or industrial, and unions affect the economy by the amount of market power they exert. Market power is often exerted by a union's influence on wages and benefits they obtain for their workers.

Commercial banks offer many services, but the main services include accepting deposits, processing payments, lending money, and issuing checks and drafts. In command economies, banks usually take less risks than in market economies. Risks involve making lending decisions, for example. Bank decision-making is based on analysis of risk and other financial analysis. In command economies, this type of analysis is not developed as it is in market economies.

In a central economy, the government does the financial and economic planning. A command economy does not promote profit motives of individuals or of private enterprise. The former Soviet Union is an example of a command economy. However, there are few command economies today. In market economies, stock markets provide opportunities for investment through the purchase and sale of stocks of public corporations.

Skill 2.6   Analyze the features of global economics (e.g., exchange rates, terms of trade, comparative advantage, less developed countries) in terms of their impact on national and international economic systems.

The theory of comparative advantage says that trade should be based on the comparative opportunity costs between two nations. The nation that can produce a good more cheaply should specialize in the production of that good and trade for the good in which it has the comparative disadvantage. In this way both nations will experience gains from trade.

A basis for trade exists if there are differing comparative costs in each country. Suppose country A can produce ten units of good X or ten units of good Y with its resources. Country B can produce 30 units of X or 10 units of Y with its resources. What are the relative costs in each country? In country A, one X costs one unit of Y, and in country B one X costs three units of Y. Good Y is cheaper in country B than it is in country A—$1/3X = 1$ Y in country B versus $1Y = 1X$ in country A. Country B has the comparative advantage in the production of Y and country A has the comparative advantage in the production of good X.

According to trade theory each country should specialize in the production of the good in which it has the comparative advantage. Country B will devote all of its resources to the production of good Y, and country A will devote its resources to the production of good X. Each country will trade for the good in which it has the comparative disadvantage.

When nations engage in trade, the traded items have to be paid for. This involves exchange rate and international currency markets. Today, the exchange rates for most currencies float. This means the exchange rate is determined by supply and demand, just like the price of any good. Governments are not required to intervene in the market, as they were when exchange rates were fixed. Under the Bretton Woods system, the U.S. dollar was quoted in terms of gold, and all other major currencies were quoted in terms of the dollar. This meant that nations were required to buy and sell currencies to maintain the par value of their currency. Situations of disequilibrium resulted from imbalances in the nation's Balance of Payments, which was an accounting statement of all of a nation's inflows and outflows. If a nation's inflows did not equal its outflows, its currency would come under pressure. A surplus in the Balance of Payments put upward pressure on the currency, and the country would have to sell its currency against the dollar to increase the supply and take the upward pressure off of the exchange rate. If there was a deficit in the Balance of Payment, there would be downward pressure on the exchange rate, and the nation would have to buy its currency against the dollar. The continued Payments imbalances resulted in one crisis after another in the world currency markets until the Bretton Woods system was ended.

Currencies have been floating since 1973. This means they adjust to trade imbalances with their values appreciating or depreciating automatically without any form of intervention. There have been no crises in the currency markets since currencies have been floating.

Global economies have an impact on less developed countries. As companies become multi-national, they seek locations where products can be manufactured more cheaply. As a result, many developing nations are selected as sites for production plants. While the facilities can bring employment to the developing area, the manufacturer may pay low wages because the cost of living in the developing area is not as high as in the developed nation. While the developing nation can have positive impacts on global economies in the areas of lower wages and increased production, the developing nations can cause the loss of jobs for employees whose jobs they replaced. Global economies can also impact the environment if the developing nation utilizing labor and facilities of a developing nation do not implement means to protect the physical and human environment.

Skill 2.7   Evaluate the functions of budgeting, saving, and credit in a consumer economy.

The part of an economy that is centered on the consumer rather than the economy between businesses is called a consumer economy. This is the part of an economy where services and finished goods are purchased by individuals for their own use. The purchase of clothing, automobiles, telephone service, personal computers, or CDs are all part of the consumer economy.

This is a crucial part of most economies, and credit plays an important role in driving it. Credit is simply a promise to pay for goods or services that have already been provided. Credit lenders such as credit card companies and banks allow borrowers to pay back these loans over time. For this service, they charge fees and interest on the balance of the loan. The money made from fees and interest finance, in part, the extension of credit to more people.

Some consumer purchases, such as automobiles and homes, are so expensive that most people would have to budget and save for many years to buy one for cash. Credit allows consumers to pay a small portion of the total cost up front and borrow the balance. Without credit, these purchases would simply be impossible for many people. With credit, a market exists for a steady stream of new houses and cars and supports construction and the auto industry. In addition, the financial services connected to the administration and collections of credit payments comprise an important part of the overall economy. Loans can be traded similar to other financial instruments such as stocks and bonds. The consumer economy is the foundation of a large portion of the overall economy.

Credit creates debt, which can have an economic downside. As can be seen, some debt is good for an economy, because it drives the services and industries tied to the consumer economy. Consumer debt becomes a problem, however, when it becomes so large that consumers cannot repay it. Some of this debt is insured by the government, such as certain home loans in the U.S., and when borrowers default, public funds are used to pay the lender. In some cases, individuals who cannot pay their debts seek legal protection by claiming bankruptcy. In these cases, the companies that provided the goods and services to that individual may never be paid, creating a loss.

COMPETENCY 3.0   KNOWLEDGE OF POLITICAL SCIENCE

Skill 3.1   Identify the features and principles of the United States Constitution, including its amendments, the separation of powers, checks and balances, and federalism.

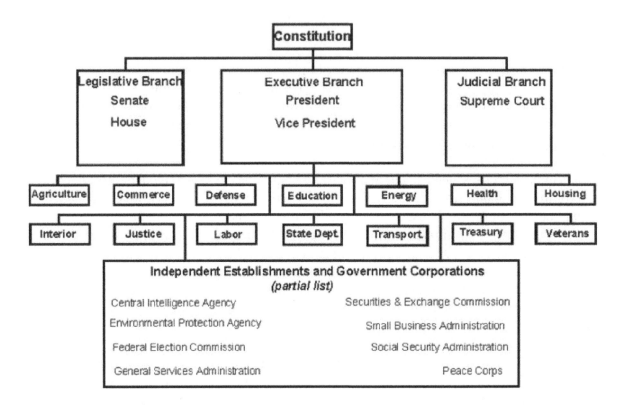

The terms "civil liberties" and "civil rights" are often used interchangeably, but there are some fine distinctions between the two terms. The term civil liberties is more often used to imply that the state has a positive role to play in assuring that all its citizens will have equal protection and justice under the law with equal opportunities to exercise their privileges of citizenship and to participate fully in the life of the nation, regardless of race, religion, sex, color or creed. The term civil rights is used more often to refer to rights that may be described as privileges and rights guaranteed by the United States Constitution and subsequent amendments and laws regarding citizens' liberties. Although the term "civil rights" has been identified with the ideal of equality and the term "civil liberties" with the idea of freedom, the two concepts are really inseparable and interacting. Equality implies the proper ordering of liberty in a society so that one individual's freedom does not infringe on the rights of others.

The beginnings of civil liberties and the idea of civil rights in the United States go back to the ideas of the ancient Greeks to the experience of the early struggle for civil rights against the British and the very philosophies that led people to come to the New World in the first place. Religious freedom, political freedom, and the right to live one's life as one sees fit are basic to the American ideal. These were embodied in the ideas expressed in the Declaration of Independence and the Constitution.

Within a few months after the adoption of the Articles of Confederation, it became apparent that there were serious defects in the system of government established for the new republic. There was a need for changes that would create a national government with adequate powers to replace the Confederation, which was actually only a league of sovereign states. In 1786, an effort to regulate interstate commerce ended in what is known as the Annapolis Convention. Because only five states were represented, this Convention was not able to accomplish definitive results. The debates, however, made it clear that foreign and interstate commerce could not be regulated by a government with as little authority as the government established by the Confederation. Congress was, therefore, asked to call a convention to provide a constitution that would address the emerging needs of the new nation.

The convention met under the presidency of George Washington, with 55 of the 65 appointed members present. A constitution was written in four months. The Constitution of the United States is the fundamental law of the republic. It is a precise, formal, written document of the extraordinary, or supreme, type of constitution. The founders of the Union established it as the highest governmental authority. There is no national power superior to it.

The foundations were so broadly laid as to provide for the expansion of national life and to make it an instrument that would last for all time. To maintain its stability, the framers created a difficult process for making any changes to it. No amendment can become valid until it is ratified by three-fourths of all of the states. The British system of government was part of the basis of the final document. But significant changes were necessary to meet the needs of a partnership of states that were tied together as a single federation, yet sovereign in their own local affairs. This constitution established a system of government that was unique and advanced far beyond other systems of its day.

There were, to be sure, differences of opinion. The compromises that resolved these conflicts are reflected in the final document. The first point of disagreement and compromise was related to the Presidency. Some wanted a strong, centralized, individual authority. Others feared autocracy or the growth of monarchy. The compromise was to give the President broad powers but to limit the amount of time, through term of office, that any individual could exercise that power. The power to make appointments and to conclude treaties was controlled by the requirement of the consent of the Senate.

The second conflict was between large and small states. The large states wanted power proportionate to their voting strength; the small states opposed this plan. The compromise was that all states should have equal voting power in the Senate, but to make the membership of the House of Representatives determined in proportion to population.

The third conflict was about slavery. The compromise was that (a) fugitive slaves should be returned by states to which they might flee for refuge, and (b) no law would be passed for 20 years prohibiting the importation of slaves.

The fourth major area of conflict was how the President would be chosen. One side of the disagreement argued for election by direct vote of the people. The other side thought the President should be chosen by Congress. One group feared the ignorance of the people; the other feared the power of a small group of people. The compromise was the Electoral College. Federalism is the division or allocation of power between a central government and local or state units of government. Under federalism, each government unit has specific powers which may not be shared but also has powers that are shared with other units of government. For example the U.S. Constitution provides that Congress shall have certain powers, such as enacting bankruptcy legislation, which are specific powers that are not shared. Examples of shared power under federalism are the power to tax and the authority to maintain roads.

The Constitution binds the states in a governmental unity in everything that affects the welfare of all. At the same time, it recognizes the right of the people of each state to independence of action in matters that relate only to them. Since the federal Constitution is the law of the land, all other laws must conform to it.

The debates conducted during the Constitutional Congress represent the issues and the arguments that led to the compromises in the final document. The debates also reflect the concerns of the Founding Fathers that the rights of the people be protected from abrogation by the government itself and the determination that no branch of government should have enough power to override the others. There is, therefore, a system of checks and balances.

The United States Constitution provides for separation of powers in the federal government. The three branches of government at the federal level, the Executive, the Legislative and the Judicial branches have different purposes and powers, and the Constitution identifies the powers as outlined below:

Legislative – Article 1 of the Constitution establishes the legislative, or lawmaking, branch of the government called Congress. It is made up of two houses, the House of Representatives and the Senate. Voters in all states elect the members who serve in each respective House of Congress. The legislative branch is responsible for making laws, raising and printing money, regulating trade, establishing the postal service and federal courts, approving the President's appointments, declaring war, and supporting the armed forces. The Congress also has the power to change the Constitution itself and to impeach (bring charges against) the President. Charges for impeachment are brought by the House of Representatives and are then tried in the Senate.

Executive – Article 2 of the Constitution creates the Executive branch of the government. This branch is headed by the President who leads the country, recommends new laws, and can veto bills passed by the legislative branch. As the chief of state, the President is responsible for carrying out the laws of the country and the treaties and declarations of war passed by the legislative branch. The President also appoints federal judges and is Commander-in-Chief of the military. Other members of the executive branch include the Vice President, who is also elected, and various cabinet members and others the President might appoint: ambassadors, presidential advisors, members of the armed forces, and other civil servants of government agencies, departments, and bureaus. Though the President appoints them, most of the positions must be approved by the legislative branch.

Judicial – Article 3 of the Constitution establishes the judicial branch of government headed by the Supreme Court. The Supreme Court has the power to rule that a law passed by the legislature or an act of the executive branch is illegal and unconstitutional. Citizens, businesses, and government officials can ask the Supreme Court to review a decision made in a lower court if someone believes that the ruling by a judge is unconstitutional. The judicial branch also includes lower federal courts known as federal district courts that have been established by the Congress. These courts try lawbreakers and review cases referred from other courts.

The Federalist Papers were written to win popular support for the new proposed Constitution. In these publications the debates of the Congress and the concerns of the founding fathers were made available to the people of the nation. In addition to providing an explanation of the underlying philosophies and concerns of the Constitution and the compromises that were made, the Federalist Papers conducted what has frequently been called the most effective marketing and public relations campaign in human history.

All these ideas found their final expression in the United States Constitution's first ten amendments, known as the Bill of Rights. In 1789, the first Congress passed these first amendments and by December 1791, three-fourths of the states at that time had ratified them. The Bill of Rights protects certain liberties and basic rights. James Madison who wrote the amendments said that the Bill of Rights does not give Americans these rights. People, Madison said, already have these rights. They are natural rights that belong to all human beings. The Bill of Rights simply prevents the governments from taking away these rights.

They are in brief:

1. Freedom of speech, press, assembly, and religion.
2. Right to keep and bear arms.
3. No quartering of soldiers in homes without consent
4. Right against unreasonable search and seizures.
5. Right against self-incrimination and being tried more than once for the same allegations.
6. Right to speedy trial
7. Right to jury trial for civil actions.
8. No cruel or unusual punishment allowed.
9. These rights shall not deny other rights the people enjoy.
10. Powers not mentioned in the Constitution shall be retained by the states or the people.

The Bill of Rights has been interpreted in different ways at different times by different interpreters. Constitutional amendments may be interpreted very strictly or very loosely. The terms of the amendments may be defined in different ways to enfranchise or to disenfranchise individuals or groups of persons.

Example: During and after Reconstruction, the interpretation of the Bill of Rights that did not include blacks in the definition of a citizen necessitated the passage of the 14th and 15th Amendments. The interpretation of these amendments was broadly interpreted by the Supreme Court in the Plessey case, resulting in the establishment of the doctrine of "separate but equal." It was not until 50 years later, in the case of Brown v. Board of Education, that a narrower interpretation resulted in a Supreme Court decision that reversed the previous interpretation.

Skill 3.2   Identify the functions of U.S. political institutions, including the executive, legislative, and judicial branches.

In the United States, the three branches of the federal government, Executive, Legislative, and Judicial, divide up the powers thus:

Legislative – Article 1 of the Constitution establishes the legislative or law-making branch of the government called the Congress. It is made up of two houses, the House of Representatives and the Senate. Voters in all states elect the members who serve in Congress. The legislative branch is responsible for making laws, raising and printing money, regulating trade, establishing the postal service and federal courts, approving the President's appointments, declaring war and supporting the armed forces. The Congress also has the power to change the Constitution itself, and to impeach (bring charges against) the President. Charges for impeachment are brought by the House of Representatives, and are then tried in the Senate.

Executive – Article 2 of the Constitution creates the Executive branch of the government, headed by the President, who leads the country, recommends new laws, and can veto bills passed by the legislative branch. As the chief of state, the President is responsible for carrying out the laws of the country and the treaties and declarations of war passed by the legislative branch. The President also appoints federal judges and is Commander-in-Chief of all the branches of the military. Other members of the Executive branch include the Vice President, also elected, and various cabinet members as he might appoint: ambassadors, presidential advisors, members of the armed forces, and other appointed and civil servants of government agencies, departments, and bureaus. Though the President appoints them, they usually must be approved by the legislative branch.

Judicial – Article 3 of the Constitution establishes the judicial branch of government headed by the Supreme Court. The Supreme Court has the power to rule that a law passed by the legislature or an act of the Executive branch is illegal and unconstitutional. Citizens, businesses, and government officials can, in an appeal capacity, ask the Supreme Court to review a decision made in a lower court. The Judicial branch also includes the lower courts known as federal district courts that have been established by the Congress. These courts try lawbreakers and review cases referred from other courts.

Skill 3.3   Identify the functions of voter behavior, political parties, interest groups, public opinion, and mass media on the electoral process in the United States.

In regard to the American political system, it is important to realize that political parties are never mentioned in the United States Constitution. In fact, George Washington himself warned against the creation of "factions" in American politics that cause "jealousies and false alarms" and the damage they could cause to the body politic. Thomas Jefferson echoed this warning, yet he would come to lead a party himself.

Americans had good reason to fear the emergence of political parties. They had witnessed how parties worked in Great Britain. Parties, called "factions" in Britain (thus Washington's warning) were made up of a few people who schemed to win favors from the government. They were more interested in their own personal profit and advantage than in the public good. Thus, the new American leaders were committed to keeping factions from forming. It was, ironically, disagreements between two of Washington's chief advisors, Thomas Jefferson and Alexander Hamilton, which spurred the formation of the first political parties in the newly formed United States of America.

The two parties that developed through the early 1790s were led by Jefferson as the Secretary of State and Alexander Hamilton as the Secretary of the Treasury. Jefferson and Hamilton were different in many ways. Not the least was their views on what should be the proper form of government of the United States. This difference helped to shape the parties that formed around them.

Hamilton wanted the federal government to be stronger than the state governments. Jefferson believed that the state governments should be stronger. Hamilton supported the creation of the first Bank of the United States. Jefferson opposed it because he felt that it gave too much power to wealthy investors who would help run it. Jefferson interpreted the Constitution strictly; he argued that nowhere did the Constitution give the federal government the power to create a national bank. Hamilton interpreted the Constitution much more loosely. He pointed out that the Constitution gave Congress the power to make all laws "necessary and proper" to carry out its duties. He reasoned that since Congress had the right to collect taxes, then Congress had the right to create a bank. Hamilton wanted the government to encourage economic growth. He favored the growth of trade, manufacturing, and the rise of cities as the necessary parts of economic growth. He favored the business leaders and mistrusted the common people. Jefferson believed that the common people, especially the farmers, were the backbone of the nation. He thought that the rise of big cities and manufacturing would corrupt American life.

At first, Hamilton and Jefferson had their disagreements only in private. But when Congress began to pass many of Hamilton's ideas and programs, Jefferson and James Madison decided to organize support for their own views. They moved quietly and very cautiously in the beginning. In 1791, they went to New York telling people that they were going to just study its wildlife. Actually, Jefferson was more interested in meeting with several important New York politicians such as its governor George Clinton and Aaron Burr, a strong critic of Hamilton.

Jefferson asked Clinton and Burr to help defeat Hamilton's program by getting New Yorkers to vote for Jefferson's supporters in the next election. Before long, leaders in other states began to organize support for either Jefferson or Hamilton. Jefferson's supporters called themselves Democratic-Republicans. Hamilton and his supporters were known as Federalists because they favored a strong federal government. The Federalists had the support of the merchants and ship owners in the Northeast and some planters in the South. Small farmers, craft workers, and some of the wealthier landowners supported Jefferson and the Democratic-Republicans.

Newspapers, then as now, influenced the growth of political parties. Newspaper publishers and editors took sides on the issues. Thus, from the very beginning, American newspapers and each new branch of the media have played an important role in helping to shape public opinion.

By the time Washington retired from office in 1796, the new political parties would come to play an important role in choosing a successor. Each party was putting up its own candidates for office. The election of 1796 was the first one in which political parties played a role, a role that, for better or worse, they have continued to play in various forms for all of American history. By the beginning of the 1800s, the Federalist Party, torn by internal divisions, began suffering a decline. With the election in 1800 of Thomas Jefferson to President, and after its leader Alexander Hamilton was killed in 1804 in a duel with Aaron Burr, the Federalist Party began to collapse. By 1816, after losing a string of important elections (Jefferson was reelected in 1804, and James Madison, a Democratic-Republican was elected in 1808), the Federalist Party ceased to be an effective political force and soon passed off the national stage.

By the late 1820s, new political parties had grown up. The Democratic-Republican Party, or simply the Republican Party, had been the major party for many years, but differences within it about the direction the country was headed in caused a split after 1824. Those who favored strong national growth took the name Whigs after a similar party in Great Britain and united around then-President John Quincy Adams. Many business people in the Northeast as well as some wealthy planters in the South supported it.

Those who favored slower growth and were more oriented toward workers and farmers went on to form the new Democratic Party, with Andrew Jackson being its first leader as well as becoming its first President.

In the mid-1850s, the slavery issue was beginning to heat up, and in 1854, those opposed to slavery, the Whigs, and some Northern Democrats opposed to slavery, united to form the Republican Party. Before the Civil War, the Democratic Party was more heavily represented in the South and was thus pro-slavery for the most part.

Thus, by the time of the Civil War, the present form of the major political parties 'had been formed. Though there would sometimes be drastic changes in ideology and platforms over the years, no other political parties would manage to gain enough strength to seriously challenge the "Big Two" parties.

In fact, they have shown themselves to adapt to the changing times. In many instances, they have managed to shut out other parties by simply adapting their platforms, such as in the 1930s during the Great Depression and in the years preceding it. The Democratic Party adapted much of the Socialist Party platform and, under Franklin Roosevelt, put much of it into effect thus managing to eliminate it as any serious threat. Since the Civil War, no other political party has managed to gain enough support to either elect substantial members to Congress or elect a President. Some have come closer than others, but barring any unforeseen circumstances, the absolute monopoly on national political debate se ems very secure in the hands of the Republican and Democratic parties.

Time will tell if this is to remain so. For history and political science both teach us that the American people are quite willing to change their support from one area or group to another— especially if it means a better way of doing things or will give them more opportunity and freedoms. As conservative as some might think Americans have become, there has always been—and likely will always be— something of the revolutionary spirit about them.

Elections

The most basic way for citizens to participate in the political process is to vote. Since the passing of the 23rd Amendment in 1965, U.S. citizens who are at least 18 years old are eligible to vote. Elections are held at regular intervals at all levels of government, allowing citizens to weigh in on local matters as well as   those of national scope.

Citizens wishing to engage in the political process to a greater degree have several paths open, such as participating in local government. Counties, states, and sometimes even neighborhoods are governed by locally-elected boards or councils that meet publicly. Citizens are usually able to address these boards, bringing their concerns and expressing their opinions on matters being considered. Citizens may even wish to stand for local election and join a governing board or seek support for higher office.

Supporting a political party is another means by which citizens can participate in the political process. Political parties endorse certain platforms that express general social and political goals, and support member candidates in election campaigns. Political parties make use of much volunteer labor, with supporters making telephone calls, distributing printed material, and campaigning for the party's causes and candidates. Political parties solicit donations to support their efforts as well. Contributing money to a political party is another form of participation citizens can undertake.

Another form of political activity is to support an issue-related political group. Several political groups work actively to sway public opinion on various issues or on behalf of a segment of American society. These groups may have representatives who meet with state and federal legislators to "lobby" them, that is, to provide them with information on an issue and persuade them to take action favorable to the lobbyists' point of view.

Public and Private Interest

In a civil society, people are certainly free to pursue business interests both private and public. Private activities are less regulated than public ones, but public activities are not discouraged or dissuaded, as long as they don't violate laws or invade other people's rights.

In America and in other countries as well, a person has the right to pursue any kind of business strategy he or she wants. The age of Internet advertising and marketing has created opportunities abound for new and different businesses. By and large, as long as these businesses don't sell or advertise illegal products or practices, the business owner is left alone by society and its government. If the business succeeds, the business owner is free to reap the rewards of his success; if the business fails, then the business owner will certainly suffer the consequences of that failure. How public that person wants to make his or her business is a personal decision. The state and federal governments make it a practice of encouraging businesses to succeed, granting them money and time to make that money back, through loans and grants, Most businesses of a significant size are required to file business announcement papers with various local, state, and federal agencies; all businesses are required, of course, to pay taxes on any income that they might earn.

Rather than discourage people from starting businesses, the American government and its various associated entities actually encourage such endeavors. Prospective business owners can find whole libraries of information encouraging them and guiding them through the sometimes rigorous practice of starting a business. Entire organizations exist just to answer questions about this process.

It's not just business that American society encourages. Americans are also free and encouraged to join non-business organizations both public and private. America is a land full of groups—religious groups, political groups, social groups, and economic groups. All these groups meet in public and in private, and the people who belong to these groups are free to associate with any groups that they choose, again as long as the practices of those groups are not illegal or harmful to other people.

Religious participation is a practice that finds extraordinary protection under the law. The First Amendment guarantees every American the right to worship as he or she sees fit, without fear of reprisal by the government. Religious organizations, however, do not, for the most part, receive funding from governments to support their efforts. The First Amendment also denies the government the right to establish a religion, meaning that it can favor no one religion over others. Entities such as parochial schools, which provide both education and religious training, routinely have to seek funding in places other than the federal or state governments.

First Amendment gives the American people the right to peaceable assembly. This certainly describes the meetings of most social organizations in America, from clubs to interest groups to veterans' organizations. Groups, made up of people with similar interests or experiences, may come together on a regular basis to discuss those interests and experiences and to pursue a joint appreciation. Striking workers, civil rights advocates, anti-war demonstrators and Ku Klux Klan marchers have all taken to the streets and sidewalks in protest or in support of their causes. There must a "clear and present danger" or an "imminent incitement of lawlessness" before government officials may restrict free-assembly rights.

One very public interest that many people pursue is politics. Theoretically, anyone who is a U.S. citizen can get on a ballot somewhere running for something. Participation in politics is encouraged in America, and more and more people are getting involved—at the local, state, and federal levels—all the time. The federal and state governments, in particular, will provide money and opportunities for candidates who reach certain thresholds of monetary support on their own.

The Media

A free press is essential to maintaining responsibility and civic-mindedness in government and in the rest of society. The broadcast, print, and electronic media in America serve as societal and governmental watchdogs, showcasing for the rest of America and for the world what kinds of brilliant and terrible things the rich, powerful, and elected are doing.

First and foremost, the media reports on the actions taken and encouraged by leaders of the government. In many cases, these actions are common knowledge. Policy debates, discussions on controversial issues, struggles against foreign powers in economic and wartime endeavors—all are fodder for media reports. The First Amendment guarantees media in America the right to report on such events, and the media reporters take full advantage of that right and privilege in striving not only to inform the American public, but also to keep the governmental leaders in check.

Owners of large companies and charities and recognizable figures in popular entertainment are continually under scrutiny for signs of questionable actions or behavior. In the same way that lawmakers are responsible for public legislative policy, many company owners are responsible for public economic policy. If a corporation is stealing money from its employees or shareholders, then those employees and shareholders and the American public at large need to know about it. Such reporting is not only informative, but also may lead to indictments, prosecutions, and jail terms for the perpetrators of such economic crimes.

Public officials will hire one person, a department of employees, or perhaps an entire business to conduct public relations, efforts intended to make the lawmakers look good in the eyes of their constituents. A public relations person or firm will have as its overreaching goal the happiness of the hiring client. They will gladly write press releases, arrange media events (including tours of schools or soup kitchens), and do everything else to keep their employer's name in the public eye in a good way. This includes making the lawmaker's position on important issues known to the public. Especially controversial issues will be embraced by lawmakers, and those lawmakers will want their constituents to know how they intend to vote those issues. It's a good idea to find out what the constituents think about these issues since the fastest way to get bad publicity or replaced at re-election time is to ignore the weight of public opinion.

Skill 3.4   Identify the elements and functions of state and local governments in the United States.

Powers delegated to the   federal government
1. To tax
2. To borrow and coin money
3. To establish postal service
4. To grant patents and copyrights
5. To regulate interstate & foreign commerce
6. To establish courts
7. To declare war
8. To raise and support the armed forces

Powers reserved to the states
1. To regulate intrastate trade
2. To establish local governments
3. To protect general welfare
4. To protect life and property
5. To ratify amendments
6. To conduct elections
7. To make state and local laws

9. To govern territories
10. To define and punish felonies and piracy on the high seas
11. To fix standards of weights and measures
12. To conduct foreign affairs

Concurrent powers of the federal government and states

1. Both Congress and the states may tax
2. Both may borrow money
3. Both may charter banks and corporations
4. Both may establish courts
5. Both may make and enforce laws
6. Both may take property for public purposes
7. Both may spend money to provide for the public welfare

Implied powers of the federal government

1. To establish banks or other corporations implied from delegated powers to tax, borrow, and regulate commerce
2. To spend money for roads, schools, health, insurance, etc., implied from powers to establish post roads, to tax to provide for general welfare and defense, and to regulate commerce
3. To create military academies, implied from powers to raise and support an armed force
4. To locate and generate sources of power and sell surplus, implied from powers to dispose of government property, commerce, and war powers
5. To assist and regulate agriculture, implied from power to tax and spend for general welfare and regulate commerce

Local governments vary widely across the country, although none of them has a judicial branch per se. Some local governments consist of a city council, of which the mayor is a member and has limited powers; in other cities, the mayor is the head of the government, and the city council consists of the chief lawmakers. Local governments have less strict requirements for people running for office than do the state and federal governments.

State governments are mirror images of the federal government, with a few important exceptions: Governors are not technically commanders-in-chief of armed forces although they can call the National Guard into action; state supreme court decisions can be appealed to federal courts; terms of state representatives and senators vary; judges, even of the state supreme courts, are elected by popular vote; governors and legislators have term limits that vary by state. Louisiana, unlike all other states operates under the Napoleonic Code; in all other states, the laws are based on English common laws.

Skill 3.5   Analyze the guiding concepts, principles, and effects of U.S. foreign policy.

There are many theories of international relations, all of which seek to describe how sovereign countries interact, or should interact, with one another. Four of the primary schools of thought in international theory are Realism, Liberalism, Institutionalism and Constructivism.

Realism is an international theory that holds the nation-state as the basic unit and recognizes no international authority above individual nations. Realism is based on the assumption that nations act only in their own self-interest to preserve their own security. Realism holds that international relations are based on the relative military and economic power between nations, and that nations are inherently aggressive.

Liberalism is often thought of as being opposed to realism in philosophy. Instead of assuming that states only act in their own interest, liberalism allows for the cooperation of several states working in common interest. Instead of the Realist belief that states act based on their capabilities, Liberalism holds that states act based on their preferences. The term Liberalism was first used critically by Realist thinkers to describe the international theories of Woodrow Wilson.

Institutionalism is a theory of international relations that holds that there is a structure to the interactions of nations that determines how they will act. The rules that nations follow in making international decisions are called institutions. Institutions can give structure, distribute power, and provide incentives for international cooperation.

Constructivism is similar to Liberalism in philosophy but recognizes the role that ideas and perceptions play in international relations. Constructivism makes note of traditional relations between countries and their relative goals, identities and perceived threats. Constructivism recognizes, for instance, that a country building up its military is likely to be taken as more of a threat by that country's traditional antagonists than by its allies.

In practice, international relations are often conducted through diplomacy. Nations that formally recognize one another, station a group of diplomats, led by an ambassador, in one another's countries to provide formal representation on international matters. Diplomats convey official information on the policies and positions of their home countries to the host countries where they are stationed. Diplomats are also involved in negotiating international agreements on issues such as trade, environmental issues, and conflict resolutions. Countries sometimes engage in informal diplomacy between private individuals when they wish to discuss common issues without taking official positions.

Diplomacy also takes place within international organizations such as the United Nations. Member nations send diplomatic representation to the U.N. and have input into forming international policy. While member countries agree to abide by U.N. resolutions as a condition of membership, in practice there is often dissent. The U.N. has the ability to impose economic and other sanctions on its members for failing to follow its decisions, but other types of enforcement have been problematic. The U.N. has the ability to raise military forces from its member countries; however, these forces have historically been limited to peacekeeping missions, not active military campaigns.

Skill 3.6   Compare various political systems in terms of elements, structures, and functions.

Forms of Government are listed below:

Anarchism - Political movement believing in the elimination of all government and its replacement by a cooperative community of individuals. Sometimes it has involved political violence such as assassinations of important political or governmental figures. The historical banner of the movement is a black flag.

Communism - A belief, as well as a political system, characterized by the ideology of class conflict and revolution, one party state and dictatorship, repressive police apparatus, and government ownership of the means of production and distribution of goods and services. Communism supports a revolutionary ideology preaching the eventual overthrow of all other political orders and the establishment of one world communist government. The historical banner of the movement is a red flag with a variation of stars and hammer and sickles, representing the various types of workers.

Dictatorship - The rule by an individual or small elite group of individuals (oligarchy) that centralizes all political control in itself. A dictator may enforce his will with a terrorist police force.

Fascism - A belief, as well as a political system, opposed ideologically to Communism, though similar in basic structure with a one-party state, centralized political control, and a repressive police system. It however tolerates private ownership of the means of production though it maintains tight overall control. Central to its belief is the idolization of the leader, a "Cult of the Personality," and most often an expansionist ideology. Examples have been German Nazism and Italian Fascism.

Monarchy - The rule of a nation by a monarch (a non-elected, usually hereditary leader), a king, queen, emperor, empress. It may or may not be accompanied by some measure of democratic open institutions and elections at various levels. A modern example is Great Britain, where it is called a constitutional monarchy.

Parliamentary System - A system of government with a legislature that usually involves a multiplicity of political parties--and often coalition politics. There is division between the head of state and head of government. Head of government is usually known as a Prime Minister who is usually the head of the largest party. The head of government and cabinet usually both sit and vote in the parliament. Head of state is most often an elected president (though in the case of a constitutional monarchy like Great Britain, the sovereign may take the place of a president as head of state). A government may fall when a majority in parliament votes "no confidence" in the government.

Presidential System - A system of government with a legislature can involve few or many political parties with no division between head of state and head of government. The President serves in both capacities. The President is elected either by direct or indirect election. A president and cabinet usually do not sit or vote in the legislature, and the president may or may not be the head of the largest political party. A president can thus rule even without a majority in the legislature. He can only be removed from office before an election for major infractions of the law.

Socialism - Political belief and system in which the state takes a guiding role in the national economy and provides extensive social services to its population. It may or may not own outright means of production, but even where it does not, it exercises tight control. It usually promotes democracy (Democratic Socialism), though the heavy state involvement produces excessive bureaucracy and usually inefficiency. Taken to an extreme, it may lead to Communism as government control increases and democratic practice decreases. Ideologically the two movements are very similar in both belief and practice, as Socialists also preach the superiority of their system to all others and that it will become the eventual natural order. It is also considered for that reason a variant of Marxism. It has used a red flag as a symbol.

The differences between democracy vs. totalitarianism and authoritarianism are an easy contrast to draw. The differences between totalitarianism and authoritarianism are not as readily apparent. Authoritarianism exists on different levels and can exist in all forms of government, at least to some extent. In the United States, for example, authoritarianism exists on some points for national security. But an authoritarian government is usually undemocratic, and the rulers do not need the consent of those they are governing. Totalitarianism (derived from the word total) is the extreme form of authoritarianism. Totalitarianism depends on authoritarianism to function. While an authoritarian regime will tolerate some pluralism; the totalitarian regime will not. The main difference between totalitarianism and authoritarianism is that totalitarianism is guided by an ideology.

Thus the totalitarian government sees itself as having a legitimate concern with all levels of human existence—not only in regard to speech or press, but even to social and religious institutions. It tries to achieve a complete conformity to its ideals. As Benito Mussolini said: "Nothing outside of the state, nothing instead of the state."

Regimes that conform to the authoritarianism can be seen throughout history. This model can be seen in the history of Central and South America, where regimes, usually representing the interests of the upper classes, came to power and instituted dictatorships that seek to concentrate all political power in a few hands. The Catholic Church in this region became an institution of opposition to the state authority.

Democracy is a much more familiar system to us because in the United States, it is the system under which we live. The term comes from the Greek "for the rule of the people." The two most prevalent types are direct and indirect democracy. Direct democracy functions when the population involved is relatively small and will usually involve all the voters in a given area coming together to vote and decide on issues that will affect them, such as the town meeting in New England. An indirect democracy involves much larger areas and populations and involves the sending of representatives to a legislative body to vote on issues affecting the people. Such a system can be comprised of a Presidential or Parliamentary system. In the United States, we follow an indirect—or representative—democracy.

Skill 3.7   Analyze the key elements of U.S. citizenship, including rights, privileges, and responsibilities.

Rights, privileges, and responsibilities are elements of U.S. citizenship. One privilege is the ability to participate in one's own government. The most basic form of participation is voting, and the responsibility that is connected with voting is to be informed before voting. Another privilege is that citizens are eligible to run for public office. Along with this privilege comes the responsibility to represent the electors as fairly as possible and to perform the duties expected of a government representative.

In the United States, citizens are guaranteed the right to free speech; the right to express an opinion on public issues. In turn, citizens have the responsibility to allow others to speak freely. At the community level, this might mean speaking at a city council hearing while allowing others with different or opposing viewpoints to have their say without interruption or comment.

The U.S. Constitution also guarantees freedom of religion. This means that the government may not impose an official religion on its citizens, and that people are free to practice their religion. The U.S. Constitution also guarantees that all citizens be treated equally by the law. In addition, federal and state laws make it a crime to discriminate against citizens based on their sex, race, religion and other factors. To ensure that all people are treated equally, citizens have the responsibility to follow these laws.

The terms "civil liberties" and "civil rights" are often used interchangeably, but there are some fine distinctions between the two terms. The term "civil liberties" refers to how people's freedoms are protected from government's abuse of power with restrictions set on how much that government can interfere with the lives of the people. The American Civil Liberties Union (ACLU) defends certain "civil liberties" that some do not believe should be civil liberties. "Civil rights" identifies equality and includes laws that prohibit private businesses, etc., from discriminating against individuals.

Although the term "civil rights" has thus been identified with the ideal of equality and the term "civil liberties" with the idea of freedom, the two concepts are really inseparable and interacting. Equality implies the proper ordering of liberty in a society so that one individual's freedom does not infringe on the rights of others.

The beginnings of civil liberties and the idea of civil rights in the United States go back to the ideas of the Greeks. The experience of the early British struggles for civil rights and to the very philosophies that led people to come to the New World in the first place. Religious freedom, political freedom, and the right to live one's life as one sees fit are basic to the American ideal. These were embodied in the ideas expressed in the Declaration of Independence and the Constitution.

All these ideas found their final expression in the United States Constitution's first ten amendments, known as the Bill of Rights. In 1789, the first Congress passed these first amendments and by December 1791, three-fourths of the states at that time had ratified them. The Bill of Rights protects certain liberties and basic rights. James Madison expressed that the majority rules the minority but that the minority needs to be protected against the majority. The Bill of Rights protects people and prevents government and others from taking away these rights.

To summarize:

The first amendment guarantees the basic rights of freedom of religion, freedom of speech, freedom of the press, and freedom of assembly.

The next three amendments came out of the colonists' struggle with Great Britain. For example, the third amendment prevents Congress from forcing citizens to keep troops in their homes. Before the Revolution, Great Britain tried to coerce the colonists to house soldiers. The second amendment guarantees the right to bear arms, and the fourth amendment protects against unreasonable search.

Amendments five through eight protect citizens who are accused of crimes and are brought to trial. Every citizen has the right to due process of law (due process being that the government must follow the same fair rules for everyone brought to trial. These rules include the right to a trial by an impartial jury, the right to be defended by a lawyer, and the right to a speedy trial.

The last two amendments limit the powers of the federal government to those that are expressly granted in the Constitution; thus, any rights not expressly mentioned in the Constitution belong to the states or to the people.

In regards to specific guarantees:

Freedom of Religion: Religious freedom has not been seriously threatened in the United States. The policy of the government has been guided by the premise that church and state should be separate. But when religious practices have been at cross purposes with prevailing attitudes or mores in the nation at particular times, restrictions have been placed on certain practices. Some of these have been restrictions against the practice of polygamy that is supported by certain religious groups. The idea of animal sacrifice that is promoted by some religious beliefs is generally prohibited. The use of mind-altering, illegal substances that some use in religious rituals has been restricted. In the United States, all recognized religious institutions are tax-exempt in following the idea of separation of church and state. Unfortunately, there have been quasi-religious groups that have tried to take advantage of this fact. All of these issues continue, and most likely will continue to occupy both political and legal considerations for some time to come.

Freedom of Speech, Press, and Assembly: These rights historically have been given wide latitude in their practices although there have been instances when these rights are limited for various reasons. The classic limitation, for instance, in regards to freedom of speech was stated by Supreme Justice Oliver Wendell Holmes: "The question in every case is whether the words used are used in such circumstances and are of such a nature as to create a clear and present danger that they will bring about the substantive evils that Congress has a right to prevent." Under Brandenburg v. Ohio, it was ruled that government cannot punish inflammatory speech unless it is directed to inciting and likely to incite imminent lawless action.

There is also a prohibition against slander, the intentional stating of a deliberate falsehood against one party by another, and libel, the printing of a known falsehood. In times of national emergency, various restrictions have been placed on the rights of press, speech—and sometimes assembly. Pornography is subject to law.

America has a number of organizations that put themselves out as champions of the fight for civil liberties and civil rights in this country, the ACLU for example. Much criticism, however, has been raised at times against these groups as to whether or not they are really protecting rights or liberties or are attempting to create "new" rights.

"Rights" come with a measure of responsibility and respect for the public order, all of which must be taken into consideration.

Overall, the American experience has been one of exemplary conduct regarding the protection of individual rights, but there too has been a lag in its practice— notably the refusal to grant full and equal rights to blacks, the very fact of their enslavement, and the second class status of women for much of American history. Yet, the country has proved itself to be largely able to change when it has not lived up to its stated ideals.

Though much effort and suffering accompanied the civil rights struggle, for example, in the end the struggle did succeed in changing the basic foundation of society profoundly. America continues its commitment to a strong tradition of freedom and liberty that was, and is, the underlying feature of American society.

How best to move forward ensuring civil liberties and civil rights for all continues to dominate the national debate. Recently, issues that seem to revolve not around individual rights, but what has been called "group rights" have been raised. At the forefront of the debate is whether some specific remedies including affirmative action, quotas, gerrymandering (redistricting), and various other forms of preferential treatment are actually fair or just as bad as the ills they are supposed to cure. At the present no easy answers seem to be forthcoming. It is a testament to the American system that it has shown itself able to enter into these debates to find solutions and then tends to come out stronger.

The fact that the United States has the longest single constitutional history in the modern era is just one reason to be optimistic about the future of American liberty.

COMPETENCY 4.0 KNOWLEDGE OF WORLD HISTORY

Skill 4.1 Identify characteristics of prehistoric cultures and early civilizations (e.g., Mesopotamian Egyptian, Indus Valley, Chinese).

Prehistory is defined as that time in the age of humans that came before written records. Because different cultures developed writing at different times, it is not a clearly defined period worldwide, but cuneiform, one of the earliest known systems of writing, appeared in Sumeria around 3200 BC. As far as we know, Egyptian hieroglyphics first appeared around the same time.

The prehistoric and ancient human eras are divided into three ages, each named after the main tool-making technology that dominated: the Stone Age, the Bronze Age and the Iron Age. In the earliest period of the Stone Age, the Paleolithic period, humans lived in improvised shelters such as caves and used crude tools. During the Mesolithic, or middle stone age, these tools were improved over time into axes, spears, the bow and arrow, boats and baskets. In the latest period of the Stone Age, the Neolithic, humans moved from hunting and gathering to agriculture as a way of life. Loose bands of people who had formed into tribes during the Mesolithic now began to think of themselves as larger groups of a common ethnicity. As working of copper and bronze developed, this signaled the beginning of the Bronze Age. The first major cities appeared, and people began to think of themselves as members of a larger state or nation. Writing and record-keeping evolved, and the historic age began.

About this time, around 3000 BC, two kingdoms in northeast Africa united creating the state of Egypt—the Egyptian unification. Egyptian advances in surveying and mathematics allowed them to lay out large building projects, such as large irrigation systems and the famous pyramids of Giza. Egyptians developed surgical skills and learned to set broken bones. The art of mummification was perfected. The Egyptian culture remained remarkably unchanged for nearly 3000 years, until Alexander the Great conquered the region in 332 bringing it under Greek influence. The Greeks held sway in Egypt until 30 BC, and this period is called the Hellenistic Age. Then Egypt became part of the Roman Empire.

About 500 years after the unification of Egypt, the great city of Ur was founded by the Sumerians of Mesopotamia, in what is now part of Iraq. The Sumerians were an agricultural people whose advances in irrigation allowed for the development of cities, where some 90 percent of them lived. Cuneiform writing emerged among the Sumerians, and they are generally credited with having invented the wheel. Sumerians dominated the Mesopotamian region until around 1900 BC when Amorites from the east gained control of the region and the city-state of Babylon grew in Babylon came to full power in the region under the king Hammurabi around 1780 BC. Hammurabi provided stability and order to the area, ruling under a set of laws now known as the Code of Hammurabi. Culture and trade flourished, and Babylonia–withstanding several changes in rulers–continued to thrive as a nation until the twelfth century BC.

As the glory of Babylonia was fading, the Canaanites were thriving along the eastern coast of the Mediterranean Sea. One group of Canaanites, the Phoenicians, came to prominence as a major seagoing, people, carrying their culture along trade routes throughout the region. The Phoenician alphabet, perhaps the earliest phonetic alphabet, was eventually adapted by the Greeks, and was the forerunner of the modern Roman alphabet. The Phoenician dominance of Mediterranean trade lasted until about 800 BC.

The Indus Valley civilization was located in present-day Pakistan and the northwest area of present-day India. The civilization developed religious practices, farming, and urban areas. It reached its peak between 2500 and 2000 BCE. Their cities were well planned and highly developed. They had developed a writing system and there is evidence they had established trade with neighboring areas in the Near East, such as Sumer. About 1800 BCE, the civilization began to decline and some towns were abandoned. About 1500 BCE, nomads from central Asia settled the Indus Valley. The language they brought with them became the dominant language, and they were involved in agriculture.

At the same time the Phoenicians were sailing the Mediterranean, the Mayan people of Central America were building their first ceremonial structures. The Mayan culture came to its peak around 300 AD, with the building of large cities dominated by huge temple pyramids. The Mayans made significant advances in the areas of astronomy and mathematics.

Around 1600 BC, the Shang Dynasty began in China, according to the earliest known written records. Over the subsequent centuries, Chinese rulers developed a bureaucracy and system of unification that culminated in 221 BC under the emperor Qin, who instituted a common form of writing, a common currency, and a unified legal code throughout the region. This high level of organization allowed Qin to undertake one of the greatest building feats ever, the construction of the Great Wall.

Skill 4.2   Evaluate the influence of ancient civilizations (e.g., Greek, Roman, Indian, Chinese) on the evolution of modern civilization.

The classical civilization of Greece reached the highest levels in man's achievements based on the foundations already laid by such ancient groups as the Egyptians, Phoenicians, Minoans, and Mycenaeans. Among the more important contributions of Greece were the Greek alphabet derived from the Phoenician letters which formed the basis for the Roman and our present-day alphabets; extensive trading and colonization resulting in the spread of the Greek civilization; the love of sports with emphasis on a sound body, leading to the tradition of the Olympic games; the rise of independent, strong city-states; the complete contrast between independent, freedom-loving Athens with its practice of pure democracy (direct, personal, active participation in government by qualified citizens) and rigid, totalitarian, militaristic Sparta; important accomplishments in drama, epic and lyric poetry, fables, myths centered around the many gods and goddesses, science, astronomy, medicine, mathematics, philosophy, art, architecture, writing about and recording historical events; the conquests of Alexander the Great spreading Greek ideas to the areas he conquered and bringing to the Greek world many ideas from Asia; and above all, the value of ideas, wisdom, curiosity, and the desire to learn as much about the world as was possible.

Ancient Greece is often called the Cradle of Western Civilization because of the enormous influence it had not only on the time in which it flourished, but on western culture ever since.

Early Greek institutions have survived for thousands of years and have influenced the entire world. The Athenian form of democracy, with each citizen having an equal vote in his own government, is the philosophy upon which all modern democracies are based. In the United States, the Greek tradition of democracy was honored in the choice of Greek architectural styles for the nation's government buildings. The modern Olympic Games are a revival of an ancient Greek tradition, and many of the events are recreations of original contests.

The works of the Greek epic poet Homer are considered the earliest in western literature, and are still read and taught today. The tradition of the theater was born in Greece, with the plays of Aristophanes and others. In philosophy, Aristotle developed an approach to learning that emphasized observation and thought, and Socrates and Plato contemplated the nature of being and the origins and ideals of government and political relations. Greek mythology has been the source of inspiration for literature into the present day.

In the field of mathematics, Pythagoras and Euclid laid the foundation of geometry, and Archimedes calculated the value of pi. Herodotus and Thucydides were the first to apply research and interpretation to written history.

In the arts, Greek sensibilities were held as perfect forms to which others might strive. In sculpture, the Greeks achieved an idealistic aesthetic that had not been perfected before that time. The Greek civilization served as an inspiration to the Roman Republic, which followed in its tradition of democracy, and was directly influenced by its achievements in art and science. Later, during the Renaissance, European scholars and artists would rediscover ancient Greece's love for dedicated inquiry and artistic expression, leading to a surge in scientific discoveries and advancements in the arts.

Rome was one of the early Italian cities conquered by the Etruscans, who ruled over Rome until 509 BC, when they were overthrown by the Roman Republic. The Etruscans had absorbed and modified Greek civilization. Elements of Greek culture such as writing, certain religious practices, and engineering skills were passed on to the Italian peoples during their rule.

The period prior to the establishment of the Republic remains a mystery to modern historians. The following has been reconstructed: Rome was composed of three tribes each divided into clans. Clans were composed of groups of families. There was a division into a class of nobles and the class of commoners very early. The nobles, called patricians (fathers) appear to have been the privileged class that functioned as an advisory council to the king and had certain political rights. There was no protective function in the government, and thus there was no army. Protection of the citizenry was the responsibility of the father of the family, who was also the priest of the religious cult of the home. The father was also a patron to commoner clients. In exchange for services to the family, these clients were given political and legal protection. The family unit, then, was composed of the family itself, free clients, and slaves (once wars of conquest began). The early kings were elected by the nobles, and ruled with supreme power in legal matters and in time of war. They were advised by the council—or the senate— which was composed of 30 senators (ten to each tribe). The religion of the early Romans was animistic–they believed that everything was inhabited by a spirit. These were not personified or anthropomorphic until just prior to the birth of the Republic. The religion absorbed a number of

Greek and Etruscan elements. The household religion was devoted to household gods, called lares and penates. They were believed to protect the household.

Ancestors were worshiped, and their death masks were maintained in an in-house chapel.

The primary factors that led to the overthrow of the last king and the establishment of the Roman Republic appear to be: 1) a desire to be free of the Etruscans; 2) a desire to put an end to the tyranny of the last king; and 3) the kind of political evolution that occurred elsewhere as the noble classes wanted to cast aside the control of the monarch and establish an aristocratic form of government.

The factors that enabled Rome to conquer Italy were:

- Geographical location in the center of the peninsula with no mountain barriers
- Sturdy citizen army and superior military tactics
- Disunity of their enemies
- Use of a superior form of imperialism, by which military veterans settled in conquered areas, providing structure and guidance that allowed self-government to local peoples
- Highly disciplined family structure and a very powerful father
- Superior form of government–the republic

The structure of the early Republic was clearly aristocratic. The nobles subjugated the commoners and dominated both the consuls and the Senate. In 450 BC a written law gave new rights to the common people: the right to popular assembly, the creation of tribunes to protect the rights of all citizens, the creation of special new officials (judges and treasury officials), who were to make government fairer and more efficient. By 287 BC, the Hortensian law allowed nobles and commoners to intermarry and permitted commoners to hold public offices.

The next 275 years or so were occupied with expansion. This involved numerous wars of conquest. By 100 BC, Rome controlled most of the Hellenistic world. This rapid conquest was one of the factors in the decline of the Republic. The republic did not have the infrastructure to absorb the conquered people. In addition, there was political decay, vast economic and social change, and military failure. In politics, the Senate refused to grant rights to the mass of the populace. A civil war erupted between rival factions. And, lacking adequate infrastructure, Rome was not able to provide good government to conquered territories. Heavy taxation of these territories, oppression by the government, and corrupt resident government officials led to decay. Critical social and economic changes included the ruin of small farmers by importing slaves from conquered areas; a vast migration of the poor to the city of Rome; a failure to encourage and invest in industry and trade; the dissatisfaction of the new business class; and a general decline in morale among all classes of citizens. At the same time, the republic experienced a vast slave uprising in southern Italy and faced the first attacks from Germanic invaders.

The end of the Republic was marked by two significant power struggles. The first was the grasp of power by the First Triumvirate in 59 BC. The Triumvirate consisted of Caesar, Pompey, and Crassus. Caesar eliminated Pompey and attempted to establish a dictatorship. Caesar made many reforms, including reducing the power of the Senate, but he was killed in the Senate in 44 BC.

The following year experienced the rise of the Second Triumvirate, composed of Octavian, Mark Antony, and Lepidus. Octavian (later called Augustus) emerged victorious from the ensuing power struggle and became ruler of Rome in 31 BC. Octavian (Augustus) established a "disguised monarchy" in which he appeared to share power with the Senate but withholding most power. He established the boundaries of Rome on the Rhine and Danube rivers, improved government, and extended citizenship rights to all Roman soldiers. The power of the emperor was gradually enlarged by his successors. The height of the empire was achieved under "the five good emperors"–Nerva, Trajan, Hadrian, Antoninus Pius, and Marcus Aurelius.

Major contributions of the Roman Empire are:

- Peace and prosperity (the Pax Romana)
- The codification of Roman law
- A unified empire that allowed much self-government to component city-states
- The introduction of the idea of separation of powers and popular sovereignty
- The development of the "science" of public administration
- Formalized methods of tax collection
- Construction of an extensive civil service program
- Tolerance and the granting of citizenship rights to all inhabitants
- Engineering and construction of excellent roads, bridges, aqueducts and sanitation systems
- Construction of massive buildings–coliseums, public baths, basilicas
- Architectural innovations in the use of vaults and arches
- Preservation of Greek artistic techniques
- Development of education
- Refinement of rhetoric
- Literature: Cicero, Caesar, Lucretius, Virgil, Juvenal, Livy, Plutarch
- Extension of philosophy in the Greek tradition

The reasons for the decline of the Roman Empire are still a matter of debate.

Political: A period of anarchy and military emperors led to war and destruction; Diocletian reconstructed the Empire, establishing a "divine-right" absolute monarchy, a new imperial bureaucracy, and new administrative divisions to lessen the burden of ruling; Diocletian also reorganized the army, and established a new efficient, but very oppressive, taxation system. Constantine reunited the Empire, but moved the capital to the East. All of this reform demoralized the city-states.

Economic: The rise of large villas owned and controlled by landlords who settled poor people on the land as hereditary tenants who lived under conditions of partial servitude; use of wasteful agricultural methods; a decline of commerce; skilled workers were bound to jobs and were forced to accept government wages and prices; corruption, lack of productivity and inadequate investment of capital; the draining of gold from the western part of the empire through unfavorable trade balances with the East.

Biological, ecological and social: Deforestation, bad agricultural methods, diseases (particularly malaria), earthquakes, immorality, and brutalization of the masses in the cities, demoralization of the upper classes. This was accompanied by the decay of pagan beliefs and Roman ideals with the rise of Christianity. The beginning of the barbarian infiltrations and invasions further weakened the sense of Roman identity. All of these factors contributed to an empire that was ill-equipped to contend with invaders.

India was the birthplace of Siddhartha Gautama (Buddha) on whose teachings Buddhism was founded. The caste system was developed in India and the major religion of Hinduism, was founded here. In India, Hinduism was a continuing influence along with the rise of Buddhism. The civilization developed industry and commerce and traded extensively with the Near East. They made outstanding advances in the fields of science and medicine as well as early advances in navigation and maritime enterprises. The Indians also discovered the principle of zero in mathematics.

The Han Dynasty in China lasted from 206 BC to 220 AD. The Dynasty was founded by the family known as the Liu clan. Within China, the period of the Han Dynasty (some 400 years) is generally considered one of the greatest periods in Chinese history. During this period China officially became a Confucian state. The empire was prosperous and commerce flourished. The empire also extended its influence, both culturally and politically, over Mongolia, Korea, Vietnam and Central Asia.

Following the death of Emperor Qin Shi Huang of the Qin Dynasty, there was widespread unrest. The resulting revolts were led by peasants, prisoners, soldiers, and descendants of the nobles of the "Six Warring States". These ongoing uprisings toppled the Qin dynasty in 206 BC. The leader of the insurgents divided the country into 19 feudal states. What followed was five years of war among the states. The struggle was essentially between Chu Han and Liu Bang. Liu Bang eventually won the struggle and became the first emperor of the Han dynasty.

The new empire maintained the administrative structure of the previous dynasty but established vassal states for the sake of political expediency. Emperor Gao (Liu Bang) divided the country into "feudal states" to appease his wartime allies. His intention, however, was to consolidate his power and then to consolidate the empire. After his death, his successors tried to rule China by combining legalist methods with the Taoist philosophical ideals. This produced a stable centralized government, revival of the agricultural sector, and the break-up of the "feudal states."

Philosophy and Religion

The classical civilization of Greece reached the highest levels in man's achievements based on the foundations already laid by such ancient groups as the Egyptians, Phoenicians, Minoans, and Mycenaeans. (See also Skill 1.1c)

The ancient Israelites and Christians created a powerful legacy of political and philosophical traditions, much of which survives to this day. In law and religion, especially, we can draw a more or less straight line from then to now.

Israel was not the first ancient civilization to have a series of laws for its people to follow. However, thanks to the staggering popularity of the Ten Commandments, we think of the Israelites in this way. This simple set of laws, some of which are not laws at all but societal instructions, maintains to this day a central role in societies the world over. Such commandments as the ones that prohibit stealing and killing were revolutionary in their day because they applied to everyone, not just the disadvantaged. In many ancient cultures, the rich and powerful were above the law because they could buy their way out of trouble and because it wasn't always clear what the laws were. Echoing the Code of Hammurabi and preceding Rome's Twelve Tables, the Ten Commandments provided a written record of laws, so all knew what was prohibited.

The civilization of Israel is also known as the first to assume a worship of just one god. The Christian communities built on this tradition, and both faiths exist and are expanding today, especially in western countries. Rather than a series of gods, each of which was in charge of a different aspect of nature or society, the ancient Israelites and Christians believed in just one god, called Yahweh (YHVH) or God. This divine being, these peoples believed, is the "one, true god," lord over all. This worship of just one god had more of a personal nature to it, and the result was that the believers thought themselves able to talk (or, more properly, pray) directly to God, whereas the peoples of Mesopotamia and Egypt thought the gods distant and unapproachable.

Modern western societies owe a tremendous debt to both the legal and religious aspects of these ancient societies.

Skill 4.3   Identify the major contributions of African, Asian, and Mesoamerican societies before 1500.

Ancient civilizations were those cultures that developed to a great degree and are considered advanced. These include the following with their major accomplishments:

The culture of Mesopotamia was autocratic in nature. The various civilizations throughout the Fertile Crescent were top-heavy, with a single ruler at the head of the government, and, in many cases, served also as the head of the religion. The people followed his strict instructions or faced the consequences, which were usually dire and often life-threatening.

The civilizations of the Sumerians, Amorites, Hittites, Assyrians, Chaldeans, and Persians controlled various areas of the land we call Mesopotamia. With few exceptions, tyrants and military leaders controlled the vast majority of aspects of society, including trade, religions, and the laws. Each Sumerian city-state (and there were several) had its own god, with the city-state's leader doubling as the high priest of worship of that local god. Subsequent cultures had a handful of gods as well although they had more of a national worship structure, with high priests centered in the capital city as advisors to the tyrant.

Trade was vastly important to these civilizations since they had access to some but not all of the things that they needed to survive. Some trading agreements led to occupation, as was the case with the Sumerians, who didn't bother to build walls to protect their wealth of knowledge. Egypt and the Phoenician cities were powerful and regular trading partners of the various Mesopotamian cultures.

- Legacies handed down to us from these early societies include:
- The first use of writing, the wheel, and banking (Sumeria)
- The first written set of laws (Code of Hammurabi)
- The first epic story (Gilgamesh)
- The first library dedicated to preserving knowledge (instituted by the Assyrian leader Ashurbanipal)
- The Hanging Gardens of Babylon (built by the Chaldean Nebuchadnezzar)

The ancient civilization of the Sumerians invented the wheel; developed irrigation through use of canals, dikes, and devices for raising water; devised the system of cuneiform writing; learned to divide time; and built large boats for trade. The Babylonians devised the famous Code of Hammurabi, a code of laws.

Egypt made numerous significant contributions including construction of the great pyramids; development of hieroglyphic writing; preservation of bodies after death; making paper from papyrus; contributing to developments in arithmetic and geometry; the invention of the method of counting in groups of 1-10 (the decimal system); completion of a solar calendar; and laying the foundation for science and astronomy.

The earliest historical record of Kush is in Egyptian sources. It describes a region upstream from the first cataract of the Nile as "wretched." This civilization was characterized by a settled way of life in fortified mud-brick villages. The people subsisted on hunting and fishing, herding cattle, and gathering grain. Skeletal remains suggest that the people were a blend of Negroid and Mediterranean peoples. This civilization appears to be the second-oldest in Africa (after Egypt).

Either the people were Egyptian or heavily influenced by Egyptians at a very early period in the development of the society. They appear to have spoken Nilo-Saharan languages. The area in which they lived is called Nubia. The capital city was Kerma, a major trading center between the northern and southern parts of Africa.

During the period of Egypt's Old Kingdom (ca. 2700-2180 BC), this civilization was essentially a diffused version of Egyptian culture and religion. When Egypt came under the domination of the Hyksos, Kush reached its greatest power and cultural energy (1700-1500 BC). When the Hyksos were eventually expelled from Egypt, the New Kingdom brought Kush back under Egyptian colonial control.

The collapse of the New Kingdom in Egypt (ca. 1000 BC), provided the second opportunity for Kush to develop independently of Egyptian control and to conquer all of the Nubian region. The capital was then moved to Napata.

For the most part, the Kushites apparently considered themselves Egyptian and inheritors of the pharoanic tradition. Their society was organized on the Egyptian model, adopting Egyptian royal titles, etc. Even their art and architecture was based on Egyptian models. But their pyramids were smaller and steeper.

In what has been called "a magnificent irony of history" the Kushites conquered Egypt in the eighth century, creating the twenty-fifth dynasty. The dynasty ended in the seventh century when Egypt was defeated by the Assyrians.

The Kushites were gradually pushed farther south by the Assyrians and later by the Persians. This essentially cut off contact with Egypt, the Middle East and Europe. They moved their capital to Meroe in about 591 BC, when Napata was conquered. Their attention then turned to sub-Saharan Africa. Free of Egyptian dominance, they developed innovations in government and other areas.

In government, the king ruled through a law of custom that was interpreted by priests. The king was elected from the royal family. Descent was determined through the mother's line (as in Egypt). But in an unparalleled innovation, the Kushites were ruled by a series of female monarchs.

The Kushite religion was polytheistic, including all of the primary Egyptian gods. There were, however, regional gods which were the principal gods in their regions. Derived from other African cultures, there was also a lion warrior god.

This civilization was vital through the last half of the first millennium BC, but it suffered about 300 years of gradual decline until it was eventually conquered by the Nuba people.

The ancient Assyrians were warlike and aggressive due to a highly organized military and used horse-drawn chariots.

The Hebrews, also known as the ancient Israelites, instituted "monotheism," which is the worship of one God, Yahweh. They migrated from Ur about 2000 BC.

The Minoans had a system of writing using symbols to represent syllables in words. They built palaces with multiple levels containing many rooms; water and sewage systems with flush toilets, bathtubs, hot and cold running water; and bright paintings on the walls.

The Mycenaeans changed the Minoan writing system to aid their own language and used symbols to represent syllables.

The Phoenicians were sea traders well-known for their manufacturing skills in glass and metals and the development of their famous purple dye. They became so proficient in the skill of navigation that they were able to sail by the stars at night. Further, they devised an alphabet using symbols to represent single sounds, which was an improved extension of the Egyptian writing system.

Asia

Skill of navigation, they were able to sail by the stars at night. Further, they devised an alphabet using symbols to represent single sounds, which was an extension of the Egyptian writing system.

In India, the caste system was developed, the principle of zero in mathematics was discovered, and the major religion of Hinduism was begun. Hinduism was a continuing influence along with the rise of Buddhism. Industry and commerce developed along with extensive trading with the Near East. Outstanding advances in the fields of science and medicine were made along with being the first to be active in navigation and maritime enterprises during this time.

China is considered by some historians to be the oldest, uninterrupted civilization in the world and was in existence around the same time as the ancient civilizations founded in Egypt, Mesopotamia, and the Indus Valley. The Chinese studied nature and weather; stressed the importance of education, family, and a strong central government; followed the religions of Buddhism, Confucianism, and Taoism; and invented such things as gunpowder, paper, printing, and the magnetic compass.

China began building the Great Wall; practiced crop rotation and terrace farming; increased the importance of the silk industry, and developed caravan routes across Central Asia for extensive trade. Also, the Chinese increased proficiency in rice cultivation and developed a written language based on drawings or pictographs (each word or character has a form different from all others).

The ancient Persians developed an alphabet; contributed the religions and philosophies of Zoroastrianism, Mithraism, and Gnosticism; and allowed conquered peoples to retain their own customs, laws, and religions.

The civilization in Japan borrowed much of its culture from China. It was the last of the classical civilizations to develop. Although Japanese used, accepted, and copied Chinese art, law, architecture, dress, and writing, the Japanese refined these into their own unique way of life, including incorporating the religion of Buddhism into their culture.

Asian Empires

The Ottoman Empire is to be noted for its ability to unite a highly varied population as it grew through conquest and treaty arrangement. This ability is to be attributed to military strength, a policy of strict control of recently invaded territories, and an Islamic-inspired philosophy that stated that all Muslims, Christians, and Jews were related because they were all "People of the Book." The major religious groups were permitted to construct their own semiautonomous communities. Conquering armies immediately repaired buildings, roads, bridges, and aqueducts or built them where needed. They also built modern sanitary facilities and linked the city to a supply structure that was able to provide for the needs of the people. This religious and ethnic tolerance was the basis upon which a heterogeneous culture was built. It quickly transformed a Turkish empire into the Ottoman Empire.

The attitude of tolerant blending and respect for diverse ethnic and cultural groups, in time produced a rich mix of people that was reflected in multi-cultural and multi-religious policies that were based on recognition and respect for different perspectives. Ottoman architecture, although influenced by Seljuk, Byzantine, and Arab styles, developed a unique style of its own.

Music was important to the elites of the empire. Two primary styles of music that developed were Ottoman classical music and folk music. Again, both styles reflect a basis in the diversity of influences that came together in the unified empire.

The Mongol Empire, founded by Genghis Khan, included the majority of the territory from Southeast Asia to central Europe during the height of the empire. One of the primary military tactics of conquest was to annihilate any cities that refused to surrender.

Government was by decree on the basis on a code of laws developed by Genghis Khan. One of the tenets of this code was that the nobility and the commoners shared the same hardship. The society, and the opportunity to advance within the society, was based on a system of meritocracy. The carefully structured and controlled society was efficient and safe for the people. Religious tolerance was guaranteed. Theft and vandalism were strictly forbidden. Trade routes and an extensive postal system were created linking the various parts of the empire. Taxes were quite onerous, but teachers, artists and lawyers were exempted from the taxes. Mongol rule, however, was absolute. The response to all resistance was collective punishment in the form of destruction of cities and slaughter of the inhabitants.

The lasting achievements of the Mongol Empire include:

- Reunification of China and expansions of its borders
- Unification of the Central Asian Republics that later formed part of the USSR
- Expansion of Europe's knowledge of the world

The Ming Dynasty in China followed the Mongol-led Yuan Dynasty. In addition to its expansion of trade and exploration of surrounding regions, the period is well-known for its highly talented artists and craftsmen. The Hongwu emperor rose from peasant origins. He distributed land to small farmers in an effort to help them support their families. To further protect these family farms, he proclaimed title of the land non-transferable. He also issued an edict by which anyone who cultivated wasteland could keep the land as his property and would never be taxed. One of the major developments of the time was the development of systems of irrigation for farms throughout the empire. Hongwu maintained a strong army by creating military settlements. During peace, each soldier was given land to farm, and if he could not afford to purchase equipment, it was provided by the government.

The legal code created during the period is generally considered one of the greatest achievements of the dynasty. The laws were written in understandable language and in enough detail to prevent misinterpretation. The law reversed previous policy toward slaves, and promised them the same protection as free citizens, and great emphasis was placed on family relations. It was clearly based on Confucian ideas. The other major accomplishment of this dynasty was the decision to begin building the Great Wall of China to provide protection from northern horsemen.

The Mogul Empire reached its height during the reign of Akbar. In the administration of the empire, Akbar initiated two notable approaches. First, he studied local revenue statistics for the various provinces within the empire. He then developed a revenue plan that matched the revenue needs of the empire with the ability of the people to pay the taxes. Although the taxes were heavy (one-third to one-half of the crop), it was possible to collect the taxes and meet the financial needs of the empire. Second, he created a rank-and-pay structure for the warrior aristocracy that was based on number of troops and obligations.

Akbar also introduced a policy of acceptance and assimilation of Hindus, allowed temples to be built, and abolished the poll tax on non-Muslims. He devised a theory of "rulership as a divine illumination" and accepted all religions and sects. He encouraged widows to remarry, discouraged marriage of children, outlawed the practice of sati, and persuaded the merchants in Delhi to recognize special market days for women who were otherwise required to remain secluded at home. He sponsored regular debates among religious and scholarly individuals with different points of view. The empire supported a strong cultural and intellectual life.

The unique style of architecture of the Mogul Empire was its primary contribution to South Asia. The Taj Mahal was one of many monuments built during this period. The culture was a blend of Indian, Iranian and Central Asian traditions. Other major accomplishments were:

- Centralized government
- Blending of traditions in art and culture
- Development of new trade routes to Arab and Turkish lands
- A unique style of architecture
- Landscape gardening
- Unique cuisine
- Creation of two languages (Urdu and Hindi) for the common people.

The Silk Road was a network of routes connecting Asia and the Mediterranean, and passing through India and the Middle East. It is named after the silk trade but was also the route for trade in other materials such as livestock, wine, and minerals. The network included overland routes as well as naval routes, extending over 8,000 miles.

The Silk Road grew out of more local trade networks that had been in use for thousands of years. The Macedonian conqueror Alexander contributed directly to the development of the Silk Road in the fourth century BC by pushing eastward and connecting Mediterranean Europe with the people of the Middle East. A short time later, in the second century BC, China sent the ambassador Zhang Qian westward to establish diplomatic and commercial ties with the civilizations of Central Asia. At the same time, the Persians had developed a system of Royal Roads throughout their region, allowing them to quickly pass information from city to city and facilitating trade. The routes opened by Alexander and Zhang Qian connected with this system of Persian roads, establishing the framework for a continuous trade route. When Rome conquered Egypt in 70 BC, Africa became a vital section of the Silk Road.

The Silk Road was not only a route for the exchange of goods. Religious, artistic, and cultural ideas moved along the routes as well. Buddhism, which originated in Central Asia, moved outward along the Silk Road toward China, Korea, and Japan where it flourished. Likewise, Islam expanded into the west. European ideas were transmitted eastward as well. Some deities recognized in the Japanese Shinto belief have nearly identical Greek counterparts.

Technology moved along the Silk Road, too. Korean printing methods and Chinese mapmaking and shipbuilding skills were brought to the Mediterranean. Advances in mathematics and astronomy in Persia and Egypt were opened to the rest of the known world.

Portions of the route through Asia were perilous, with bands of marauders attacking travelers and looting shipments. The expansion of the Mongol Empire in the thirteenth and fourteenth centuries stabilized this region, strengthening the connection between east and west. It was during this time that Marco Polo became the first European to travel the Silk Road to China and to bring back a description of what he encountered. As the fifteenth century approached, the Mongol Empire crumbled, however, destabilizing the road once again. This, along with the increased Muslim control over the central portion of the Silk Road, prompted Europeans to seek other routes to the prosperous Asian trade. They began to look to the west, for a route by sea.

Africa

The civilizations in Africa south of the Sahara were developing the refining and use of iron, especially for farm implements and later for weapons. Trading was overland using camels and at important seaports. The Arab influence was extremely important, as was their later contact with Indians, Christian Nubians, and Persians. In fact, their trading activities were probably the most important factor in the spread of and assimilation of different ideas and stimulation of cultural growth.

Bantu-speaking people currently populate most of sub-Equatorial Africa. Their exact patterns of migration are not known for certain, but linguistic evidence suggests that they originated in west and North Africa sometime in the second millennium BC moving eastward and southward.

The dominance of the Bantu language in Africa leads historians to believe that this was one of the largest migrations in human history. Evidence points to its beginning around 1000 BC and lasting until about 1100 AD, taking place in several waves.

Along with the spread of their language, the Bantu also introduced iron-working and agricultural advances wherever they settled. Their superior technology and common language allowed their communities to thrive and supported further expansion.
The Bantu migration has shaped the present population of Africa, as well. The modern language of Swahili, which is spoken throughout most of southern Africa, is a Bantu language.

The Americas

The people who lived in the Americas before Columbus arrived had a thriving, connected society. The civilizations in North America tended to spread out more and were in occasional conflict but maintained their sovereignty for the most part. The South American civilizations, however, tended to migrate into empires, with the strongest city or tribe assuming control of the lives and resources of the rest of the nearby peoples.

Native Americans in North America had a spiritual and personal relationship with the various spirits of nature and a keen appreciation of the ways of woodworking and metalworking. Various tribes dotted the landscape of what is now the United States. They struggled against one another for control of resources such as food and water but had no concept of ownership of land since they believed they were living on the land with the permission of the Spirits. The North Americans mastered the art of growing many crops and, to their credit, were willing to share that knowledge with the various Europeans who eventually showed up. Artwork made of hides, beads, and jewels was popular at this time.

Early residents of North America had large concentrations of people and houses, but they didn't have the kind of large civilization centers like the cities of elsewhere in the world nor an exact system of writing.

Earlier empires of South America included the Aztec, Incan, and Mayan civilizations. One of the earliest people of record was the Olmecs, who left behind little to prove their existence except a series of huge carved figures.

The Aztecs dominated Mexico and Central America. They weren't the only people living in these areas, just the most powerful ones. The Aztecs had many enemies, some of whom were only too happy to help Hernán Cortés precipitate the downfall of the Aztec society. The Aztecs had access to large numbers of metals and jewels, and they used metals to make weapons and jewels to trade for items they didn't already possess. The Aztecs didn't do a whole lot of trading; rather, they conquered neighboring tribes and demanded tribute from them; this was the source of much of the Aztec riches. The Aztecs also believed in a handful of gods and believed that these gods demanded human sacrifice in order to continue to smile on the Aztecs. The center of Aztec society was the great city of Tenochtitlan, which was built on an island so as to be easier to defend. The city boasted a population of 300,000 at the time of the arrival of the conquistadors. Tenochtitlan was known for its canals and its pyramids, none of which survives today.

The Inca Empire stretched across a vast period of territory down the western coast of South America and was connected by a series of roads. A series of messengers ran along these roads, carrying news and instructions from the capital, Cusco, another large city along the lines of—but not as spectacular as— Tenochtitlan. The Incas are known for inventing the quipu, a string-based device that provided them with a method of keeping records. The Inca Empire, like the Aztec Empire, was very much a centralized state, with all income going to the state coffers and all trade going through the emperor as well. The Incas worshiped the dead, their ancestors, and nature, and they often took part in what we could consider strange rituals, such as treating the mummies of dead rulers as still alive.

The most advanced Native American civilization was the Maya, who lived primarily in Central America. The Mayans were the only Native American civilization to develop writing, which consisted of a series of symbols that has still not been deciphered. The Mayans also built huge pyramids and other stone figures and sculptures, mostly of the gods they worshiped. The Mayans are most famous, however, for their calendars and for their mathematics. The Mayan calendars are a complex system of distinct calendars. The Mayans also invented the idea of zero. Mayan worship resembled the practices of the Aztec and Inca and was characterized by the building of pyramids. The Mayans traded heavily with their neighbors.

Skill 4.4   Identify the major contributions of the Middle Ages, the Renaissance, and the Reformation period to Western civilization.

Middle Ages

The period between the division of the Roman Empire in the fifth century AD and the Renaissance in the sixteenth century is called the Middle Ages. This was a period of migration and conquest throughout Europe, as Germanic tribes extended their hold into former Roman territories. Among these tribes, the Franks rose to prominence, under Charles Martel.

In the seventh century, the prophet Muhammad began to spread his teachings in the East, and the Islamic faith was born. Within a century of the death of Muhammad, an Islamic nation had spread from Arabia to the west, including Egypt and the Middle East, to the region that is now Spain. The Franks repelled the Islamic invasion of Europe in 732 AD.

The conflict between the Christian West and the Islamic East continued to grow, culminating in the eleventh century with the first Crusade, a Christian military campaign to take control of Jerusalem and the Holy Land. Several more Crusades took place through the following centuries as Jerusalem and other areas changed hands between Christian and Islamic control. While usually bloody and devastating, the Crusades did connect cultures and contribute to trade routes throughout the region.

As trade and travel increased, more cities sprang up and began to grow in the west. Craft workers in the cities developed their skills to a high degree, eventually organizing guilds to protect the quality of the work and to regulate the buying and selling of their products. City government developed and flourished, centered on strong town councils, and a mercantile class began to grow and exert its influence. The city-states of Italy, which were to figure so importantly in the coming Renaissance, began to flourish.

As Catholic knights were marching in the First Crusade, the Song Dynasty of China was reaching its high point. During this period in China, significant advances in ironworking and agriculture led to the development of large cities– the largest in the world at this time. Trade increased, and a mercantile class developed. Chinese printing technology allowed for widespread communication, and an efficient bureaucracy was consolidated. Chinese engineers developed gunpowder and methods of mass-producing iron objects such as ploughs (plows) and swords.

Feudalism arose in the West during the Middles Ages as an economic and political system. Noble landowners, called lords, granted land to individuals, called vassals, who were allowed to keep the proceeds from farming the land in exchange for loyalty and military service. Nobles themselves were granted land by the monarch. As monarchs grew in power and nationalism took hold, the feudal system proved to be a cumbersome way to raise an army. Less and less land was available for the nobility to support vassals, and the practice largely fell out of use.

The Christian church grew to be a central power in the Middle Ages, centered in the cities of Rome and Constantinople. In 1054, these two factions of the church split over the question of the authority of the Roman patriarch, the Pope, over the four patriarchs of the Eastern Church. The Western Church, under the Pope, survives today as the Roman Catholic Church. The Eastern Church is now referred to as the Eastern Orthodox Church.

In the middle of the fourteenth century, the Black Plague, a fatal disease, swept through Europe with devastating quickness. As thousands of people died, farms were abandoned and trade routes closed. For the survivors of the Plague, new opportunities arose out of the shortage of labor. Faith in alchemists and the clergy diminished as neither had been able to cure the disease. The stage was set for the coming rebirth of culture and learning.

Renaissance

The word "Renaissance" literally means "rebirth" and refers to the rekindling of interest in the learning of classical Greece and Rome that reached its peak in the sixteenth century in Italy. Centered in the Italian city-state of Florence, the Renaissance saw tremendous developments in the fields of art, science, medicine, and literature.

In art, perhaps the most striking development was the introduction of realistic perspective in painting, which opened a new age in artistic expression. The lifelike sculptures of Michelangelo and the realistic drawings of Leonardo da Vinci are prominent examples of this awakening to the expressive possibilities of art.

Leonardo da Vinci also contributed to the field of science, inventing several devices. Galileo took his newly invented telescope and pointed it skyward, discovering four of the moons of Jupiter and establishing that they moved in orbit around the planet. Andrea Vesalius made extensive studies of human anatomy, laying the groundwork for later advances in medicine. In the field of literature, Boccaccio carried on the tradition of Middle Age Italian writers Dante and Petrarch.

Outside of Italy, Cervantes and William Shakespeare were completing their great works. Gutenberg developed a system of printing from moveable type, and Thomas More advanced social philosophy with the publication of Utopia

The Roman Catholic Church played an important, influential role throughout the period of the Renaissance, often commissioning artists to decorate church buildings such as the famous ceiling of the Sistine Chapel. The Church played a limiting role as well, punishing scientists such as Galileo when their findings seemed to challenge official church doctrine.

Throughout the rest of Europe, dissatisfaction with the Roman Church was growing over questions of doctrine and practice. Nationalist feelings were on the rise, and monarchs and other political leaders were becoming less and less willing to submit to the political authority of the

Church. The result of these and other social factors was a change in the religious structure called the Reformation.

The Reformation period consisted of two phases: the Protestant Revolution and the Catholic Reformation.

The Protestant Revolution began in Germany in 1517 when Martin Luther posted a document outlining his opposition to the selling of indulgences by the Church. Indulgences were partial forgiveness of time a person would have to spend in purgatory after death before entering Heaven. This dissent sparked a debate that led to the eventual formation of a new, "Protestant" church. The movement spread to Switzerland, led by John Calvin (Jean Cauvin), and to England, where King Henry VIII was eager to escape the Catholic prohibition against divorce.

In response to the growing Protestant movements, the Church undertook a series of changes known as the Catholic Reformation. These reforms increased religious tolerance by the Church in an attempt to slow the growth of the new protestant churches.

The foundation laid by the great thinkers of the Renaissance was built upon in the next centuries by the European philosophers Rene Descartes and Immanuel Kant. This Age of Reason, as it is called, is usually thought of as signaling the beginning of modern philosophical thought. The Age of Enlightenment, beginning in the eighteenth century, took this advance in rational thought even further in the writings of Voltaire and David Hume. The Age of Reason and Age of Enlightenment are sometimes considered together as an era of continuous development in ethics, logic and philosophy and are considered a major turning point between the Renaissance and modern thought.

Six major results of the Reformation include:

- Religious freedom
- Religious tolerance
- More opportunities for education
- Power and control of rulers limited
- Increase in religious wars
- An increase in fanaticism and persecution.

Skill 4.5   Identify the social, cultural, political, and economic characteristics of African, Asian, and eastern European societies from 1500 to 1900.

Africa

During the fifteenth century, Portuguese mariners explored the west coast of Africa where African rules had laid the foundations for the Akan and Benin states. Sailors from the Swahili city-states in East Africa helped Vasco da Gama understand local monsoon winds and finish his voyage to India.

The area known today as the Republic of Benin was the site of an early African kingdom known as Dahomey. By the seventeenth century, the kingdom included a large part of West Africa. The kingdom was economically prosperous because of slave-trading relations with Europeans, primarily the Dutch and Portuguese, who arrived in the fifteenth century. The coastal part of the kingdom was known as "the Slave Coast.

In the 1500s, the Portuguese established the first trading posts in East Africa, the Ottomans conquered Egypt, and the Songhay destroyed the Mali Empire. In the later 1500s, Portugal established a colony in Angola and the Songhay Empire fell to Morocco.

In the 1600s, the slave trade affected African politics and society, and populations grew because of the introduction of food crops from the Americas. Two million slaves were exported during this time and some were taken to the English colony at Jamestown. A Dutch colony was established at the Cape of Good Hope in 1652.

By the late 1600s, the area known today as the Republic of Benin was the site of an early African kingdom known as Dahomey and included a large part of West Africa. The kingdom was economically prosperous because of slave-trading relations with Europeans, primarily the Dutch and Portuguese, who had arrived in the fifteenth century. The coastal part of the kingdom was known as "the Slave".

Islamic influence spread in North Africa and the slave trade flourished, with over 13.5 million people transported from Africa. In 1779 and 1780, the Boers and Bantu fought a war in southern Africa. Also during the late 1700s, the British took over the Cape of Good Hope and Napoleon occupied Egypt.

The slave trade provided economic stability for the kingdom for almost 300 years. The continuing need for human sacrifices caused a decrease in the number of slaves available for export. As many colonial countries declared the trade of slaves illegal, demand for slaves subsided steadily until 1885 when the last Portuguese slave ship left the coast. With the decline of the slave trade, the kingdom began a slow disintegration. The French took over in 1892.

Asia

West Asia: In 1453, the Ottoman Turks laid siege to the city of Constantinople. After the capture, the city was renamed Istanbul and it became the Islamic capital. The Ottoman navy ruled the Mediterranean Sea until 1571, and Muslims dominated commercial shipping.

In the early nineteenth century policy of modernization based on European customs, architecture and legislation. The rise of nationalism throughout Europe also affected the empire and former sovereign states that had been conquered began to express nationalistic goals. These developments marked the beginning of the end for the empire. Despite several attempts to reform the government, economic depression and political unrest plagued the declining state.

South and Southeast Asia: In the 1500s, Turks invaded northern India, creating the Mughal dynasty of Muslim rulers. Portugal gained control of the Spice Islands, and Burma remained the leading power in Southeast Asia, conquering Siam (present-day Thailand) and Laos. English and Dutch trading companies consolidated their holdings in the Indian Ocean and founded trading centers in Southeast Asia.

East Asia: In 1600s, a Manchu army defeated the Ming dynasty and established the Qing dynasty which endured until the early 1900s. Japan introduced a centralized government and China and Japan carefully controlled foreign trade.

The Chinese Revolution was a response to imperial rule under the Qing Dynasty. The failure of the dynasty to modernize and liberalize and the violent repression of dissidents had moved the reformers toward revolution. The most popular of the numerous revolutionary groups was led by Sun Yat-sen. His movement was supported by Chinese who were living outside China and by students in Japan. He won the support of regional military officers. He favored nationalism and wanted to oust the Manchus. He favored democracy and wanted to establish a popularly elected government and equalize the ownership of land and the tools of production.

After the revolution, Sun Yat-sen was elected the first Provisional President of the new Republic of China. A second revolution began in 1913. This resulted in the flight to Japan of Sun and his followers.

Eastern Europe: Poland dominated Eastern Europe until Ivan III claimed the title "tsar" in 1472 and began Russian expansion. Until the early years of the twentieth century, Russia was ruled by a succession of Tsars. Society was essentially feudalistic and was structured in three levels. The top level was held by the Tsar. The second level was composed of the rich nobles who held government positions and owned vast tracts of land. The third level of the society was composed of the remaining people who lived in poverty as peasants or serfs. There was discontent among the peasants. There were several unsuccessful attempts to revolt during the nineteenth century, but they were quickly suppressed. In 1905 and 1917 there were revolutions, however, that were quite different. The causes of the 1905 Revolution were discontent with the social structure, the living conditions of the peasants, and with working conditions despite industrialization.

A trade union leader organized a protest and over 150,000 peasants joined a demonstration outside the Tsar's Winter Palace. Before the demonstrators even spoke, the palace guard opened fire on the crowd. This destroyed the people's trust in the Tsar. Tsar Nicholas II created a constitutional monarchy, extended some civil rights, and gave Parliament limited legislative power but in a very short period of time disbanded the parliament and violated the promised civil liberties. This violation fomented the 1917 Revolution.

The 1917 Russian Revolution resulted in the abdication of Tsar Nicholas II and the establishment of a democratic government. The Bolsheviks did away with the provisional democratic government and set up the world's first Marxist state. Support for and strength of the Bolsheviks existed mainly in the cities. After two or three years of civil war, fighting foreign invasions, and opposing other revolutionary groups, the Bolsheviks were finally successful in making possible a type of "pre-Utopia" for the workers and the people.

In Western Europe, the following are examples of events in the societies. For example: Renaissance

Art - The more important artists were Giotto and his development of perspective in paintings; Leonardo Da Vinci was not only an artist but also a scientist and inventor; Michelangelo was a sculptor, painter, and architect; and others include Raphael, Donatello, Titian, and Tintoretto

Political philosophy - the writings of Machiavelli

Literature - the writings of Petrarch and Boccaccio Science - Galileo

Medicine - The work of Brussels-born Andrea Vesalius earned him the title of "father of anatomy" and had a profound influence on the Spaniard Michael Servetus and the Englishman William Harvey

In Germany, Gutenberg's invention of the printing press with movable type facilitated the rapid spread of Renaissance ideas, writings and innovations, thus ensuring the enlightenment of most of Western Europe. Contributions were also made by Durer and Holbein in art and by Paracelsus in science and medicine.

The effects of the Renaissance in the Low Countries can be seen in the literature and philosophy of Erasmus and the art of van Eyck and Breughel the Elder. Rabelais and de Montaigne in France also contributed to literature and philosophy. In Spain, the art of El Greco and de Morales flourished as did the writings of Cervantes and De Vega. In England, Sir Thomas More and Sir Francis Bacon wrote and taught philosophy and were inspired by Vesalius.

William Harvey made important contributions in medicine. The greatest talent was found in literature and drama and given to mankind by Chaucer, Spenser, Marlowe, Jonson, and the incomparable Shakespeare.

The Renaissance ushered in a time of curiosity, learning, and incredible energy sparking the desire for trade to procure these new, exotic products and to find better, faster, cheaper trade routes to get to them. The work of geographers, astronomers and mapmakers made important contributions and many studied and applied the work of such men as Hipparchus of Greece, Ptolemy of Egypt, Tycho Brahe of Denmark, and Fra Mauro of Italy.

Skill 4.6   Evaluate the significant scientific, intellectual, and philosophical contributions of the Age of Reason through the Age of Enlightenment.

The period from the 1700s to the 1800s was characterized in Western countries by opposing political ideas of democracy and nationalism. This resulted in strong nationalistic feelings and people of common cultures asserting their belief in the right to have a part in their government. The Scientific Revolution and the Age of Enlightenment were two of the most important movements in the history of civilization, resulting in a new sense of self-examination and a wider view of the world than ever before. The Age of Enlightenment is also called the Age of Reason.

The Scientific Revolution was, above all, a shift in focus from belief to evidence. Scientists and philosophers wanted to see the proof, not just believe what other people told them. It was an exciting time, if you were a forward-looking thinker.

A Polish astronomer, Nicolaus Copernicus, began the Scientific Revolution. He crystallized a lifetime of observations into a book that was published about the time of his death. Copernicus argued that the Sun, not the Earth, was the center of a solar system and that other planets revolved around the Sun, not the Earth. This flew in the face of established (Church-mandated) doctrine. The Church still wielded tremendous power at this time, including the power to banish people or sentence them to prison or even death.

The Danish astronomer Tycho Brahe was the first to catalog his observations of the night sky, of which he recorded thousands. Building on Brahe's data, German scientist Johannes Kepler instituted his theory of planetary movement, embodied in his famous Laws of Planetary Movement. Using Brahe's data, Kepler also confirmed Copernicus's observations and argument that the Earth revolved around the Sun.

The most famous defender of this idea was Galileo Galilei, an Italian scientist who conducted many famous experiments in the pursuit of science. He is most well-known, however, for his defense of the heliocentric (sun-centered) idea. He wrote a book comparing the two theories, but most readers could tell easily that he favored the new one. He was convinced of this mainly because of what he had seen with his own eyes. He had used the relatively new invention of the telescope to see four moons of Jupiter. They certainly did not revolve around the Earth, so why should everything else? His ideas were not at all favored with the Church, which continued to assert its authority in this and many other matters. The Church was still powerful enough at this time, especially in Italy, to order Galileo to be placed under house arrest.

Galileo died under house arrest, but his ideas didn't die with him. Picking up the baton was an English scientist named Isaac Newton, who became perhaps the most famous scientist of all. He is known as the discoverer of gravity and a pioneering voice in the study of optics (light), calculus, and physics.

More than any other scientist, Newton argued for (and proved) the idea of a mechanistic view of the world: You can see how the world works and prove how the world works through observation; if you can see these things with your own eyes, they must be so. Up to this time, people believed what other people told them; this is how the Church was able to keep control of people's lives for so long. Newton, following in the footsteps of Copernicus and Galileo, changed all that.

The Enlightenment was a period of intense self-study that focused on ethics and logic. More so than at any time before, scientists and philosophers questioned cherished truths, widely held beliefs, and their own sanity in an attempt to discover why the world worked—from within. "I think, therefore I am" was one of the famous sayings of that day. It was uttered by Rene Descartes, a French scientist-philosopher whose dedication to logic and the rigid rules of observation were a blueprint for the thinkers who came after him.

One of the giants of the era was England's David Hume. Hume, a pioneer of the doctrine of empiricism (believing things only when you've seen the proof for yourself), was also a prime believer in the value of skepticism. In other words, he was naturally suspicious of things other people told him and constantly set out to discover the truth for himself. These two related ideas influenced great many thinkers after Hume and his writings.

Immanuel Kant of Germany was both a philosopher and a scientist. He took a definitely scientific view of the world. He wrote the movement's most famous essay, "Answering the Question: What Is Enlightenment?" and he answered his famous question with the motto "Dare to Know." For Kant, the human being was a rational being capable of hugely creative thought and intense self-evaluation. He encouraged all to examine themselves and the world around them. He believed that the source of morality lay not in nature or in the grace of God but in the human soul itself. He believed that man believed in God for practical, not religious or mystical, reasons.

Also prevalent during the Enlightenment was the idea of the "social contract," the belief that government existed because people wanted it to, that the people had an agreement with the government that they would submit to it as long as it protected them and didn't encroach on their basic human rights. This idea was first made famous by the Frenchman Jean-Jacques Rousseau but was also adopted by England's John Locke and America's Thomas Jefferson. John Locke was one of the most influential political writers of the 17th century who put great emphasis on human rights and put forth the belief that when governments violate those rights people should rebel. He wrote the book Two Treatises of Government in 1690, which had tremendous influence on political thought in the American colonies and helped shaped the U.S. Constitution and Declaration of Independence.

Skill 4.7   Identify the causes, effects, events, and significant individuals associated with the Age of Exploration.

The Age of Exploration actually had its beginnings centuries before exploration actually took place. The rise and spread of Islam in the seventh century and its subsequent control over the holy city of Jerusalem led to the European so-called Holy Wars, the Crusades, to free Jerusalem and the Holy Land from this control. Even though the Crusades were not a success, those who survived and returned to their homes and countries in Western Europe brought back with them new products such as silks, spices, perfumes, new and different foods—luxuries that were unheard of and that gave new meaning what may have to colorless, drab, dull lives.

New ideas, new inventions, and new methods also went to Western Europe with the returning Crusaders, and from these new influences was the intellectual stimulation which led to the period known as the Renaissance. The revival of interest in classical Greek art, classical Greek architecture, classical Greek literature—and developments in science, astronomy, medicine along with increased trade between Europe and Asia—and the invention of the printing press helped to push the spread of knowledge and stimulated more global exploration.

For many centuries, mapmakers made many maps and charts, which in turn stimulated curiosity and the seeking of more knowledge. At the same time, the Chinese were using the magnetic compass in their ships. Pacific islanders were going from island to island, covering thousands of miles in open canoes navigating by sun and stars. Arab traders were sailing all over the Indian Ocean in their dhows. The trade routes between Europe and Asia were slow, difficult, dangerous, and very expensive. Between sea voyages on the Indian Ocean and Mediterranean Sea and the camel caravans in central Asia and the Arabian Desert, the trade was still controlled by the Italian merchants in Genoa and Venice. It would take months and even years for the exotic luxuries of Asia to reach the markets of Western Europe. A faster, cheaper way had to be found. A way had to be found which would bypass traditional routes and end the control of the Italian merchants.

Prince Henry of Portugal (also called the Navigator) encouraged, supported, and financed the Portuguese seamen who led in the search for an all-water route to Asia. A shipyard was built along with a school that taught navigation. New types of sailing ships were built which would carry the seamen safely through the ocean waters. Experiments were conducted in newer maps, newer navigational methods, and newer instruments. These included the astrolabe and the compass enabling sailors to determine direction as well as latitude and longitude for exact location. Although Prince Henry died in 1460, the Portuguese kept on, sailing and exploring Africa's west coastline. In 1488, Bartholomew Diaz and his men sailed around Africa's southern tip and headed toward Asia. Diaz wanted to push on but turned back because his men were discouraged and weary from the long months at sea, extremely fearful of the unknown, and unwilling to travel any further.

However, the Portuguese were finally successful ten years later in 1498 when Vasco da Gama and his men, continuing the route of Diaz, rounded Africa's Cape of Good Hope, sailing across the Indian Ocean, reaching India's port of Calicut (Calcutta). Although, six years earlier, Columbus had reached the New World and an entire hemisphere, da Gama had proved Asia could be reached from Europe by sea.

Columbus' first trans-Atlantic voyage proved his theory that Asia could be reached by sailing west. It could be done—but only after figuring how to go around or across or through the landmass in between. Long after Spain dispatched explorers and her famed conquistadors to gather the wealth for the Spanish monarchs and their coffers, the British were searching valiantly for the "Northwest Passage," a land-sea route across North America and open sea to the wealth of Asia. It wasn't until after the Lewis and Clark Expedition when Captains Meriwether Lewis and William Clark proved conclusively that there simply was no Northwest Passage.

However, this did not deter exploration and settlement. Spain, France, and England along with some participation by the Dutch led the way with expanding Western European civilization in the New World. These three nations had strong monarchial governments and were struggling for dominance and power in Europe. With the defeat of Spain's mighty Armada in 1588, England became undisputed mistress of the seas. Spain lost its power and influence in Europe and it was left to France and England to carry on the rivalry, leading to eventual British control in Asia as well.

Spain's influence was in Florida, the Gulf Coast from Texas all the way west to California and south to the tip of South America and to some of the islands of the West Indies. French control centered from New Orleans north to what is now northern Canada including the entire Mississippi Valley, the St. Lawrence Valley, the Great Lakes, and the land that was part of the Louisiana Territory. A few West Indies islands were also part of France's empire. England settled the eastern seaboard of North America, including parts of Canada and from Maine to Georgia. Some West Indies islands also came under British control. The Dutch had New Amsterdam for a period of time but later ceded it into British hands.

For each of these three nations—Spain, France, and especially England—the land claims extended partly or all the way across the continent, no matter that others claimed the same land. The wars for dominance and control of power and influence in Europe eventually extended to the Americas, especially North America.

The importance of the Age of Exploration was not just the discovery and colonization of the New World, but better maps and charts and newer and more accurate navigational instruments increased knowledge and great wealth. Furthermore, new and different foods and other items previously unknown in Europe were introduced. A new hemisphere became accessible as a refuge from poverty and persecution—a place to start a new and better life. The proof that Asia could be reached by sea and that the earth was round meant that ships and sailors would not sail off the edge of a flat earth and disappear forever into nothingness.

Skill 4.8   Assess the social, political, and economic effects of the Industrial Revolution.

The Industrial Revolution, which began in Great Britain and spread elsewhere, was the development of power-driven machinery (fueled by coal and steam) leading to the accelerated growth of industry with large factories replacing homes and small workshops as work centers. The lives of people changed drastically, and a largely agricultural society changed to an industrial one. In Western Europe, the period of empire and colonialism began. The industrialized nations seized and claimed parts of Africa and Asia in an effort to control and provide the raw materials needed to feed the industries and machines in the "mother country." Ultimately coal and steam were replaced by electricity and internal combustion.

A reason for European imperialism was the harsh, urgent demand for the raw materials needed to fuel and feed the great Industrial Revolution. These resources were not available in the huge quantity so desperately needed, which necessitated (and rationalized) the partitioning of the continent of Africa and parts of Asia. In turn, these colonial areas would purchase the finished manufactured goods. Europe in the nineteenth century was densely populated. Populations were growing, but resources were not. The people of many European countries were agitating for rights as never before. To address these concerns, European powers began to look elsewhere for relief.

One of the main places for European imperialist expansion was Africa. Britain, France, Germany, and Belgium took over countries in Africa and claimed them as their own. The resources (including people) were then shipped back to the mainland and claimed as colonial gains. The Europeans went about "civilizing the savages," reasoning that their technological superiority gave them the right to rule and "educate" the peoples of Africa.

Southeast Asia was another area of European expansion at this time, mainly by France. So, too, was India, colonized by Great Britain. These two nations combined with Spain to occupy countries in Latin America. Spain also seized the rich lands of the Philippines. As a result of all this activity, a whole new flood of goods, people, and ideas began to come back to Europe, and a whole group of people began to travel to these colonies, to oversee the colonization and to "help bring the people up" to the European level. European leaders could also assert their authority in these colonies as they could not back home. The continent of Africa was controlled by France, Great Britain, Italy, Portugal, Spain, Germany, and Belgium—except Liberia and Ethiopia. In Asia and the Pacific Islands, only China, Japan, and present-day Thailand (Siam) kept their independence. The others were controlled by the strong European nations.

Italy and Germany each were united into single nations from many smaller states. There were ultimately revolutions in Austria and Hungary, the Franco-Prussian War, the dividing of Africa among the strong European nations, interference and intervention of Western nations in Asia, and the breakup of Turkish dominance in the Balkans.

Although there was a marked degree of industrialization before and during the Civil War, at the end of that war, industry in America was small. After the war, dramatic changes took place. Machines replaced hand labor, extensive nationwide railroad service made possible the wider distribution of goods, invention of new products made them available in large quantities, and large amounts of money flowed in from bankers and investors for expansion of business operations. American life was definitely affected by this phenomenal industrial growth. Cities became the centers of this new business activity resulting in mass population movements and tremendous growth. This new boom in business resulted in huge fortunes for some Americans and extreme poverty for many others. The discontent this caused resulted in a number of new reform movements from which came measures to control the power and size of big businesses and to help the poor.

Of course, industry before, during, and after the Civil War was centered mainly in the North, especially the tremendous industrial growth. This resulted in larger migration of blacks from South to North. The late 1800s and early 1900s saw the increasing buildup of military strength and the U.S. becoming a world power.

The use of machines in industry enabled workers to produce a large quantity of goods much faster than by hand. With the increase in business, hundreds of workers were hired and assigned to perform a certain job in the production process. This was a method of organization called "division of labor" and by increasing the rate of production, businesses lowered prices for their products, making the products affordable for more people. As a result, sales and businesses were increasingly successful and profitable.

A great variety of new products or inventions became available such as the typewriter, the telephone, barbed wire, the electric light, the phonograph, and the gasoline automobile. From this list, the one that had the greatest effect on America's economy was the automobile.

The increase in business and industry was greatly affected by the many rich natural resources that were found throughout the nation. Industrial machines were powered by abundant water supply. The construction industry as well as the manufacturing industry that created products made from wood depended heavily on lumber from the forests. Coal and iron ore were needed in abundance for the steel industry, which profited and grew because of the use of steel in skyscrapers, automobiles, bridges, railroad tracks, and machines. Other minerals such as silver, copper, and petroleum played a large role in industrial growth, especially petroleum, from which gasoline was refined as fuel for the increasingly popular automobile.

Between 1870 and 1916, more than 25 million immigrants came into the United States, adding to the phenomenal population growth. This tremendous growth aided business and industry in two ways. The number of consumers increased, creating a greater demand for products, thus enlarging the markets for the products. With increased production and expanding business, more workers were available for newly created jobs.

The completion of the nation's transcontinental railroad in 1869 contributed greatly to the nation's economic and industrial growth. Some of the benefits of using the railroads were that raw materials were shipped quickly by the mining companies and finished products were sent to all parts of the country. Many wealthy industrialists and railroad owners saw tremendous profits steadily increasing due to this improved method of transportation. At the same time, the process of building the transcontinental railroad was tainted with fraud in regard to the Union Pacific Railroad and the construction company, Crédit Mobilier of America.

As business grew, methods of sales and promotion were developed. Salespersons went to all parts of the country promoting the various products, opening large department stores in the growing cities, offering varied products at reasonable, affordable prices. People who lived too far from the cities to shop there had the advantage of using a mail order service, buying what they needed from catalogs furnished by the companies. The developments in communication—telephone and telegraph—increased the efficiency and prosperity of big business.

Investments in corporate stocks and bonds resulted from business prosperity. As individuals began investing heavily in eager desire to share in the profits, their investments made available the needed capital for companies to expand their operations. From this, banks increased in number throughout the country, making loans to businesses and significant contributions to economic growth. At the same time, during the 1880s, government made little effort to regulate businesses. This gave rise to monopolies where larger businesses overpowered their smaller competitors and assumed complete control of their industries.

Some owners in the same business would join or merge to form one company. Others formed what were called "trusts," a type of monopoly in which rival businesses were controlled but not formally owned. Monopolies had some good effects on the economy. Out of them grew the large, efficient corporations, which made important contributions to the growth of the nation's economy. Also, the monopolies enabled businesses to keep their sales steady and avoid sharp fluctuations in price and production. The downside of monopolies was that some business leaders acquired so much power, they were able to take advantage of smaller businesses. Those who had little or no competition would require their suppliers to supply goods at a low cost, sell the finished products at high prices, and reduce the quality of the product to save money. The monopolies would perform "price fixing."

During the late 1800s and early 1900s, significant reforms and changes and changes were made in the areas of politics, society, and the economy. There was a growing need to reduce the levels of poverty and improve living conditions. Also, large businesses needed to be regulated and governmental reforms were needed to eliminate corruption and respond to the people's needs. Until 1890, there was very little success, but from 1890 on, the reformers gained increased public support and were able to achieve some influence in government. Since some of the reformers referred to themselves as "progressives," the period of 1890 to 1917 is referred to by historians as the Progressive Era.

Skilled laborers were organized into a labor union called the American Federation of Labor in an effort to gain better working conditions and wages for its members. Farmers joined organizations such as the National Grange and Farmers Alliances. Farmers were producing more food than people could afford to buy. This was the result of new farmlands rapidly sprouting on the plains and prairies and development and availability of new farm machinery and newer and better methods of farming. They tried selling their surplus abroad but faced stiff competition from other nations selling the same farm products. Other problems contributed significantly to the farmers' situation. Items they needed for daily life were highly priced. Having to borrow money to carry on farming activities kept them constantly in debt. Higher interest rates, shortage of money, falling farm prices, dealing with the so-called middlemen, and the increasingly high charges by the railroads to haul farm products to large markets all contributed to the desperate need for reform to relieve the plight of American farmers.

Direct results of the Industrial Revolution—particularly as they affected industry, commerce, and agriculture—included:

- Enormous increases in productivity
- Huge increases in world trade
- Specialization and division of labor
- Standardization of parts and mass production
- Growth of giant business conglomerates and monopolies
- A new revolution in agriculture facilitated by the steam engine, machinery, chemical fertilizers, processing, canning, and refrigeration

The political results included:

- Growth of complex government by technical experts
- Centralization of government, including regulatory administrative agencies
- Advantages to democratic development including 1) extension of franchise to the middle class—and later to all elements of the population; 2) mass education to meet the needs of an industrial society; 3) development of media of public communication including radio, television, and cheap newspapers
- Dangers to democracy included the risk of manipulation of the media of mass communication, facilitation of dictatorial centralization and totalitarian control, subordination of the legislative function to administrative directives, efforts to achieve uniformity and conformity, and social impersonalization.

The economic results were numerous:

- The conflict between free trade and low tariffs and protectionism
- The issue of free enterprise against government regulation
- Struggles between labor and capital, including the trade-union movement
- The rise of socialism
- The rise of the utopian socialists
- The rise of Marxian or "scientific socialism"

The social results of the Industrial Revolution include:

- Increased population, especially in industrial centers
- Advances in science applied to agriculture, sanitation and medicine
- Growth of great cities
- Disappearance of differences between city dwellers and farmers
- Faster tempo of life and increased stress from the monotony of the work routine
- The emancipation of women
- The decline of religion
- Rise of scientific materialism
- Darwin's theory of evolution

Skill 4.9   Identify the causes, effects, events, and significant individuals associated with the Age of Revolution.

The period from the 1700s to the1800s was characterized in Western countries by opposing political ideas of democracy and nationalism. This resulted in strong nationalistic feelings and people of common cultures asserting their belief in the right to have a part in their government.

The American Revolution resulted in the successful efforts of the English colonists in America to win their freedom from Great Britain. After more than one hundred years of mostly self-government, the colonists resented the increased British meddling and control. They declared their freedom, won the Revolutionary War with aid from France, and formed a new independent nation.

The French Revolution was the revolt of the middle and lower classes against the gross political and economic excesses of the rulers and the supporting nobility. It ended with the establishment of the First Republic in a series of French Republics. Conditions leading to the Revolution included extreme taxation, inflation, lack of food, and total disregard for the very poor living standards of the people on the part of the rulers, nobility, and the Church.

The American Revolution and the French Revolution were similar yet different, liberating their people from unwanted government interference and installing a different kind of government. They were both fought for the liberty of the common people, and they both were built on writings and ideas that embraced such an outcome. Both Revolutions proved that people could expect more from their government and that such rights as self-determination were worth fighting for—and dying for.

The American colonists were striking back against British unwanted taxation and other sorts of "government interference." The French people were starving and, in many cases, destitute. They rebelled against an autocratic regime that cared more for high fashion and "courtly love" than food and health for the people.

- The American Revolution involved a year-long campaign, of bloody battles, skirmishes, and stalemates. The French Revolution was bloody to a degree but mainly an overthrow of society and its outdated traditions.
- The American Revolution resulted in a representative government, which marketed itself as a beacon of democracy for the rest of the world. The French Revolution resulted in a consulship, a generalship, and then an emperor—probably not what the perpetrators of the Revolution had in mind when they first rose against King Louis XVI and Queen Marie-Antoinette.

The major turning point for Latin America, already unhappy with Spanish restrictions on trade, agriculture, and the manufacture of goods, was Napoleon's move into Spain and Portugal. Napoleon's imprisonment of King Ferdinand VII made the local agents of the Spanish authorities feel that they were agents of the French. Conservative and liberal locals joined forces, declared their loyalty to King Ferdinand, and formed committees (juntas). Between May of 1810 and July of 1811, the juntas in Argentina, Chile, Paraguay, Venezuela, Bolivia, and Colombia all declared independence. Fighting erupted between Spanish authorities in Latin America and the members and followers of the juntas. In Mexico City another junta declared loyalty to King Ferdinand and independence.

Society in Latin America was sharply distinguished according to race and the purity of Spanish blood. Miguel Hidalgo, a 60-year-old priest and enlightened intellectual, disregarded the racial distinctions of the society. He had been fighting for the interests of the Indians and part Indian/part white citizens of Mexico, including a call for the return of land stolen from the Indians. He called for an uprising in 1810.

Simon Bolivar had been born into Venezuela's wealthy society and educated in Europe. With Francisco de Miranda, he declared Venezuela and Columbia to be republics and removed all Spanish trading restrictions. These leaders also removed taxes on the sale of food, ended payment of tribute to the government by the local Indians, and prohibited slavery. In March 1812 Caracas was devastated by an earthquake. When the Spanish clergy in Caracas proclaimed the earthquake God's act of vengeance against the rebel government, they then provided support for the Spanish government officials, who quickly regained control.

When Ferdinand was returned to power in 1814, it was no longer possible for the rebel groups to claim to act in his name. Bolivar was driven to Colombia, where he gathered a small army that returned to Venezuela in 1817. As his army grew, Spain became concerned, and the military moved into the interior of Venezuela. This action aroused the local people to active rebellion. As he freed slaves, Bolivar gained support and strength. Realizing that he did not have the strength to take Caracas, he moved his people to Colombia. Bolivar's forces defeated the Spanish and organized "Gran Colombia" (which included present-day Ecuador, Colombia and Panama), and he became president in 1819. When Ferdinand encountered difficulties in Spain, the soldiers assembled to be transported to the Americas revolted. Several groups in Spain joined the revolt and together, drove Ferdinand from power. Bolivar took advantage of the opportunity and took his army back into Venezuela. In 1821, Bolivar defeated the Spanish, took Caracas, and established Venezuelan freedom from Spanish rule.

In Peru, San Martin took his force into Lima amid celebration. Bolivar provided assistance in winning Peru's independence in 1822. Bolivar now controlled Peru. By 1824, Bolivar had combined forces with local groups and rid South America of Spanish control.

In 1807, Queen Maria of Portugal fled to escape Napoleon. The royal family sailed to Brazil, where they were welcomed by the local people. Rio de Janeiro became the temporary capital of Portugal's empire. Maria's son Joao ruled as regent. He opened Brazil's trade with other nations; gave the British favorable tax rates in gratitude for their assistance against Napoleon; and opened Brazil to foreign scholars, visitors and immigrants. In 1815, he made Brazil a kingdom that was united with Portugal. By 1817 there was economic trouble in Brazil along with unrest over repression (such as censorship). This discontent became a rebellion that was repressed by Joao's military.

When Napoleon's forces withdrew from Portugal, the British asked Joao to return. Liberals took power in Portugal and in Spain and both drafted liberal constitutions. By 1821, Joao decided to return to Portugal as a constitutional monarch. He left his oldest son Pedro on the throne in Brazil. When Portugal tried to reinstate economic advantages for Portugal and restrict Brazil, resistance began to grow. Pedro did not want to be controlled by Portugal and was labeled a rebel. When he learned that Portuguese troops had been sent to arrest him, he prohibited the landing of the ship, sent it back to Portugal, and declared independence in 1922. In a little more than a month he was declared Emperor of Brazil.

Until the early years of the twentieth century Russia was ruled by a succession of Czars. The Czars ruled as autocrats or, sometimes, despots. Society was essentially feudalistic and was structured in three levels. The top level was held by the Czar. The second level was composed of the rich nobles who held government positions and owned vast tracts of land. The third level of the society was composed of the remaining people, who lived in poverty as peasants or serfs.

There was discontent among the peasants. There were several unsuccessful attempts to rebel during the nineteenth century, but they were quickly suppressed. The Russian Revolutions of 1905 and 1917, however, were quite different.

The causes of the 1905 Revolution were:

- Discontent with the social structure
- Discontent with the living conditions of the peasants
- Discontent with working conditions despite industrialization
- General discontent aggravated by the Russo-Japanese War (1904-1905) with inflation and rising prices. Peasants who had been able to eke out a living began to starve.

- Many fighting troops killed in battles as Russia lost a war to Japan (Russo-Japanese War) because of poor leadership, lack of training, and inferior weaponry
- Czar Nicholas II refused to end the war despite setbacks.
- In January 1905 Port Arthur fell.

A trade union leader, Father Gapon, organized a protest to demand an end to the war, industrial reform, more civil liberties, and a constituent assembly. Over 150,000 peasants joined a demonstration outside the Czar's Winter Palace. Before the demonstrators even spoke, the palace guard opened fire on the crowd. This destroyed the people's trust in the Czar. Illegal trade unions and political parties formed and organized strikes to gain power.

The strikes eventually brought the Russian economy to a halt. This led Czar Nicholas II to sign the October Manifesto, which created a constitutional monarchy, extended some civil rights, and gave the Parliament limited legislative power. In a very short period of time, the Czar disbanded the Parliament and violated the promised civil liberties. This violation further stirred discontent and rebellion.

Causes of the 1917 Revolution were:

- The violation of the October Manifesto
- Defeats on the battlefields during WWI caused discontent, loss of life, and a popular desire to withdraw from the war.
- The Czar continued to appoint unqualified people to government posts and handle the country with general incompetence.
- The Czar also listened to his wife's (Alexandra) advice. She was strongly influenced by Rasputin. This caused increased discontent among all level of the social structure.
- WWI had caused another surge in prices and scarcity of many items. Most of the peasants could not afford to buy bread.

Workers in Petrograd went on strike in 1917 over the need for food. The Czar again ordered troops to suppress the strike. This time, however, the troops sided with the workers. The revolution then took a unique direction. The Parliament created a provisional government to rule the country. The military and the workers also created their own governments, called soviets (popularly elected local councils). The Parliament was composed of nobles, who soon lost control of the country when they failed to comply with the wishes of the populace. The result was chaos.

The political leaders who had previously been driven into exile returned. Lenin, Stalin, and Trotsky won the support of the peasants with the promise of "Peace, Land, and Bread." The Parliament, on the other hand, continued the country's involvement in the war. Lenin and the Bolshevik Party gained the support of the Red Guard and together overthrew the provisional government. In short order, they had complete control of Russia and established a new communist state.

The most significant differences between the 1905 and 1917 revolutions were the 1) formation of political parties and their use of propaganda, and 2) the support of the military and some of the nobles in 1917.

Declaration of Independence and the Declaration of the Rights of Man

Jean-Jacques Rousseau (1712-1778) was one of the most famous and influential political theorists before the French Revolution. His most important and most studied work is The Social Contract (1762). He was concerned with what should be the proper form of society and government. However, unlike Hobbes, Rousseau did not view the state of nature as one of absolute chaos. The problem as Rousseau saw it was that the natural harmony of the state of nature was due to people's intuitive goodness not to their actual reason. Reason only developed once a civilized society was established.

Rousseau's most direct influence was upon the French Revolution (1789-1815). The Declaration of the Rights of Man and of the Citizen (1789), explicitly recognized the sovereignty of the general will as expressed in the law. In contrast to the American Declaration of Independence, it contains explicit mention of the obligations and duties of the citizen, such as assenting to taxes in support of the military or police forces for the common good. In modern times, ideas such as Rousseau's have often been used to justify the ideas of authoritarian and totalitarian socialist systems.

The three most basic rights guaranteed by the Declaration of Independence are "life, liberty, and the pursuit of happiness." The first one is self-explanatory: Americans are guaranteed the right to live their lives in America. The second one is basic as well: Americans are guaranteed the right to live their lives free in America. (This principle, however, has been violated many times, most notably with Native Americans and African-Americans.) The last basic right is more esoteric, but no less important: Americans are guaranteed the right to pursue a happy life. First and foremost, they are allowed the ability to make a life for themselves in America, "the Land of Opportunity." That happiness also extends to the pursuit of life free from oppression or discrimination, two things that, again, African-Americans, women, and non-white Americans have suffered from to varying degrees throughout the history of the country.

The Declaration of Independence is an outgrowth of both ancient Greek ideas of democracy and individual rights, and the ideas of the European Enlightenment and the Renaissance, especially the ideology of the political thinker John Locke. Thomas Jefferson (1743-1826), author of the Declaration, borrowed much from Locke's theories and writings. John Locke was one of the most influential political writers of the seventeenth century. He put great emphasis on human rights and put forth the belief that when governments violate those rights, people should rebel. He wrote the book "Two Treatises of Government" in 1690, which had tremendous influence on political thought in the American colonies and helped shape the U.S. Constitution and Declaration of Independence.

Essentially, Jefferson applied Locke's principles to the contemporary American situation. Jefferson argued that the currently reigning King George Ill had repeatedly violated the rights of the colonists as subjects of the British Crown. Disdaining the colonial petition for redress of grievances (a right guaranteed by the Declaration of Rights of 1689), the King seemed bent upon establishing an "absolute tyranny" over the colonies. Such disgraceful behavior itself violated the reasons for which government had been instituted. The American colonists were left with no choice. "It is their right, it is their duty, to throw off such a government, and to provide new guards for their future security," wrote Thomas Jefferson.

By 1776, the colonists and their representatives in the Second Continental Congress realized that things were past the point of no return. The Declaration of Independence was drafted and declared July 4, 1776. George Washington labored against tremendous odds to wage a victorious war. The turning point in the Americans' favor occurred in 1777 with the American victory at Saratoga. This victory was supported by the French decision to align itself with the Americans against the British. With the aid of Admiral de Grasse and French warships blocking the entrance to Chesapeake Bay, British General Cornwallis trapped at Yorktown, Virginia, surrendered in 1781 and the war was over. The Treaty of Paris officially ending the war was signed in 1783.

The Declaration of the Rights of Man and of the Citizen is a document created by the French National Assembly, issued in 1789. It sets forth the "natural, inalienable and sacred rights of man." It proclaims the following rights:

- Men are born and remain free and equal in rights. Social distinctions may only be founded upon the general good.
- The aim of all political association is the preservation of the natural and imprescriptible rights of man: liberty, property, security, and resistance to oppression.
- All sovereignty resides essentially in the nation. No body or individual may exercise any authority which does not proceed directly from the nation.
- Liberty is the freedom to do everything which injures no one else; hence the exercise of these rights has no limits except those which assure to the other members of the society the enjoyment of the same rights. These limits can only be determined by law.
- Law can only prohibit such actions as are hurtful to society.
- Law is the expression of the general will. Every citizen has a right to participate in the formation of law. It must be the same for all. All citizens, being equal in the eyes of the law, are equally eligible to all dignities and to all public positions and occupations, according to their abilities.
- No person shall be accused, arrested, or imprisoned except in the cases and according to the forms prescribed by law.
- The law shall provide for such punishments only as are strictly and obviously necessary.
- All persons are held innocent until they have been declared guilty. If it is necessary to arrest a person, all harshness not essential to the securing of the prisoner's person shall be severely repressed by law.
- No one shall be disquieted on account of his opinions, including religious views, provided their manifestation does not disturb the peace.
- The free communication of ideas and opinions is one of the most precious of the rights of man.

- The security of the rights of man and of the citizen requires public military force. These forces are, therefore, established for the good of all and not for the personal advantage of those to whom they shall be entrusted.
- A common contribution is essential for the maintenance of the public forces and for the cost of administration. This should be equitably distributed among all the citizens in proportion to their means.
- All the citizens have a right to decide, either personally or by their representatives, as to the necessity of the public contribution.
- Society has the right to require of every public agent an account of his administration.
- A society in which the observance of the law is not assured nor the separation of powers defined has no constitution at all.

Since property is an inviolable and sacred right, no one shall be deprived thereof except where public necessity, legally determined, shall clearly demand it, and then only on condition that the owner shall have been previously and equitably indemnified.

Skill 4.10   Evaluate the impact of imperialism and nationalism on global social, political, geographic, and economic development.

Imperialism is a government's policy of extending authority or rule over foreign countries or obtaining and holding colonies and dependencies.

Before World War I, France, Great Britain, Italy, Portugal, Spain, Germany, and Belgium controlled the entire continent of Africa except Liberia and Ethiopia. In Asia and the Pacific Islands, only China, Japan, and present-day Thailand (Siam) kept their independence. The other areas were controlled by the strong European nations.

One reason for European imperialism was the urgent demand for the raw materials needed to fuel and feed the great Industrial Revolution. These resources were not available in the huge quantities needed, which necessitated (and rationalized) the partitioning of the continent of Africa and parts of Asia.

In turn, these colonial areas would purchase the finished manufactured goods. Europe in the nineteenth century was a crowded place. Populations were growing, but resources were not. The peoples of many European countries were also agitating for rights as never before. To address these concerns, European powers began to look elsewhere for relief.

One of the main places for European imperialist expansion was Africa. Britain, France, Germany, and Belgium took over countries in Africa and claimed them as their own. The resources (including people) were then shipped back to the mainland and claimed as colonial gains. The Europeans felt they were "civilizing the savages," reasoning that their technological superiority gave them the right to rule and "educate" the peoples of Africa.

Southeast Asia was another area of European expansion with France in Vietnam, Spain in the Philippines, and Great Britain in Burma, Malaysia, and Singapore.

Nationalism is most simply defined as the belief that the nation is the basic unit of human association, and that a nation was a well-defined group of people sharing a common identity. Beginning in the late eighteenth century, nationalistic thought grew throughout the world reaching its peak during the nineteenth century, particularly in Europe.

Of course once a group of people determines that it is a nation, the issue of borders arises, which can result in conflict between nations. As borders are fixed, alliances between nations are drawn to protect national territory. Such was the case throughout Europe in the nineteenth century when growing nationalism contributed to a tangled web of treaties and alliances that unraveled in the World War I.

Growing nationalism within the formerly independent states that made up the empire of Austria-Hungary—as well as that country's nationalistic imperialist ambitions—led to the tense conditions that erupted with the assassination of Archduke Ferdinand, sparking the first hostilities of World War I.

Afterward, Adolf Hitler came to power promising to reunite the various German-speaking peoples of Europe into one nation. His aggressive nationalism sparked World War II.

Skill 4.11   Analyze the causes and effects of political transformations and military conflicts in the 20th Century.

Genocide is defined by the Convention on the Prevention and Punishment of the Crime of Genocide (CPPCG):

Article II: In the present Convention, genocide means any of the following acts committed with intent to destroy, in whole or in part, a national, ethnical, racial or religious group, as such:

a. Killing members of the group;
b. Causing serious bodily or mental harm to members of the group;
c. Deliberately inflicting on the group conditions of life calculated to bring about its physical destruction in whole or in part;
d. Imposing measures intended to prevent births within the group;
e. Forcibly transferring children of the group to another group.

Notable instances of genocide have occurred throughout history and throughout the world.

In the United States, efforts to claim and expand the territory of the new nation and its perceived rights to settle the nation led to the attempted extermination of the Native American peoples. To be sure, many died from diseases introduced by European settlers against which the Native Americans had no acquired or natural resistance. The Native Americans were, however, systematically pushed west—out of the way of progress and national development. They were relocated to undesirable lands where many starved. The most systematic efforts, however, occurred in the Indian Wars when entire villages and tribes were wantonly slaughtered. The massacre at Wounded Knee (1890) is a memorable example of this policy.

During the reign of the Ottoman Empire, the government of the Young Turks, 1915-1917 forced the mass evacuation of over one million Armenians. Many died or were executed in the process. This is referred to as the Armenian Genocide, and indeed the term was coined to describe the event. The Armenians were Christians in a Muslim empire. When the Russians defeated the Ottoman Empire in 1915, the Young Turks placed the blame on the Armenians.

The Holocaust was an effort at ethnic cleansing of Germany and Europe by Adolf Hitler and the Nazi government. Millions of Jews and other "undesirables" were gathered from throughout Europe as the German army advanced and sent to concentration camps where they were either used for medical experimentation, slave labor, or exterminated. Most of the world was slow to believe that this kind of genocide could be occurring, and therefore slow to respond. Hundreds of thousands of Jews were murdered in the gas chambers of the camps.

The genocides in Bosnia-Herzegovina and Rwanda were two sides of the same story, one of the oldest in the world, that of one ethnic group trying to eliminate another solely because of its ethnicity. The disparity between the number of people killed in these two modern genocides in no way reflects any difference in ferocity with which these people were murdered.

The Bosnian Genocide, as it is usually called, took place during the Bosnian War, which lasted from 1992 to 1995. It was part of a larger conflict that stemmed from the breakup of Yugoslavia, which was itself a confederation of ethnic societies held together by not much more than an iron fist for most of its life. Bosnia-Herzegovina and Serbia were once and again their own countries, and their ethnic conflict stretched back for ages. With modern weapons, however, the "ethnic cleansing" that the Serbs practiced on their Bosnian neighbors reached new heights of efficiency.

The worst group of mass murders on record is that at Srebrenica, in 1992, when, international observers estimate, Serbs murdered more than 8,000 Bosnians. The people of Bosnia-Herzegovina say that Srebrenica was just one of many such instances of genocide. Some reports have deaths numbering in the hundreds of thousands, with millions forced to flee their homes.

Serbia also maintained detainment camps during this war that practiced cruel and unusual punishment of prisoners. Photos of some of these detainees made the rounds in international circles during the war, strengthening Bosnia's case against Serb oppression.

As more and more details of the Serb atrocities leaked out, the international outcry over such events grew stronger and stronger. United Nations forces were eventually sent to restore order.

In the end, Serbia was made to stop its "cleansing." The reason given for such atrocities was multi-faceted, but they were all facets of the same basic cause: one ethnic group determined to stamp out another.

The same was true in Rwanda, where Hutus systematically murdered close to a million Tutsis. This staggering number included fellow Hutus who were sympathetic to the Tutsi cause. Most shocking of all, this genocide took place in about 100 days, in the spring and summer of 1994. Perhaps world opinion was too much divided over how to respond to the Serbian problem;

perhaps no one cared "because it's only Africa." Whatever the reason, it took other nations of the world a relatively long time to respond to such savagery.

The Rwandan Genocide was more a matter of geography and economics, as Hutus coveted land owned and worked by Tutsis. Rwanda then, as now, was also a densely populated country, but only in certain areas. The ownership of much of those areas was in dispute, a dispute that spanned centuries of cohabitation and colonization.

International opinion eventually focused on Rwanda, however, and the killings were brought to a halt—not before the aforementioned million people died, however. Again, the impetus for the killings was competing ethnicities.

Another tremendously oppressive ethnic conflict is taking place in the Darfur region of Sudan. An organized campaign of Janjaweed militia has been persecuting members of ethnic groups Fur, Zaghawa, and Massalit, among others. Some estimates put the death toll higher than two million and the number of displaced people higher than four million. The killing goes on in Darfur, with little repercussion from the outside world.

The African genocides fly in the face of Pan-Africanism, the belief that all Africans are one and that they should expand their solidarity under that maxim. The philosophy is a rather old one that has seen new life in recent decades, most notably in Ethiopia and South Africa. Many social scientists argue that if this doctrine were followed, such genocides as those in Rwanda and Sudan would not take place. These social scientists would argue that Africans should respect the lives, intentions, and ethnicities of their fellow Africans.

The same sort of cultural nationalism can be found in the doctrine of Pan Arabism, which is the call for Arab peoples to unite as Arabs and put political, ethnic, and religious differences behind them in favor of a unity based on joint heritage and shared tradition. This doctrine was in force much more prominently in the early days of Islam and saw its zenith during the Crusades. Even then, though, divides in the Muslim world were deep for many Arabs. Those rifts have widened as the centuries have gone by, and many social scientists question whether Pan-Arabism would gain many adherents in the modern, fragmented world. Indeed, many would argue that Pan-Africanism is more likely to succeed than Pan-Arabism, simply because of geography.

See also Skills 5.10, 5.11 and 5.12.

Skill 4.12   Analyze major contemporary global political, social, economic, and geographic issues and trends.

At the turn of the twenty-first century, the world witnessed unprecedented strides in communications, a major expansion of international trade, and significant international diplomatic and military activity.

Globalism is defined as the principle of the interdependence of all the world's nations and their peoples. Within this global community, every nation, in some way to a certain degree, is dependent on other nations. Since no one nation has all of the resources needed for production, trade with other nations is required to obtain what is needed for production, to sell what is produced or to buy finished products, and to earn money to maintain and strengthen the nation's economic system.

Developing nations receive technical assistance and financial aid from developed nations. Many international organizations have been created to promote and encourage cooperation and economic progress among member nations. Through the elimination of barriers to trade such as tariffs, trade is stimulated, resulting in increased productivity, economic progress, cooperation, and understanding on diplomatic levels.

Nations not part of an international trade organization not only must make economic decisions of what to produce, how and for whom, but must also deal with the problem of tariffs and quotas on imports. Regardless of international trade memberships, economic growth and development are vital and affect all trading nations. Businesses, labor, and governments share common interests and goals in a nation's economic status. International systems of banking and finance have been devised to assist governments and businesses in setting the policy and guidelines for the exchange of currencies.

The global economy had its origins in the early twentieth century, with the advent of the airplane, which made travel and trade easier and less time-consuming than ever. With the recent advent of the Internet, the world might be better termed a global neighborhood.

The speed of airplanes results in not only shorter tourist trips but also shorter trade trips, meaning that goods (especially perishable foods) can travel farther and wider than ever before. Being able to ship goods quickly and efficiently means that businesses can conduct business overseas much more efficiently than they ever could.

Trucks, trains, and ships carry cargo all over the world. Trains travel faster than ever, as do ships. Roads are more prevalent and usually in better repair than they have ever been, making truck and even car travel not the dead-end option that it once was.

With all of this capability has come increasing demand. People traditionally had exchanged goods using their own means of transportation or from traders who lived nearby. As technology improved, trade routes expanded and imports from overseas grew. This demand feeds the economic imperative of creating more supply—and vice versa. As more people discover goods from overseas, the demand for those foreign goods increases. Because people can get goods from overseas with relative ease, they continue to get them and demand more. Suppliers are only too happy to supply the goods.

An incredible increase in demand for something is not always a good thing, however, especially if what is being demanded is in limited supply. The precious rainforests are disappearing at an alarming rate, especially in South America and Indonesia. Not only do rainforests provide products, but they are an essential part of the global weather system.

Nonrenewable resources such as coal and oil are in worldwide demand these days, and the supplies won't last forever. Making it easier to ship goods all over the world has made demand grow at an unbelievable rate, raising concerns about supply. Because resources like this have a limited supply (even though the day when that limit is reached seems far away still), they are in danger of becoming extinct without being replaced.

Globalization has also brought about welcome and unwelcome developments in the field of epidemiology. Vaccines and other cures for diseases can be shipped relatively quickly all around the world. For example, this has made it possible for HIV vaccines to reach the remotest areas of the world, for example. Unfortunately, the preponderance of global travel has also meant that the threat of spreading a disease to the world by an infected person traveling on an international flight is quite real.

Technology contributed to globalization with the development of the Internet. Instant communication between people thousands of miles apart is possible just by plugging in a computer and connecting to the Internet. The Internet is an extension of the telephone and cell phone revolutions; all three are developments in communications that have brought faraway places closer together. All three allow people to communicate no matter the distance. This communication can facilitate friendly chatter, remote business meetings, and distant trade opportunities. Cell phones and the Internet are often required to do business nowadays. Computer programs enable the tracking of goods and receipts quickly and efficiently.

Globalization has also brought financial and cultural exchange on a worldwide scale. Many businesses have investments in countries around the world. Financial transactions are conducted using a variety of currencies. The cultures of the countries of the world are increasingly viewed by people throughout the world via multimedia developments. Not only goods but also belief systems, customs, and practices are being exchanged.

With this exchange of money, goods, and culture has come an increase in immigration. Many people who live in less-developed nations see what is available in other places and want to move there, in order to fully take advantage of all that those more-developed nations have to offer. This can create an increase in immigration. Depending on the numbers of people who want to immigrate and the resources available, this could become a problem. The technological advances in transportation and communications have made such immigration easier than ever.

Contemporary political and social issues include health care reform, illegal drugs, homeland security, the threat of terrorism, illegal immigrants, same sex marriage, gun control, and unrest and wars in the Middle East.

Skill 4.13   Identify major world religions and ideologies.

Judaism: Judaism is the oldest of the Western world's three monotheistic religions. It grew out of the ancient religion of the Hebrews or Israelites. This early religion shared a number of common elements and primordial stories with neighboring peoples, especially the Mesopotamian and Babylonian cultures. Judaism's sacred writing, the Hebrew Scripture, is generally referred to as Tanakh. It consists of 24 books which are divided into three sections: the Teachings or Law (Torah, also known as the Five Books of Moses or the Pentateuch); Prophets (Envois); and Writings (Ketuvim).

The word and law of God were transmitted orally for many generations prior to the writing of the Hebrew Scripture. The Mishnah is the collection of the oral tradition. The Gemara is a collection of commentary by the rabbis (teachers). The tradition of living interpretation and commentary continued through the centuries. Halakah is the tradition of interpretation of law, history and practice. Kabbalah is a body of Jewish mystical literature. Kabbalah arose from a movement in France in the eleventh century that discovered an esoteric system of symbolic interpretation of scripture.

Judaism is centered in belief in a single, all-powerful, all-seeing, and all-knowing God. Judaism says that God chose the Hebrew people from all the people of the earth and entered into a covenant with them. "I will be your God, and you will be my people." This covenant implies special privileges, but it also implies certain obligations of the people. The life of the people is to be structured around the promises and commandments of God. The Law provides the structure of religious practice and daily life. The Law is the guide for making ethical choices that reflect and demonstrate their unique character as the chosen people of God. Failure to act in accordance with God's law is a willful act, called sin. Sin destroys the proper relationship between the person and God. It is, however, possible to return from willful rebellion and restore the broken relationship with God. Judaism is also marked by a strong sense of communal identity and sin can be either individual or communal.

The Jewish people, as the chosen people of God, are to remain separate or apart from other peoples in several ways. First, the Jews are to avoid marriage to persons outside the faith. Second, they are to observe certain dietary restrictions The rules for kosher (ritually correct) food preparation and consumption are quite detailed, and include prohibitions against eating certain animals, including pork and shellfish, specifications for the slaughter and butchering of meat, and a prohibition against mixing meat and dairy products. Third, Jews shall not marry foreigners which protects the faith of the community against other influences and conflicting ideas. Fourth is the circumcision of all males (both an act of obedience to the covenant and an indication of the separateness of the people).

Among devout Jews, special times for prayer are at dawn, noon, dusk, and, for some, bedtime. The Jewish Sabbath is observed from sunset on Friday until sunset on Saturday. The Sabbath is a day of rest. Many observant Jews gather on the Sabbath for worship in synagogues, where a rabbi leads them in readings from the Scriptures, prayer and singing. The Jewish religious calendar is based on a lunar calendar, so the dates of religious holidays vary from year to year. With the exception of the New Year observance and the Day of Atonement, most holidays are based on either seasonal or historical events. The frequent prohibitions against idolatry in Hebrew Scripture reflect a deep and abiding concern that no limited entity or belief be mistaken for the one true God by God's chosen people.

The basic beliefs of Judaism are:

1. There is one and only one God with whom each believer has direct personal experience and to whom prayers may be addressed.
2. God is the ultimate authority and possesses final dominion over the universe, which He created.

3. Life is holy.
4. The Torah is a guide to correct living and a source of continued revelation of the word of God.
5. Group worship and prayer are indispensable elements of a righteous life.
6. Jews share a broad common diversity and a sense of collective purpose and responsibility to one another.

Today, there are three basic branches or schools of Jewish belief and practice.

Orthodox Judaism is the most rigorous and the smallest branch. This group conducts worship in Hebrew and interprets the Law very strictly and literally.

Reform Judaism, which originated in the 18th century, attempted to integrate Judaism into the mainstream European culture. Law, doctrine, and ritual are more liberally interpreted, and dietary laws generally are not observed.

Conservative Judaism combines doctrinal reform with traditional observance. Attempts to retain much of the old orthodoxy, while not losing touch with contemporary culture, has made Conservative Jews somewhat reluctant to embrace most of the changes of Reform Judaism.

Christianity: Christianity grew out of Judaism and its belief that God would send a Messiah ("anointed one") who would establish the Kingdom of God on earth. The Christian Bible says that Jesus of Nazareth appeared in the early years of the first century BC, preaching repentance in preparation for the arrival of the Kingdom of God. His brief (about three years) ministry of teaching, preaching, healing, and miracles gathered followers from among the common and the despised of his day, as well as non-Jews and the wealthy. This ministry was confined to the areas of Galilee and northwest Palestine. According to Christian writings, Jesus eschewed the separatism of Judaism and reached out to the poor, the sick, and the social outcasts. He preached a Kingdom of God not of this world, which ran contrary to Jewish expectation of a political Messiah who would establish an earthly kingdom. As the movement grew, the teachings of Jesus were perceived as a danger to the political order by both the Jews and the Roman government. Jesus was handed over to the authorities by one of his closest followers, arrested, tried, and crucified. According to Christian belief, Jesus rose from the dead on the third day, appeared to his disciples, and then ascended to heaven.

Christians believe that Jesus was the Son of God who died on the cross as an offering and sacrifice that saved humankind from sin. Those who believe in him will be saved. Christian scripture (the Bible) consists of two major parts: the Old Testament, which is an adoption of the Hebrew Scripture, and the New Testament, which consists of 27 books.

As an outgrowth of Judaism, Christianity accepts many of the beliefs, though not the practices of Judaism. Fundamental beliefs of Christianity are: (1) one God who is the creator and redeemer of humankind; (2) God is all-knowing, all-powerful, and all-present; and (3) Jesus Christ is the unique Son of God who is the savior of humankind.

The doctrine of the Trinity teaches that the one God has three natures through/by which God is active in the world: God the Father, the creator and governor of creation, is the judge of humankind; God the Son (Jesus) is God in the flesh, who came among humankind to save them from sin; and God the Holy Spirit is the invisible presence of God for believers to provide strength, faith and guidance.

Christians observe Sunday as the Sabbath because Jesus was believed to have risen from the dead on a Sunday morning. Christian worship consists of the reading of scripture, the proclamation of the word of God, prayer, and the observance of the Sacraments. The Roman Catholic and Eastern Orthodox churches recognize seven sacraments: baptism, confirmation, marriage, ordination, anointing and absolution of the sick and dying, the confession of sins, and the Eucharist or Holy Communion. Protestant churches recognize only two sacraments: baptism and Holy Communion. Christians believe that each human being has an eternal soul that will be judged by God after death. The soul will then be "rewarded" or punished according to one's faith and actions in life. Roman Catholics and Eastern Orthodox also believe in the existence of a purgatory, which is a state in which some souls are purified for entry to heaven.

Christian ethics are based on the Ten Commandments of the Old Testament and the teachings of Jesus, which include the "Golden Rule" (Do unto others as you would have them do unto you") and a broadening of the application of the commandments. Until 1054 there was one Christian Church. In 1054 the Eastern Orthodox Church split from the Roman Catholic Church over several issues of belief and practice. In the sixteenth century, several reformers split from the Roman Catholic Church, again over issues of belief and practice, in what is known as the Protestant Reformation.

Islam: In about 610 CE a prophet named Mohammed came to some prominence with a new religion called Islam (translates to "submission to the will of God"). The new religion came from the same source of Judaism and Christianity, and Islam recognizes both religions. After early persecution, the religion began to gain adherents. The teachings of Islam are in a holy book, the Qur'an, which instructs Muslims on ways of life, including worship, morality, and behavior. Muslims observe five prayers a day, have a month of fasting (Ramadan), and practice charity and giving alms as a part of their religion. During the month of pilgrimage, many Muslims travel to Mecca for a spiritual journey.

Hinduism: Hinduism is unique among the major religions of the world in that it has no identifiable founder, no single theological system, no single code of ethics, and no central religious organization. Modern Hinduism evolved from an ancient religion called Vedism, which dates from around 1500 BC. Hinduism is expressed in many forms, most of which are "henotheistic"–recognizing a single God that is manifested or expressed in other gods and goddesses.

Hinduism recognizes several sacred writings: The Vedas are the chants of the priestly class of the Aryan ("noble") people who introduced Vedism into the Indian subcontinent; the four central texts – the Rig Veda ("hymn knowledge"), the Yajur Veda ("ceremonial knowledge"), the Sama Veda ("chant knowledge") and the Atharva Veda ("knowledge from Atharve," a Vedic teacher); the Brahmana and Aranyakas, which are ceremonial rules that were later added to the other

Vedas; and the Upanishads, which is a collection of poetry and prose that explores the basic philosophical and spiritual concepts of Hinduism. The Upanishads teach that spiritual mastery is achievable by all who practice correct meditation and discipline. Two other important Hindu texts are the Ramayana and the Mahabharata, which include the Bahagavad Gita. The Bhagavad Gita teaches that duty (dharma) and action are equal to prayer and sacrifice as paths to spiritual perfection.

Hinduism is a diverse religion. Beliefs and practices vary from one school to another. Central beliefs are:

1. Worship is an individual or family matter.
2. Atman and Brahman are generally understood as "Soul" and "divine spirit". Brahman is the course and substance of all existence; when it is understood as the "self" of humans, it is called Atman.
3. The spiritual goal of Hinduism is to understand and experience that there is no difference between one's self and the rest of the universe.
4. Maya, which is used to describe the world, comes from the concepts of magic and matter and is often translated "illusion". This belief is that the world has a single spiritual nature and is not divided into "things."
5. Karma is the moral consequence of every act in the course of human life.
6. Samsara is the cycle of birth and rebirth in life. The path of the soul through rebirth is determined by the individual's karma.
7. Moksha, which means "liberation" or "freedom," refers to the soul breaking free of the endless cycle of rebirth in life. Moksha is attained by freeing oneself of egotism and anger and losing one's sense of individuality in maya. The ultimate goal of Hinduism is the achievement of recognition that one's self is indistinguishable from Brahman.

In addition, Hindus also believe in pursuing worldly goals, including religious and social duty, economic security and power, and pleasure, all of this according to one's place in society. The caste system provides the framework of society and this process. The society is divided into four major "castes" that are defined by social standing and occupation. These are the priestly class; the aristocratic protectors of society; the class of merchants, landowners and moneylenders; and the laborers. Those outside the caste system were the "Untouchables."

Yoga is an active path to spiritual perfection. Evolving around the cults of anthropomorphic gods, there are three major theistic traditions. Vishnu is the force of preservation, Shiva is a god of destruction, and Brahma is the creative force. Hindus honor a number of incarnations of these gods, including Rama and Krishna. Hindus believe that all living things share a common element of Brahman, and thus are to be respected. Some animals are understood to be manifestations of certain deities. The most honored animal is the cow.

Buddhism: Buddhism was developed and taught by Siddhartha Gautama in what is now Nepal around 563 BC. Upon consideration of the suffering of people in the world, he traveled widely, studying and meditating. He experienced "enlightenment" and thus earned the name Buddha, which means "the awakened one" or "the enlightened one." He then created an order of monks and taught the Buddhist philosophy of escape from life's cycle of suffering through compassion, nonviolence, and moderate living.

The central written text of Buddhism is called the Tipitaka, the "three baskets" or collections of Buddhist thought. Although these were not written down until many years after the death of the Buddha, these texts are accepted as his exact words. The three baskets are: the sutras, which are the teachings in the form of dialogues and sermons; the vinaya, which are the rules for monastic life; and the abhidharma, a systematic ordering of the lessons of the sutras.

A number of beliefs and ideas are shared with Hinduism, from the context of which Buddhism arose. These include nonviolence and the cycle of birth and rebirth. The idea of nirvana is quite similar to moksha in the Hindu tradition, which is an escape from the cycle of rebirth. However, Buddhism teaches that nothing is permanent, including the universal spirit or the self. The Buddha taught that there is constant change in the universe and that all things will, in time, decay and disappear. Because nothing can endure unchanged forever, desire is infinite and insatiable. Peace and enlightenment are thus possible only by renouncing desire and accepting that existence is not permanent.

The Three Jewels of Buddhism are the three things that are the heart of Buddhist belief: 1) the Buddha is the model of what all humans should aspire to be or become; 2) the overarching Buddhist worldview and way of life; and 3) the community of Buddhist nuns and monks.

The Four Noble Truths summarize the Buddhist worldview: 1) all life involves suffering; 2) suffering is caused by desire; 3) desire can be overcome; and 4) the way to overcome desire is to follow the eightfold path.

The Noble Eightfold Path summarizes the steps one should practice simultaneously to understand the universe, to live compassionately, and to achieve peace and enlightenment – 1) right views; 2) right intentions; 3) right speech; 4) right conduct; 5) right work; 6) right effort; (7) right meditation; and 8) right contemplation.

The major schools or branches of Buddhism are:

- Theravada Buddhism (Doctrine of the Elders) adheres most closely to the earliest practices. The monastic life has special importance in this branch. The ideal is a person who has attained perfect enlightenment and the end of all desire.

- Mahayana Buddhism (Greater Vehicle) focuses on compassion for others over personal progress toward enlightenment. The ideal of this branch is the "bodhisattva" – an enlightened person who postpones entry into Nirvana to help others.

- Vajrayana Buddhism (Tantric Buddhism) emphasizes ritual, including the use of mantras (chants) hand gestures, mandalas (icons of the universe) and prayer wheels.

- Confucianism: is a Chinese religion based on the teachings of the Chinese philosopher Kung Fu-Tzu (translated, Confucius). There is no clergy, no organization, and no belief in a deity or in life after death. Confucius took a code of ethics and the teaching of a scholarly tradition and systematized it. The teachings of Confucius were written down in the Analects. These writings deal with individual morality and ethics and with the correct exercise of power by rulers.

Confucianism is essentially a "humanitarian ethical system" built on five key values: 1) Ren, reciprocal human feeling; 2) Yi, righteousness; 3) Li, propriety, which includes ritually correct behavior; 4) Zhi, knowledge; and 5) Xin, trustworthiness. These five values enable one to exercise the virtues of Xiao, filial piety; and Wen, civilization.

Confucianism was primarily a philosophical and ethical system until about the first century AD, when Buddhism was introduced into China. It gradually began to take on aspects of a religion.

Taoism: a native Chinese religion with worship of more deities than almost any other religion. It is believed to have been founded by Lao Tzu, who was a contemporary of Confucius. The word Tao means path or way. The central writing of Taoism is the Tao Te Ching (The Way and its Power). The 81 brief chapters, in poetry, discuss the nature of the Tao, which is the source and essence of all being. Primary Taoist concepts, practices and beliefs are: 1) Tao is the first cause of the universe and the force that flows through all life; 2) the goal of each believer is to develop harmony with the Tao; 3) there are many gods, which are manifestations of the one Tao; 4) answers to life's problems are to be sought through inner meditation and outward observation; 5) time is cyclical, not linear; 6) health and vitality are to be strengthened; 7) the five main organs and orifices of the body correspond to the five parts of the universe–fire, water, metal, earth, wood; 8) the development of virtue is the chief goal of believers; 9) the three "Jewels" to be cultivated in life are moderation, humility and compassion; 10) humans should allow nature to take its course; 11) one should carefully consider each action in advance; 12) one should be kind to others; and 13) people are compassionate by nature. A basic Taoist symbol is the Yin and Yang. It represents the balance and the essential unity of opposites in the universe.

Shinto: Shinto is a native religion of Japan that developed from native folk beliefs and involved the worship of spirits and demons in animals, trees, and mountains. According to its belief, deities created Japan and its people, which resulted in worshipping the emperor as a god. Shinto was strongly influenced by Buddhism and Confucianism but never has had strong doctrines on salvation or life after death.

There are "Four Affirmations" in Shinto: 1) tradition and the family (the family is the primary mechanism for preserving traditions); 2) love of nature (nature is sacred. To be in contact with nature is to be close to the gods, who reside in natural objects); 3) physical cleanliness; and 4) "Matsuri" (the honor and worship of the Kami and the ancestral spirits. Morality in Shinto is defined by what is in the best interest of the group.

COMPETENCY 5.0   KNOWLEDGE OF AMERICAN HISTORY

Skill 5.1   Evaluate the impact of the Age of Exploration on the Americas.

The Meeting of Three Worlds: Africa, Europe, and the Americas

The Age of Exploration actually had its beginnings centuries before exploration actually took place. The rise and spread of Islam in the seventh century and its subsequent control over the holy city of Jerusalem led to the European so-called Holy Wars, the Crusades, to free Jerusalem and the Holy Land from this control. Even though the Crusades were not a success, those who survived and returned to their homes and countries in Western Europe brought back with them new products such as silks, spices, perfumes, and new and different foods. New ideas, inventions, and methods also went to Western Europe with the returning Crusaders, and from these new influences was the intellectual stimulation which led to the period known as the Renaissance.

Colonization and Settlement (1585-1763)

The part of North America claimed by France was called New France and consisted of the land west of the Appalachian Mountains. This area of claims and settlement included the St. Lawrence Valley, the Great Lakes, the Mississippi Valley, and the entire region of land westward to the Rocky Mountains. They established the permanent settlements of Montreal and New Orleans, thus giving them control of the two major gateways into the heart of North America, the vast, rich interior. The St. Lawrence River, the Great Lakes, and the Mississippi River along with its tributaries made it possible for the French explorers and traders to roam at will, virtually unhindered in exploring, trapping, trading, and furthering the interests of France.

Most of the French settlements were in Canada along the St. Lawrence River. Only scattered forts and trading posts were found in the upper Mississippi Valley and Great Lakes region. The rulers of France originally intended New France to have vast estates owned by nobles and worked by peasants who would live on the estates in compact farming villages—the New World version of the Old World's medieval system of feudalism. However, it didn't work out that way. Each of the nobles wanted his estate to be on the river for ease of transportation. The peasants working the estates wanted the prime waterfront location, also. The result of all this real estate squabbling was that New France's settled areas wound up mostly as a string of farmhouses stretching from Quebec to Montreal along the St. Lawrence and Richelieu Rivers.

In the non-settled areas in the interior were the French fur traders. They made friends with the friendly tribes of Indians, spending the winters with them getting the furs needed for trade. In the spring, they would return to Montreal in time to take advantage of trading their furs for the products brought by the cargo ships from France, which usually arrived at about the same time. Most of the wealth for New France and its "Mother Country" was from the fur trade, which provided a livelihood for many, many people. Manufacturers and workmen back in France, ship-owners and merchants, as well as the fur traders and their Indian allies all benefited. However, the freedom of roaming and trapping in the interior was a strong enticement for the younger, stronger men and resulted in the French not strengthening the areas settled along the St. Lawrence.

Into the eighteenth century, the rivalry with the British was growing stronger and stronger. New France was united under a single government and enjoyed the support of many Indian allies. The French traders were very diligent in not destroying the forests and driving away game upon which the Indians depended for life. It was difficult for the French to defend all of their settlements as they were scattered over half of the continent. However, by the early 1750s, in Western Europe, France was the most powerful nation. Its armies were superior to all others and its navy was giving the British stiff competition for control of the seas. The stage was set for confrontation in both Europe and America.

Spanish settlement had its beginnings in the Caribbean with the establishment of colonies on Hispaniola (at Santo Domingo which became the capital of the West Indies), Puerto Rico, and Cuba. There were a number of reasons for Spanish involvement in the Americas, to name just a few:

- spirit of adventure
- desire for land
- expansion of Spanish power, influence, and empire
- desire for great wealth
- expansion of Roman Catholic influence and conversion of native peoples

The first permanent settlement in what is now the United States was in 1565 at St. Augustine, Florida. A later permanent settlement in the southwestern United States was in 1609 at Santa Fe, New Mexico. At the peak of Spanish power, the area in the United States claimed, settled, and controlled by Spain included Florida and all land west of the Mississippi River—quite a piece of choice real estate. Of course, France and England also lay claim to the same areas. Nonetheless, ranches and missions were built, and the Indians who came in contact with the Spaniards were introduced to animals, plants, and seeds from the Old World that they had never seen before. Animals brought in included horses, cattle, donkeys, pigs, sheep, goats, and poultry.

Barrels were cut in half and filled with earth to transport and transplant trees bearing apples, oranges, limes, cherries, pears, walnuts, olives, lemons, figs, apricots, almonds

Even sugar cane and flowers made it to America along with bags of seeds of wheat, barley, rye, flax, lentils, rice, and peas.

All Spanish colonies belonged to the King of Spain. He was considered an absolute monarch with complete or absolute power and claimed rule by divine right, the belief being God had given him the right to rule, and he answered only to God for his actions. His word was final and the law. The people had no voice in government. The land, the people, the wealth all belonged to him to use as he pleased. He appointed personal representatives or viceroys to rule for him in his colonies. They ruled in his name with complete authority. Since the majority of them were friends and advisers, they were richly rewarded with land grants, gold and silver, privileges of trading, and the right to operate the gold and silver mines.

For the needed labor in the mines and on the plantations, Indians were used first as slaves. However, they either rapidly died out due to a lack of immunity from European diseases or escaped into nearby jungles or mountains. As a result, African slaves were brought in, especially to the islands of the West Indies. Some historians state that Latin American slavery was less harsh than in the later English colonies in North America. Three reasons for this are:

- The following of a slave code based on ancient Roman laws
- The efforts of the Roman Catholic Church to protect and defend slaves because of efforts to convert them
- The existence of less prejudice because of racial mixtures in parts of Spain controlled at one time by dark-skinned Moors from North Africa

Regardless, slavery was still slavery and was very harsh—cruelly denying dignity and human worth and leading to desperate resistance.

Spain's control over her New World colonies lasted more than 300 years, longer than England or France. To this day, Spanish influence remains in names of places, art, architecture, music, literature, law, and cuisine. The Spanish settlements in North America were not commercial enterprises but were for protection and defense of the trading and wealth from their colonies in Mexico and South America. The Russians hunted seals along the Pacific coast; the English moved into Florida and into the Appalachians; and the French traders and trappers made their way from Louisiana and other parts of New France into Spanish territory. The Spanish never realized or understood that self-sustaining economic development and colonial trade were so important. Consequently, the Spanish settlements in the U.S. never really prospered.

The treasure and wealth found in Spanish New World colonies went back to Spain to be used to buy whatever goods and products were needed instead of setting up industries to make what was needed. As the amount of gold and silver was depleted, Spain could not pay for the goods needed and was unable to produce goods for themselves. Also, at the same time, Spanish treasure ships at sea were being seized by English and Dutch "pirates" taking the wealth to the coffers of their own countries.

Before 1763, England was rapidly becoming the most powerful of the three major Western European powers. Its thirteen colonies, located between the Atlantic and the Appalachians, physically occupied the least amount of land. Moreover, it is interesting that even before the Spanish Armada was defeated, two Englishmen, Sir Humphrey Gilbert and his half-brother Sir Walter Raleigh, were unsuccessful in their attempts to build successful permanent colonies in the New World. Nonetheless, the thirteen English colonies were successful, and by the time they had gained their independence from Britain, they were more than able to govern themselves. They had a rich historical heritage of law, tradition, and documents leading the way to constitutional government conducted according to laws and customs. The settlers in the British colonies highly valued individual freedom, democratic government, and getting ahead through hard work.

Skill 5.2 **Analyze the social, cultural, political, and economic development of the Americas during the colonial period.**

The English colonies, with only a few exceptions, were considered commercial ventures to make a profit for the crown or the company or whoever financed its beginnings. One was strictly a philanthropic enterprise and three others were primarily for religious reasons but the other nine were started for economic reasons. Settlers in these unique colonies came for different reasons:

- religious freedom
- political freedom
- economic prosperity
- land ownership

The colonies were divided generally into the three regions of New England, Middle Atlantic, and Southern. The culture of each was distinct and affected attitudes, ideas towards politics, religion, and economic activities. The geography of each region also contributed to its unique characteristics.

The New England colonies consisted of Massachusetts, Rhode Island, Connecticut, and New Hampshire. Life in these colonies was centered on the towns. Farming was done was by each family on its own plot of land, but a short summer growing season and limited amount of good soil gave rise to other economic activities such as manufacturing, fishing, shipbuilding, and trade. The vast majority of the settlers shared similar origins, coming from England and Scotland. Towns were carefully planned and laid out the same way. The form of government was the town meeting, where all adult males met to make the laws. The legislative body, the General Court, consisted of an upper and lower house. Metacom, called King Philip by New Englanders, was the leader of the Wampanoags near Plymouth colony, and he led many Indians into a revolt against the colonists of southern New England in 1675.

The Middle or Middle Atlantic colonies included New York, New Jersey, Pennsylvania, Delaware, and Maryland. New York and New Jersey were at one time the Dutch colony of New Netherland, and Delaware at one time was New Sweden. These five colonies, from their beginnings were considered "melting pots" with settlers from many different nations and backgrounds. The main economic activity was farming, with the settlers scattered over the countryside cultivating large farms. The Indians were not as much of a threat as in New England, so the colonists did not have to settle in small farming villages. The soil was very fertile, the land was gently rolling, and a milder climate provided a longer growing season.

These farms produced a large surplus of food, not only for the colonists themselves but also for sale. This colonial region became known as the "breadbasket" of the New World and the New York and Philadelphia seaports were constantly filled with ships being loaded with meat, flour, and other foodstuffs for the West Indies and England.

There were other economic activities such as shipbuilding, iron mines, and the production of paper, glass, and textiles. The legislative body in Pennsylvania was unicameral or consisted of one house. In the other four colonies, the legislative bodies had two houses. Units of local government were in counties and towns.

The Southern colonies were Virginia, North and South Carolina, and Georgia. Virginia was the first permanent successful English colony, and Georgia was the last. The year 1619 was a very important year in the history of Virginia and the United States with three very significant events. First, sixty women were sent to Virginia to marry and establish families; second, twenty Africans, the first of thousands, arrived; and third, the Virginia colonists were granted the right to self-government and began by electing their own representatives to the House of Burgesses, their own legislative body.

The major economic activity in this region was farming. The soil was very fertile and the climate mild, with a long growing season. The large plantations that eventually required large numbers of slaves were located in the coastal or tidewater areas. Although the wealthy slave-owning planters set the pattern of life in this region, most of the people lived inland away from coastal areas. They were small farmers and very few, if any, owned slaves.

The settlers in these four colonies came from diverse backgrounds and cultures. Virginia was colonized mostly by people from England while Georgia was started as a haven for debtors from English prisons. Pioneers from Virginia settled in North Carolina while South Carolina welcomed people from England and Scotland, French Protestants, Germans, and emigrants from islands in the West Indies. Products from farms and plantations included rice, tobacco, indigo, cotton, corn and wheat. Other economic activities included lumber, naval stores (tar, pitch, rosin, and turpentine) from the pine forests, and fur trade on the frontier. Cities such as Savannah and Charleston were important seaports and trading centers.

In the colonies, the daily life of the colonists differed greatly between the coastal settlements and the inland or interior. The Southern planters and the people living in the coastal cities and towns had a way of life similar to that of towns in England. The influence was seen and heard in the way people dressed and talked, the architectural styles of houses and public buildings, and the social divisions or levels of society. Both the planters and city dwellers enjoyed an active social life and had strong emotional ties to England.

On the other hand, life inland on the frontier had marked differences. All facets of daily living—clothing, food, and home, economic and social activities—were all connected to what was needed to sustain life and survive in the wilderness. Everything was produced within the colonies. The people were self-sufficient, extremely individualistic, and independent. There were few, if any, levels of society or class distinctions as nearly all considered themselves equal to all others, regardless of station in life. The roots of equality, independence, individual rights and freedoms were extremely strong and well-developed. People were not judged by their fancy dress, expensive house, eloquent language, or titles following their names.

Skill 5.3   **Identify the causes, significant individuals, and effects of the events associated with the Revolutionary era.**

The War for Independence occurred due to a number of changes, the two most important ones being economic and political. By the end of the French and Indian War in 1763, Britain's American colonies were thirteen out of a total of 33 scattered around the earth. Like all other countries, Britain strove for having a strong economy and a favorable balance of trade. To have that delicate balance a nation needs wealth, self-sufficiency, and a powerful army and navy. The overseas colonies would provide raw materials for the industries in the Mother Country, be a market for the finished products by buying them and assist the Mother Country in becoming powerful and strong (as in the case of Great Britain). By having a strong merchant fleet, it would be a school for training the Royal Navy and provide bases of operation for the Royal Navy.

So between 1607 and 1763, at various times for various reasons, the British Parliament enacted different laws to assist the government in getting and keeping this trade balance. One series of laws required that most of the manufacturing be done only in England and prohibited exporting any wool or woolen cloth from the colonies as well as the manufacture of beaver hats or iron products. The colonists weren't particularly concerned as they had no money and no highly skilled labor to set up any industries anyway.

The Navigation Acts of 1651 put restrictions on shipping and trade within the British Empire, requiring that it was allowed only on British ships. This increased the strength of the British merchant fleet and greatly benefited the American colonists. Since they were British citizens, they could have their own vessels, building and operating them as well. By the end of the war in 1763, the shipyards in the colonies were building one-third of the merchant ships under the British flag. There were quite a number of wealthy, colonial merchants.

The Navigation Act of 1660 restricted the shipment and sale of colonial products to England only. In 1663 another Navigation Act stipulated that the colonies had to buy manufactured products only from England and that any European goods going to the colonies had to go to England first. These acts were a protection from enemy ships and pirates—and from competition from European rivals.

The New England and Middle Atlantic colonies at first felt threatened by these laws as they had started producing many of the products being produced in Britain. They soon found new markets for their goods and began what was known as a triangular trade. Colonial vessels started the first part of the triangle by sailing for Africa loaded with kegs of rum from colonial distilleries. On Africa's West Coast, the rum was traded for either gold or slaves. The second part of the triangle was from Africa to the West Indies where slaves were traded for molasses, sugar, or money. The third part of the triangle was home, bringing home sugar or molasses (to make more rum), gold, and silver.

The major concern of the British government was that the trade violated the 1733 Molasses Act. Planters had wanted the colonists to buy all of their molasses in the British West Indies, but these islands could give the traders only about one-eighth of the amount of molasses needed for distilling the rum. The colonists were forced to buy the rest of what they needed from the French,

Dutch, and Spanish islands, thus evading the law by not paying the high duty on the molasses bought from these islands. If Britain had enforced the Molasses Act, economic and financial chaos and ruin would have occurred. Nevertheless, for this Act and all the other mercantile laws, the government followed the policy of "salutary neglect," deliberately failing to enforce the laws.

In 1763, after the war, money was needed to pay the British war debt, for the defense of the empire, and to pay for the governing of 33 colonies scattered around the earth. It was decided to adopt a new colonial policy and pass laws to raise revenue. It was reasoned that the colonists were subjects of the king and since the king and his ministers had spent a great deal of money defending and protecting them (this especially for the American colonists), it was only right and fair that the colonists should help pay the costs of their defense. The earlier laws passed had been for the purposes of regulating production and trade which generally put money into colonial pockets. These new laws would take some of that rather hard-earned money out of their pockets, and it would be done, in colonial eyes, unjustly and illegally.

Before 1763, except for trade and supplying raw materials, the colonies had been left pretty much to themselves. England looked on the colonies merely as part of an economic or commercial empire. Little consideration was given as to how they were to conduct their daily affairs, so the colonists became very independent, self-reliant, and extremely skillful at handling those daily affairs. This, in turn, gave rise to leadership, initiative, achievement, and vast experience. In fact, there was a far greater degree of independence and self-government in the British colonies in America than could be found in Britain or the major countries on the Continent or any other colonies anywhere. There were a number of reasons for this:

1. The religious and scriptural teachings of previous centuries put forth the worth of the individual and equality in God's sight. Keep in mind that freedom of worship and from religious persecution were major reasons to live in the New World.
2. European Protestants, especially Calvinists, believed and taught the idea that government originates from those governed, that rulers are required to protect individual rights, and that the governed have the right and privilege to choose their rulers.
3. Trading companies put into practice the principle that their members had the right to make the decisions and shape the policies affecting their lives.
4. The colonists believed and supported the idea that a person's property should not be taken without his consent, based on that treasured English document, the Magna Carta, and English common law.
5. From about 1700 to 1750, population increases in America came about through immigration and generations of descendants of the original settlers. The immigrants were mainly Scots-Irish who hated the English, Germans who cared nothing about England, and black slaves who knew nothing about England. The descendants of many of the original settlers had never been out of America at any time.
6. In America, as new towns and counties were formed, there began the practice of representation in government. Representatives to the colonial legislative assemblies were elected from the district in which they lived, chosen by qualified property-owning male voters, and represented the interests of the political district from which they were elected. However, each of the thirteen colonies had a royal governor appointed by the king representing his interests in the colonies. Nevertheless, the colonial legislative assemblies

controlled the purse strings, having the power to vote on all issues involving money to be spent by the colonial governments.

Thomas Paine (1737-1809), the great American political theorist, wrote: "These are the times that try men's souls" in his 16-part pamphlet The Crisis. Paine's authoring of Common Sense was an important step in spreading information to the American colonists about their need for independence from Great Britain.

Contrary to this was the governmental set up in England. Members of Parliament were not elected to represent their own districts. They were considered representative of classes, not individuals. If some members of a professional or commercial class or some landed interests were able to elect representatives, then those classes or special interests were represented. It had nothing at all to do with numbers or territories. Some large population centers had no direct representation at all, yet the people there considered themselves represented by men elected from their particular class or interest somewhere else. Consequently, it was extremely difficult for the English to understand why the American merchants and landowners claimed they were not represented because they themselves did not vote for a member of Parliament.

The colonists' protest of "no taxation without representation" was meaningless to the English. Parliament represented the entire nation, was completely unlimited in legislation, and had become supreme; and the colonists were incensed at the English attitude of "of course you have representation—everyone does." The colonists considered their colonial legislative assemblies equal to Parliament, totally unacceptable in England, of course. There were two different environments: the older traditional British system in the "mother country" and new ideas and different ways of doing things in America. In a new country, a new environment has little or no tradition, institutions, or vested interests. New ideas and traditions grew extremely fast pushing aside what was left of the old ideas and old traditions. By 1763, Britain had changed its perception of its American colonies to their being a "territorial" empire. The stage was set and the conditions right for a showdown.

In 1763, Parliament decided to have a standing army in North America to reinforce British control. In 1765, the Quartering Act was passed requiring the colonists to provide supplies and living quarters for the British troops. In addition, efforts by the British were made to keep the peace by establishing good relations with the Indians. Consequently, a proclamation was issued which prohibited any American colonists from making any settlements west of the Appalachians until provided for through treaties with the Indians.

The Sugar Act of 1764 required efficient collection of taxes on any molasses brought into the colonies. The Act also gave British officials free license to conduct searches of the premises of anyone suspected of violating the law. The colonists were taxed on newspapers, legal documents, and other printed matter under the Stamp Act of 1765. Although a stamp tax was already in use in England, the colonists would have none of it, and after the ensuing uproar of rioting and mob violence, Parliament repealed the tax.

Of course, great exultation, jubilance, and wild joy resulted when news of the repeal reached America. However, what the celebrators did not notice was the small, quiet Declaratory Act attached to the repeal. This Act plainly and unequivocally stated that Parliament still had the right to make all laws for the colonies. It denied their right to be taxed only by their own colonial legislatures— a very crucial, important piece of legislation. Other acts leading up to armed conflict included the Townshend Acts passed in 1767 taxing lead, paint, paper, and tea brought into the colonies. This increased anger and tension resulting in the British sending troops to New York City and Boston.

In Boston, mob violence provoked retaliation by the troops thus bringing about the deaths of five people and the wounding of eight others. The so-called Boston Massacre shocked Americans and British alike. Subsequently, in 1770, Parliament voted to repeal all the provisions of the Townshend Acts with the exception of the tea tax. In 1773, the tax on tea sold by the British East India Company was substantially reduced, fueling colonial anger once more. This gave the company an unfair trade advantage and forcibly reminded the colonists of the British right to tax them. Merchants refused to sell the tea; colonists refused to buy and drink it; and a shipload of it was dumped into Boston Harbor—the Boston Tea Party.

In 1774, the passage of the Quebec Act extended the limits of that Canadian colony's boundary southward to include territory located north of the Ohio River. However, the punishment for Boston's Tea Party came in the same year with the Intolerable Acts. Boston's port was closed; the royal governor of the colony of Massachusetts was given increased power, and the colonists were compelled to house and feed the British soldiers. The propaganda activities of the patriot organizations Sons of Liberty and Committees of Correspondence kept the opposition and resistance before everyone. Delegates from twelve colonies met in Philadelphia September 5, 1774, in the First Continental Congress. They opposed acts of lawlessness and wanted some form of peaceful settlement with Britain. They maintained American loyalty to the mother country and affirmed Parliament's power over colonial foreign affairs.

They insisted on repeal of the Intolerable Acts and demanded ending all trade with Britain until this took place. The reply from King George III, the last king of America, was an insistence of colonial submission to British rule—or be crushed. With the start of the Revolutionary War April 19, 1775, the Second Continental Congress began meeting in Philadelphia May 10th that year to conduct the business of war and government for the next six years.

The British had been extremely lax and totally inconsistent in enforcement of the mercantile or trade laws passed in the years before 1754. The government itself was not particularly stable, so actions against the colonies occurred in anger with an attitude of moral superiority, that they knew how to manage America better than the Americans did themselves. Of course, this points to a lack of sufficient knowledge of conditions and opinions in America. The colonists had been left on their own for nearly 150 years, and by the time the Revolutionary War began, they were quite adept at self-government and adequately handling the affairs of their daily lives. The Americans equated ownership of land or property with the right to vote. Property was considered the foundation of life and liberty, and in the colonial mind and tradition, these went together.

Therefore when an indirect tax on tea was made, the British felt that since it wasn't a direct tax, there should be no objection to it. The colonists viewed any tax, direct or indirect, as an attack on their property. They felt that as a representative body, the British Parliament should protect

British citizens, including the colonists, from arbitrary taxation. Since they felt they were not represented, Parliament, in their eyes, gave them no protection. So, war began. August 23, 1775, George III declared that the colonies were in rebellion and warned them to stop.

By 1776, the colonists and their representatives in the Second Continental Congress realized that things were past the point of no return. The Declaration of Independence was drafted and declared July 4, 1776. George Washington labored against tremendous odds to wage a victorious war. The turning point in the Americans' favor occurred in 1777 with the American victory at Saratoga. This victory decided the French to align themselves with the Americans against the British. With the aid of Admiral de Grasse and French warships blocking the entrance to Chesapeake Bay, British General Cornwallis, trapped at Yorktown, Virginia, surrendered in 1781, and the war was over. The Treaty of Paris officially ending the war was signed in 1783.

During the war, and after independence was declared, the former colonies now found themselves independent states. The Second Continental Congress was conducting a war with representation by delegates from thirteen separate states. The Congress had no power to act for the states or to require them to accept and follow its wishes. A permanent united government was needed. On November 15, 1777, the Articles of Confederation were adopted, creating a league of free and independent states.

Skill 5.4   Identify the causes, significant individuals, and effects of the events associated with the Constitutional era and the early republic.

Articles of Confederation - This was the first political system under which the newly independent colonies tried to organize themselves. It was drafted on November 15, 1777, ratified by the thirteen states, and took effect on March 1, 1781.

The newly independent states were unwilling to give too much power to a national government. They were already fighting Great Britain. They did not want to replace one harsh ruler with another. After many debates, the form of the Articles was accepted. Each state agreed to send delegates to the Congress. Each state had one vote in the Congress. The Articles gave Congress the power to declare war, appoint military officers, and coin money. The Congress was also responsible for foreign affairs. The Articles of Confederation limited the powers of Congress by giving the states final authority. Although Congress could pass laws, at least nine of the thirteen states had to approve a law before it went into effect. Congress could not pass any laws regarding taxes. To get money, Congress had to ask each state for it, and no state could be forced to pay.

Thus, the Articles created a loose alliance among the thirteen states. The national government was weak, in part, because it did not have a strong chief executive to carry out laws passed by the legislature. This weak national government might have worked if the states were able to establish peaceful relations with one another. However, many different disputes arose, and there was no way of settling them. Thus, the delegates went to meet again to try to amend the Articles; instead they ended up creating a new Constitution that would resolve these earlier shortcomings.

The central government of the new United States of America consisted of a Congress of two to seven delegates from each state, with each state having just one vote. The government under the

Articles solved some of the postwar problems but had major weaknesses. Some of its powers included borrowing and coining money, directing foreign affairs, declaring war and making peace, building and equipping a navy, regulating weights and measures, and asking the states to supply men and money for an army. The delegates to Congress had no real authority as each state carefully guarded its own interests and limited powers under the Articles. Also, the delegates to Congress were paid by their states and had to vote as directed by their state legislatures. The weaknesses were the lack of power to regulate finances or trade, to enforce treaties, or provide military power. Something better and more efficient was needed.

In May of 1787, delegates from all states except Rhode Island began meeting in Philadelphia. At first, they met to revise the Articles of Confederation as instructed by Congress; but they soon realized that much more was needed. Abandoning the instructions, they set out to write a new Constitution, a new document, the foundation of all government in the United States and a model for representative government throughout the world.

The first order of business was the agreement among all the delegates that the convention would be kept secret. No discussion of the convention outside of the meeting room would be allowed. They wanted to be able to discuss, argue, and agree among themselves before presenting the completed document to the American people.

The delegates were afraid that if the people were aware of what was taking place before it was completed, the entire country would be plunged into argument and dissension. It would be extremely difficult, if not impossible, to settle differences and come to an agreement. Between the official notes kept and the complete notes of future President James Madison, an accurate picture of the events of the Convention is part of the historical record.

The delegates went to Philadelphia representing different areas and different interests. They all agreed on a strong central government but not one with unlimited powers. They also agreed that no one part of government could control the rest. It would be a republican form of government (sometimes referred to as representative democracy) in which the supreme power was in the hands of the voters who would elect the men who would govern for them.

Of course, when work was completed and the document was presented, nine states needed to approve for it to go into effect. There was no lack of discussion, arguing, debating, and haranguing. The opposition had three major objections:

1. The states seemed as if they were being asked to surrender too much power to the national government.
2. The voters did not have enough control and influence over the men who would be elected by them to run the government.
3. There was a lack of a "bill of rights" guaranteeing hard-won individual freedoms and liberties.

Eleven states finally ratified the document and the new national government went into effect. It was no small feat that the delegates were able to produce a workable document that satisfied all opinions, feelings, and viewpoints. The separation of powers of the three branches of government and the built-in system of checks and balances to keep power balanced were the basic tenets to safeguard against corruption in government. The Constitution provided for the individuals and the states an organized central authority to keep a young, inexperienced nation on track.

The system of government was so flexible, it has continued in its basic form to this day. In 1789, the Electoral College unanimously elected George Washington as the first President of the United States.

Of the newly created government, Benjamin Franklin said, "Thus I consent, Sir, to this Constitution because I expect no better, and because I am not sure that it is not the best." This might be true, considering that the Constitution has lasted, through civil war, foreign wars, depression, and social revolution for over 200 years. It is truly a living document because of its ability to remain strong while allowing itself to be changed with changing times.

The Constitution of the United States

Ratification of the U.S. Constitution was by no means a foregone conclusion. The representative government had powerful enemies, especially those who had seen firsthand the failure of the Articles of Confederation. The strong central government had powerful enemies, including some of the guiding lights of the American Revolution.

Those who wanted to see a strong central government were called Federalists, because they wanted to see a federal government reign supreme. Among the leaders of the Federalists were Alexander Hamilton and John Jay. These two men, along with James Madison, wrote a series of letters to New York newspapers, urging that the state ratify the Constitution. These became known as the Federalist Papers.

In the Anti-Federalist camp were Thomas Jefferson and Patrick Henry. These men and many others like them were worried that a strong national government would descend into the kind of tyranny that they had worked so hard to abolish. In the same way, they wrote a series of arguments against the Constitution called the Anti-Federalist Papers.

In the end, both sides achieved most of what they wanted. The Federalists established their strong national government, which was held in place by the famous "checks and balances." The Anti-Federalists achieved the Bill of Rights, the first ten Amendments to the Constitution, a series of laws that protect some of the most basic of human rights. The states that had been in doubt for ratification of the Constitution signed on when the Bill of Rights was promised.

Skill 5.5   Evaluate the impact of westward expansion on the social, cultural, political, and economic development of the emerging nation.

In the United States, territorial expansion occurred in the expansion westward under the banner of "Manifest Destiny, the belief in the divinely given right of the nation to expand westward and incorporate more of the continent into the nation. This belief had been expressed at the end of the Revolutionary War with the demand that Britain cede all lands east of the Mississippi River to

America. The goal of expanding westward was further confirmed with the Northwest Ordinance (1787) and the Louisiana Purchase (1803). Manifest Destiny was the justification of the Mexican-American War (1846-48), which resulted in the annexation of Texas and California, as well as much of the southwest. Due to the U.S. involvement in the War with Mexico, the Spanish-American War, and support of the Latin American colonies of Spain in their revolt for independence, the Spanish colonies were successful in their fight for independence and self-government.

After the U.S. purchased the Louisiana Territory, Jefferson appointed Captains Meriwether Lewis and William Clark to explore it, to find out exactly what had been bought. The Corps of Discovery went all the way to the Pacific Ocean, returning two years later with maps, journals, and artifacts. This led the way for future explorers to make available more knowledge about the territory and resulted in the Westward Movement and the later belief in the doctrine of Manifest Destiny. The U.S. and Britain had shared the Oregon country. By the 1840s, with the increase in the free and slave populations and the demand of the settlers for control and government by the U.S., the conflict had to be resolved. In a treaty, signed in 1846, by both nations, a peaceful resolution occurred with Britain giving up its claims south of the 49th parallel.

The Red River cession was the next acquisition of land and came about as part of a treaty with Great Britain in 1818. It included parts of North and South Dakota and Minnesota. In 1819, Florida, both east and west, was ceded to the U.S. by Spain along with parts of Alabama, Mississippi, and Louisiana. Texas was annexed in 1845, and after the war with Mexico in 1848, the government paid $15 million for what would become the states of California, Utah, and Nevada, and parts of four other states.

In 1846, the Oregon Country was ceded to the U.S., which extended the western border to the Pacific Ocean. The northern U.S. boundary was established at the 49th parallel. The states of Idaho, Oregon, and Washington were formed from this territory. In 1853, the Gadsden Purchase rounded out the present boundary of the 48 conterminous states with payment to Mexico of $10 million for land that makes up the present states of New Mexico and Arizona.

In the American Southwest, the results were exactly the opposite. Spain had claimed this area since the 1540s, had spread northward from Mexico City, and in the 1700s, had established missions, forts, villages, towns, and very large ranches. After the purchase of the Louisiana Territory in 1803, Americans began moving into Spanish territory. A few hundred American families in what is now Texas were allowed to live there but had to agree to become loyal subjects to Spain. In 1821, Mexico successfully revolted against Spanish rule, won independence, and chose to be more tolerant towards the American settlers and traders.

The Mexican government encouraged and allowed extensive trade and settlement, especially in Texas. Many of the new settlers were southerners and brought with them their slaves. Slavery was outlawed in Mexico and technically illegal in Texas, although the Mexican government rather looked the other way.

Friction increased between land-hungry Americans swarming into western lands and the Mexican government, which controlled these lands. The clash was not only political but also cultural and economic. The Spanish influence permeated all parts of southwestern life: law, language, architecture, and customs. By this time, the doctrine of Manifest Destiny was in the hearts and on the lips of those seeking new areas of settlement and a new life. Americans were demanding U.S. control of not only the Mexican Territory but also Oregon. Peaceful negotiations with Great Britain secured Oregon but it took two years of war to gain control of the southwestern U.S.

In addition, the Mexican government owed debts to U.S. citizens whose property was damaged or destroyed during its struggle for independence from Spain. By the time war broke out in 1845, Mexico had not paid its war debts. The government was weak, corrupt, irresponsible, tom by revolutions, and financially insolvent. Mexico was also bitter over American expansion into Texas and the 1836 revolution, which resulted in Texas independence. In the 1844 Presidential election, the Democrats pushed for annexation of Texas and Oregon, and after winning, they started the procedure to admit Texas to the Union.

When statehood occurred, diplomatic relations between the U.S. and Mexico ended. President Polk wanted U.S. control of the entire Southwest, from Texas to the Pacific Ocean. He sent a diplomatic mission with an offer to purchase New Mexico and Upper California but the Mexican government refused to even receive the diplomat. Consequently, in 1846, each nation claimed aggression on the part of the other, and war was declared. The treaty signed in 1848 and a subsequent one in 1853 completed the southwestern boundary of the United States, reaching to the Pacific Ocean, as President Polk wished.

Frontier Life

Settlers were lured by what they perceived as unpopulated places with land for the taking. However, when they arrived, they found that the lands were populated by earlier settlers of Spanish descent and Native Americans, who did not particularly welcome the newcomers. These original and earlier inhabitants frequently clashed with those who were moving west. Despite having signed treaties with the United States government years earlier, virtually all were ignored and broken as westward settlement accelerated and the government was called upon to protect migrating settlers. This led to a series of wars between the United States and the various Native American Nations that were deemed hostile. Although the bloodshed during these encounters was great, it paled compared to the number of Native Americans who had died from epidemics of deadly diseases for which they had no resistance. Eventually, the government sought to relocate inconveniently located peoples to Indian reservations, and to Oklahoma, which lacked the needed resources needed and was geographically remote from their homelands.

The post-Reconstruction era represents a period of great transformation and expansion for the United States, both economically and geographically, particularly for the South, recovering from the devastation of the Civil War and migration west of the Mississippi River. Great numbers of former slaves moved west, away from their former masters, lured by the promise of land. White migration was also spurred by similar desires for land and resources, leading to boom economies of cotton, cattle and grain, starting in Kansas and spreading westward.

Although industrial production grew fastest in the South during this period, it was still predominantly agricultural, featuring land tenancy and sharecropping, which did not really advance the freed slaves economically, since most of the land was still owned by the large plantation landowners. The economic chasm dividing white landowners and black freedmen only widened as the tenants sank further into debt to their landlords.

Westward movement of significant populations from the eastern United States originated with the discovery of gold in the West in the 1840s and acquired greater momentum after the Civil War. The justification for this westward expansion, at the expense of the previous inhabitants was that it was America's "Manifest Destiny" to "tame" and settle the continent from coast-to-coast.

Another major factor affecting the opening of the West to migration of Americans and displacement of native peoples was the expansion of the railroad. The transcontinental railroad was completed in 1869, joining the West Coast with the existing rail infrastructure terminating at Omaha, Nebraska, its westernmost point. This not only enabled unprecedented movement of people and goods, it also hastened the near extinction of bison, which the Indians of the Great Plains, in particular, depended on for their survival.

Skill 5.6   Identify the social, cultural, political, and economic characteristics of the antebellum period.

The drafting of the Constitution, its ratification and implementation, united thirteen different, independent states into a union under one central government. Two crucial compromises of the convention concerning slaves pacified Southerners, especially the slave owners, but the issue of slavery was not settled. From then on, sectionalism became stronger and more apparent each year, putting the entire country on a collision course.

Slavery in the English colonies began in 1619 when 20 Africans arrived in the colony of Virginia at Jamestown. From then on, slavery had a foothold, especially in the agricultural South, where a large amount of slave labor was needed for the extensive plantations. Free men refused to work for wages on the plantations when land was available for settling on the frontier. Therefore, in the plantation owners' minds, slave labor was the only recourse left. If it had been profitable to use slaves in New England and the Middle Colonies, then without doubt slavery would have been more widespread. However, it came down to whether or not slavery was profitable. It was in the South, but not in the other two colonial regions.

The West was involved in the controversy as well as the North and South. By 1860, the country was made up of these three major regions. The people in all three sections or regions had a number of beliefs and institutions in common. Of course, there were major differences since each region had its own unique characteristics.

The North, along with agriculture, was becoming industrial with factories that employed women and children in the towns and cities that were growing at a fast rate. The South was agricultural, eventually becoming increasingly dependent on the one crop of cotton. In the West, restless pioneers moved into new frontiers seeking land, wealth, and opportunity. Many were from the

South and were slave owners, bringing their slaves with them. So between these three different parts of the country, the views on tariffs, public lands, internal improvements at federal expense, banking and currency, and the issue of slavery were decidedly, totally different.

This period of U.S. history was a period of compromises, breakdowns of the compromises, desperate attempts to restore and retain harmony among the three sections, short-lived intervals of the uneasy balance of interests, and ever-increasing conflict.

At the Constitutional Convention, one of the slavery compromises concerned counting slaves for deciding the number of representatives for the House and the amount of taxes to be paid. Southerners pushed for counting the slaves for representation but not for taxes. The Northerners pushed for the opposite. The resulting compromise, sometimes referred to as the "three-fifths compromise," was that both groups agreed that three-fifths of the slaves would be counted for both taxes and representation.

The other compromise over slavery was part of the disputes over how much regulation the central government would control over commercial activities such as trade with other nations and the slave trade. It was agreed that Congress would regulate commerce with other nations including taxing imports. Southerners were worried about taxing slaves coming into the country and the possibility of Congress prohibiting the slave trade altogether. The agreement reached allowed the states to continue importation of slaves for the next 20 years until 1808, at which time Congress would make the decision as to the future of the slave trade. During the 20-year period, no more than $10 per person could be levied on slaves coming into the country.

These two "slavery' compromises were a necessary concession to have Southern support and approval for the new document and new government. Many Americans felt that the system of slavery would eventually die out in the U.S., but by 1808, cotton was becoming increasingly important in the primarily agricultural South and the institution of slavery had become firmly entrenched in Southern culture. It is evident that as early as the Constitutional Convention, active antislavery feelings and opinions were very strong, leading to extremely active antislavery groups and societies.

Democracy is loosely defined as "rule by the people," either directly or through representatives. Associated with the idea of democracy are freedom, equality, and opportunity. The basic concept of democracy existed in the thirteen English colonies with the practice of independent self-government. The right of qualified persons to vote, hold office and actively participate in their own government is sometimes referred to as "political" democracy. "Social" and "economic" democracy pertain to the idea that all have the opportunity to get an education, choose their own careers, and live as free men every day, all equal in the eyes of the law.

Three concepts of democracy were basic reasons why people came to the New World and the practices of these concepts continued through the colonial and revolutionary periods. They were extremely influential in the shaping of the new central government under the Constitution. As the nation extended its borders into the lands west of the Mississippi, thousands of settlers streamed into this part of the country. They brought with them ideas and concepts and adapted them to the development of the unique characteristics of the region. Equality for everyone, as stated in the

Declaration of Independence, did not yet apply to women, minority groups, black Americans, or American Indians. Voting rights and the right to hold public office were restricted in varying degrees in each state. All of these factors decidedly affected the political, economic, and social life of the country and all three were focused in the attitudes on slavery in the three sections of the country.

The first serious clash between North and South occurred during 1819-1820 when James Monroe was in office as President, and it concerned admitting Missouri as a state. In 1819, the U.S. consisted of twenty-one states: eleven free states and ten slave states. The Missouri Territory allowed slavery, and, if admitted, would cause an imbalance in the number of U.S. Senators. Alabama had already been admitted as a slave state, and that had balanced the Senate with the North and South with North and South each having 22 senators. The first Missouri Compromise resolved the conflict by approving admission of Maine as a free state along with Missouri as a slave state. This continued to keep a balance of power in the Senate with the same number of free and slave states.

An additional provision of this compromise was that with the admission of Missouri, slavery would not be allowed in the rest of the Louisiana Purchase territory north of latitude 36 degrees 30'. This was acceptable to the Southern congressmen since it was not profitable to grow cotton on land north of this latitude line anyway. It was thought that the crisis had been resolved, but in the next year, it was discovered that in its state constitution, Missouri discriminated against the free blacks. Anti-slavery supporters in Congress went into an uproar, determined to exclude Missouri from the Union. Henry Clay, known as the Great Compromiser, then proposed a second Missouri Compromise. His proposal stated that the Constitution of the United States guaranteed protections and privileges to citizens of states and that Missouri's proposed constitution could not deny these to any of its citizens. The acceptance in 1820 of this second compromise opened the way for Missouri's statehood—a temporary reprieve only.

The issue of tariffs also was a divisive factor during this period, especially between 1829 and 1833. The Embargo Act of 1807 and the War of 1812 had completely cut off the source of manufactured goods for Americans, so it was necessary to build factories to produce what was needed. After 1815 when the war had ended, Great Britain proceeded to get rid of its industrial rivals by unloading its goods in America. To protect and encourage its own industries and their products, Congress passed the Tariff of 1816, which required high duties to be levied on manufactured goods coming into the United States. Southern leaders, such as John C. Calhoun of South Carolina, supported the tariff with the assumption that the South would develop its own industries.

For a brief period after 1815, the nation enjoyed the "Era of Good Feelings." People were moving into the West; industry and agriculture were growing; a feeling of national pride united Americans in their efforts and determination to strengthen the country. However, over-speculation in stocks and lands for quick profits backfired. Cotton prices were rising so many Southerners bought land for cultivation at inflated prices. Manufacturers in the industrial North purchased land to build more plants and factories as an attempt to have a part of this prosperity. Settlers in the West rushed to buy land to reap the benefits of the increasing prices of meat and grain. To have the money for all of these economic activities, all of these groups were borrowing heavily from the banks, and the banks encouraged this by giving loans on insubstantial security.

In late 1818, the Bank of the United States and its branches stopped renewal of personal mortgages and required state banks to immediately pay their bank notes in gold, silver, or in national bank notes. The state banks were unable to do this, so they closed their doors and were unable to do any business at all. Since mortgages could not be renewed, people lost all their properties, and foreclosures were rampant throughout the country. At the same time as all of this was occurring, cotton prices collapsed in the English market. Its high price had caused the British manufacturers to seek cheaper cotton from India for their textile mills. With the fall of cotton prices, the demand for American manufactured goods declined, revealing how fragile the economic prosperity had been.

In 1824, a higher tariff was passed by Congress, favoring the financial interests of the manufacturers in New England and the Middle Atlantic States. In addition, the 1824 tariff was closely tied to the presidential election of that year. Before becoming law, Calhoun had proposed the high tariffs in an effort to get Eastern business interests to vote with the agricultural interests in the South, who opposed it. Supporters of candidate Andrew Jackson sided with whichever side served their best interests. Jackson himself would not be involved in any of this scheming.

The bill became law, to Calhoun's surprise, due mainly to the political maneuvering of Martin van Buren and Daniel Webster. By the time the higher 1828 tariff was passed, feelings were extremely bitter in the South, who believed that the New England manufacturers greatly benefited from it. Vice-President Calhoun, also speaking for his home state of South Carolina, promptly declared that if any state felt that a federal law was unconstitutional, that state could nullify it. In 1832, Congress took the action of lowering the tariffs to a degree but not enough to please South Carolina, which promptly declared the tariff null and void, and threatened to secede from the Union.

In 1833, Congress lowered the tariffs again, this time at a level acceptable to South Carolina. Although President Jackson believed in states' rights, he also firmly believed in and determined to keep the preservation of the Union. A constitutional crisis had been averted, but sectional divisions were getting deeper and more pronounced. The abolition movement was growing rapidly, becoming an important issue in the North.

The slavery issue was at the root of every problem, crisis, event, decision, and struggle from then on. The next crisis involved the issue concerning Texas. By 1836, Texas was an independent republic with its own constitution. During its fight for independence, Americans were sympathetic to and supportive of the Texans and some recruited volunteers who crossed into Texas to help the struggle. Problems arose when the state petitioned Congress for statehood. Texas wanted to allow slavery but Northerners in Congress opposed admission to the Union because it would disrupt the balance between free and slave states and give Southerners in Congress increased influence. There were others who believed that granting statehood to Texas would lead to a war with Mexico, which had refused to recognize Texas independence. For the time being, statehood was put on hold.

The slavery issue flared again not to be done away with until the end of the Civil War. It was obvious that the newly acquired territory would be divided up into territories and later become states. In addition to the two factions of Northerners who advocated prohibition of slavery and of Southerners who favored slavery existing there, a third faction arose supporting the doctrine of "popular sovereignty". Popular sovereignty stated that people living in territories and states should be allowed to decide for themselves whether or not slavery should be permitted. In 1849, California applied for admittance to the Union and the furor began.

The result was the Compromise of 1850, a series of laws designed as a final solution to the issue. Concessions made to the North included the admission of California as a free state and the abolition of slave trading in Washington, D.C. The laws also provided for the creation of the New Mexico and Utah territories. As a concession to Southerners, the residents there would decide whether to permit slavery when these two territories became states. In addition, Congress authorized implementation of stricter measures to capture runaway slaves.

A few years later, Congress took up consideration of new territories between Missouri and present-day Idaho. Again, heated debate over permitting slavery in these areas flared up. Those opposed to slavery used the Missouri Compromise to prove their point showing that the land being considered for territories was part of the area the Compromise had designated as banned to slavery. On May 25, 1854, Congress passed the infamous Kansas-Nebraska Act, which nullified this provision, created the territories of Kansas and Nebraska, and provided for the people of these two territories to decide for themselves whether to permit slavery. Feelings were so deep and divided that any further attempts to compromise would meet with little, if any, success. Political and social turmoil swirled everywhere. Kansas was called "Bleeding Kansas" because of the extreme violence and bloodshed throughout the territory because two governments existed there, one pro-slavery and the other anti-slavery.

The Supreme Court in 1857 handed down a decision guaranteed to cause explosions throughout the country. Dred Scott was a slave whose owner had taken him from slave state Missouri, then to free state Illinois, into Minnesota Territory, free under the provisions of the Missouri Compromise, then finally back to slave state Missouri. Abolitionists pursued the dilemma by presenting a court case, stating that since Scott had lived in a free state and free territory, he was in actuality a free man. Two lower courts had ruled before the Supreme Court became involved, one ruling in favor and one against. The Supreme Court in 1857 handed down an explosive decision when it decided that residing in a free state and free territory did not make Scott a free man because Scott (and all other slaves) was not a U.S. citizen or state citizen of Missouri. Therefore, he did not have the right to sue in state or federal courts. The Court went a step further and ruled that the old Missouri Compromise was now unconstitutional because Congress did not have the power to prohibit slavery in the Territories.

Anti-slavery supporters were stunned. They had just formed the new Republican Party, and one of its platforms was keeping slavery out of the Territories. Now, according to the decision in the Dred Scott case, this basic party principle was unconstitutional. The only way to ban slavery in new areas was by a Constitutional amendment, requiring ratification by three-fourths of all states. At this time, this was out of the question because the supporters would be unable to get a majority due to Southern opposition.

In 1858, Abraham Lincoln and Stephen A. Douglas were running for the office of U.S. Senator from Illinois and participated in a series of debates, which directly affected the outcome of the 1860 presidential election. Douglas, a Democrat, was up for re-election and believed that if he won the race, he had a good chance of becoming President in 1860. Lincoln, a Republican, was not an abolitionist but believed that slavery was wrong morally. He firmly believed in and supported the Republican Party principle that slavery must not be allowed to extend any further.

Douglas, on the other hand, had originated the doctrine of "popular sovereignty" and was responsible for supporting and getting through Congress the inflammatory Kansas-Nebraska Act. In the course of the debates, Lincoln challenged Douglas to show that popular sovereignty reconciled with the Dred Scott decision. Either way he answered Lincoln, Douglas would lose crucial support from one group or the other. If he supported the Dred Scott decision, Southerners would support him, but he would lose Northern support. If he stayed with popular sovereignty, Northern support would be his, but Southern support would be lost. His reply to Lincoln stated that Territorial legislatures could exclude slavery by refusing to pass laws supporting it, and that gave him enough support and approval to be re-elected to the Senate. But it cost him the Democratic nomination for President in 1860.

Southerners came to the realization that Douglas supported popular sovereignty but not necessarily for the expansion of slavery. Two years later, Lincoln received the nomination of the Republican Party for President.

In 1859, abolitionist John Brown and his followers seized the federal arsenal at Harper's Ferry in what is now West Virginia. His purpose was to take the guns stored in the arsenal, give them to slaves nearby, and lead them in a widespread rebellion. Colonel Robert E. Lee of the United States Army captured him and his men and, after being found guilty at trial, he was hanged. Southerners supposed that the majority of Northerners approved of Brown's actions, but in actuality, most of them were stunned and shocked. Southern newspapers took great pains to quote a small but well-known minority of abolitionists who applauded and supported Brown's actions. This merely served to widen the gap between the two sections.

The final straw came with the election of Lincoln to the Presidency the next year. Due to a split in the Democratic Party, there were four candidates from four political parties. With Lincoln receiving a minority of the popular vote and a majority of electoral votes, the Southern states, one by one, voted to secede from the Union as they had promised they would do if Lincoln and the Republicans were victorious.

Skill 5.7   Identify causes, significant individuals, and effects of the events associated with the American Civil War and Reconstruction eras.

The slavery issue flared again not to be done away with until the end of the Civil War. It was obvious that newly acquired territory would be divided up into territories and later become states. Factions of Northerners advocated prohibition of slavery and Southerners favored slavery. A third faction arose supporting the doctrine of popular sovereignty which stated that people living in territories and states should be allowed to decide for themselves whether or not slavery should be permitted. In 1849, California applied for admittance to the Union and the furor began.

The result was the Compromise of 1850, a series of laws designed as a final solution to the issue. Concessions made to the North included the admission of California as a free state and the abolition of slave trading in Washington, D.C. The laws also provided for the creation of the New Mexico and Utah territories. As a concession to Southerners, the residents there would decide whether to permit slavery when these two territories became states. In addition, Congress authorized implementation of stricter measures to capture runaway slaves.

A few years later, Congress took up consideration of new territories between Missouri and present-day Idaho. Again, heated debate over permitting slavery in these areas flared up. Those opposed to slavery used the Missouri Compromise to prove their point showing that the land being considered for territories was part of the area the Compromise had been designated as banned to slavery. On May 25, 1854, Congress passed the infamous Kansas-Nebraska Act which nullified the provision creating the territories of Kansas and Nebraska. This provided for the people of these two territories to decide for themselves whether or not to permit slavery to exist there. Feelings were so deep and divided that any further attempts to compromise would meet with little, if any, success. Political and social turmoil swirled everywhere. Kansas was called "Bleeding Kansas" because of the extreme violence and bloodshed throughout the territory because two governments existed there, one pro-slavery and the other anti-slavery.

The Supreme Court decided that residing in a free state and free territory did not make Scott a free man because Scott (and all other slaves) was not an U.S. citizen or a state citizen of Missouri. Therefore, he did not have the right to sue in state or federal courts. The Court went a step further and ruled that the old Missouri Compromise was now unconstitutional because Congress did not have the power to prohibit slavery in the Territories.

It is ironic that South Carolina was the first state to secede from the Union and the first shots of the war were fired on Fort Sumter in Charleston Harbor. Both sides quickly prepared for war. The North had more in its favor: a larger population; superiority in finances and transportation facilities; manufacturing, agricultural, and natural resources. The North possessed most of the nation's gold, had about 92% of all industries, and almost all known supplies of copper, coal, iron, and various other minerals. Most of the nation's railroads were in the North and mid-West, men and supplies could be moved wherever needed; food could be transported from the farms of the mid-West to workers in the East and to soldiers on the battlefields. Trade with nations overseas could go on as usual due to control of the navy and the merchant fleet. The Northern states numbered 24 and included western (California and Oregon) and border (Maryland, Delaware, Kentucky, Missouri, and West Virginia) states.

The Southern states numbered eleven and included South Carolina, Georgia, Florida, Alabama, Mississippi, Louisiana, Texas, Virginia, North Carolina, Tennessee, and Arkansas, making up the Confederacy. Although outnumbered in population, the South was completely confident of victory. They knew that all they had to do was fight a defensive war and protect their own territory. The North had to invade and defeat an area almost the size of Western Europe. They figured the North would tire of the struggle and gave up. Another advantage of the South was that a number of its best officers had graduated from the U.S. Military Academy at West Point and had had long years of army experience. Many had exercised varying degrees of command in the Indian Wars and the war with Mexico. Men from the South were conditioned to living outdoors and were more familiar with horses and firearms than men from northeastern cities. Since cotton was such an important crop, Southerners felt that British and French textile mills were so dependent on raw cotton that they would be forced to help the Confederacy in the war.

The South had specific reasons and goals for fighting the war, more so than the North. The major aim of the Confederacy never wavered: to win independence, the right to govern themselves as they wished, and to preserve slavery. The Northerners were not as clear in their reasons for conducting war. At the beginning, most believed, along with Lincoln, that preservation of the Union was paramount. Only a few extremely fanatical abolitionists looked on the war as a way to end slavery. However, by war's end, more and more northerners had come to believe that freeing the slaves was just as important as restoring the Union.

The war strategies for both sides were relatively clear and simple. The South planned a defensive war, wearing down the North until it agreed to peace on Southern terms. One exception was to gain control of Washington, D.C., go north through the Shenandoah Valley into Maryland and Pennsylvania and drive a wedge between the Northeast and mid-West, interrupt the lines of communication, and end the war quickly. The North had three basic strategies:

1. Blockade the Confederate coastline in order to cripple the South;
2. Seize control of the Mississippi River and interior railroad lines to split the Confederacy in two; and
3. Seize the Confederate capital of Richmond, Virginia, driving southward joining up with Union forces coming east from the Mississippi Valley.

The South won decisively until the Battle of Gettysburg, July 1 - 3, 1863. Until Gettysburg, Lincoln's commanders, McDowell and McClellan, were less than desirable; Burnside and Hooker, not what was needed. Lee, on the other hand, had many able officers; he depended heavily on Jackson and Stuart. Jackson died at Chancellorsville and was replaced by Longstreet. Lee decided to invade the North and depended on J.E.B. Stuart and his cavalry to keep him informed of the location of Union troops and their strengths. Four things worked against Lee at Gettysburg:

1. The Union troops gained the best positions and the best ground first, making it easier to make a stand there.
2. Lee's move into Northern territory put him and his army a long way from food and supply lines. They were more or less on their own.
3. Lee thought that his Army of Northern Virginia was invincible and could fight and win under any conditions or circumstances.
4. Stuart and his men did not arrive at Gettysburg until the end of the second day of fighting, and by then, it was too little too late. He and the men had had to detour around Union soldiers, and he was delayed getting the information Lee needed.

Consequently, he made the mistake of failing to listen to Longstreet and following the strategy of regrouping back into Southern territory to the supply lines. Lee felt that regrouping was retreating and almost an admission of defeat. He was convinced the army would be victorious. Longstreet was concerned about the Union troops occupying the best positions and felt that regrouping to a better position would be an advantage. He was also concerned about the distance from supply lines.

It was not the intention of either side to fight there, but the fighting began when a Confederate brigade stumbled into a unit of Union cavalry while looking for shoes. The third and last day Lee launched the final attempt to break Union lines. General George Pickett sent his division of three brigades under Generals Garnet, Kemper, and Armistead against Union troops on Cemetery Ridge under command of General Winfield Scott Hancock. Union lines held, and Lee and the defeated Army of Northern Virginia made their way back to Virginia. Although Lincoln's commander George Meade successfully turned back a Confederate charge, he and the Union troops failed to pursue Lee and the Confederates. Yet, this battle was the turning point for the North. After this, Lee never again had the troop strength to launch a major offensive.

The day after Gettysburg, on July 4, Vicksburg, Mississippi, surrendered to Union General Ulysses Grant, thus severing the western Confederacy from the eastern part. In September 1863, the Confederacy won its last important victory at Chickamauga. In November, the Union victory at Chattanooga made it possible for Union troops to go into Alabama and Georgia, splitting the eastern Confederacy in two. Lincoln gave Grant command of all Northern armies in March of 1864. Grant led his armies into battles in Virginia while Phil Sheridan and his cavalry did as much damage as possible. In a skirmish at a place called Yellow Tavern, Virginia, Sheridan's and Stuart's forces met, with Stuart being fatally wounded. The Union won the Battle of Mobile Bay and in May 1864, William Tecumseh Sherman began his march to successfully demolish Atlanta, then on to Savannah. He and his troops turned northward through the Carolinas to Grant in Virginia. On April 9, 1865, Lee formally surrendered to Grant at Appomattox Courthouse, Virginia.

The Civil War took more American lives than any other war in history, the South losing one-third of its soldiers in battle compared to about one-sixth for the North. More than half of the deaths were caused by disease and the horrendous conditions of field hospitals. Both sides paid a tremendous economic price, but the South suffered more severely from direct damages. Destruction was pervasive with towns, farms, trade, industry, lives, and homes of men, women, and children all destroyed and an entire Southern way of life lost. The deep resentment, bitterness, and hatred that remained for generations gradually lessened as the years went by, but legacies of it surface and remain to this day.

The South had no voice in the political, social, and cultural affairs of the nation, lessening to a great degree the influence of the more traditional Southern ideals. The Northern Yankee Protestant ideals of hard work, education, and economic freedom became the standard of the United States and helped influence the development of the nation into a modem, industrial power.

The effects of the Civil War were tremendous. It changed the methods of waging war and has been called the first modern war. It introduced weapons and tactics that, when improved later, were used extensively in wars of the late 1800s and 1900s. Civil War soldiers were the first to fight in trenches, first to fight under a unified command, first to wage a defense called "major cordon defense," a strategy of advance on all fronts. They were also the first to use repeating and breech-loading weapons. Observation balloons were first used during the war along with submarines, ironclad ships, and mines. Telegraphy and railroads were put to use first in the Civil War. It was considered a modern war because of the vast destruction and was "total war," involving the use of all resources of the opposing sides. Perhaps it could not have ended other than the total defeat and unconditional surrender of one side or the other.

By executive proclamation and constitutional amendment, slavery was officially and finally ended. There remained deep prejudice and racism, which still raises its ugly head today. But the Union was preserved, and the states were finally truly united. Sectionalism, especially in the area of politics, remained strong for another 100 years but not to the degree and with the violence as existed before 1861. It has been noted that the Civil War may have been American democracy's greatest failure because from 1861 to 1865, calm reason—basic to democracy— fell to human passion. Yet, democracy did survive. The victory of the North established that no state has the right to end or leave the Union. Because of unity, the U.S. became a major global power. Lincoln never proposed to punish the South. He was most concerned with restoring the South to the Union in a program that was flexible and practical rather than rigid and unbending. He did not feel that the states had succeeded in leaving the Union but that they had left the 'family circle" for a short time. His plans consisted of two major steps:

- All Southerners taking an oath of allegiance to the Union promising to accept all federal laws and proclamations dealing with slavery would receive a full pardon. The exceptions were men who had resigned from civil and military positions in the federal government to serve in the Confederacy, those who were part of the Confederate government, those in the Confederate army above the rank of lieutenant, and Confederates who were guilty of mistreating prisoners of war and blacks.

- A state would be able to write a new constitution, elect new officials, and return to the Union fully equal to all other states on certain conditions. First, a minimum number of persons (at least 10% of those who were qualified voters in their states before secession from the Union who had voted in the 1860 election) must take an oath of allegiance.

As the war dragged on to its bloody, destructive conclusion, Lincoln was eager to get the states restored to the Union. He showed flexibility in his thinking as he made changes to his Reconstruction program to make it as easy and painless as possible. Of course, Congress had final approval of many actions, and it would be interesting to know how differently things might have turned out if Lincoln had lived to see some or all of his benevolent policies, supported by fellow moderates, put into action. Unfortunately, it didn't turn out that way. After Andrew Johnson became President and the Radical Republicans gained control of Congress, the harsh measures of radical Reconstruction were implemented.

The economic and social chaos in the South after the war was unbelievable with starvation and disease rampant, especially in the cities. The U.S. Army provided some relief of food and clothing for both white and blacks, but the major responsibility fell to the Freedmen's Bureau. Though the bureau agents to a certain extent helped southern whites, their main responsibility was to the freed slaves. They were to assist the freed slaves to become self-supporting and to protect them from being taken advantage of by others. Northerners looked on it as a real, honest effort to help the South out of the chaos it was in. Most white Southerners charged the Bureau with causing racial friction, deliberately encouraging the freed slaves to consider former owners as enemies.

As a result, as southern leaders began to be able to restore life as it had once been, they adopted a set of laws known as "Black Codes," containing many of the provisions of the prewar "slave codes." There were certain improvements in the lives of freed slaves, but the codes denied basic civil rights. In short, except for the condition of freedom and a few civil rights, white Southerners made every effort to keep the freed slaves in a way of life subordinate to theirs.

Radicals in Congress pointed out these illegal actions by white Southerners as evidence that they were unwilling to recognize, accept, and support the complete freedom of black Americans and could not be trusted. Therefore, Congress drafted its own program of Reconstruction, including laws that would protect and further the rights of blacks. Three amendments were added to the Constitution: the Thirteenth Amendment of 1865 outlawed slavery throughout the entire United States. The Fourteenth Amendment of 1868 made blacks American citizens. The Fifteenth Amendment of 1870 gave black Americans the right to vote and made it illegal to deny anyone the right to vote based on race.

Federal troops stationed throughout the South protected Republicans who took control of Southern governments. Bitterly resentful, many white Southerners fought the new political system by joining a secret society called the Ku Klux Klan, using violence to keep black Americans from voting and getting equality. Between 1866 and 1870, all of the states had returned to the Union, but Northern interest in Reconstruction was fading. Reconstruction officially ended when the last Federal troops left the South in 1877. It can be said that Reconstruction had a limited success as it set up public school systems and expanded legal rights of black Americans. Nevertheless, white supremacy came to be in control again, and its bitter fruitage remains.

Lincoln and Johnson had considered the conflict of Civil War as a "rebellion of individuals," but Congressional Radicals, such as Charles Sumner in the Senate, considered the Southern states as complete political organizations. He considered them in the same position as any unorganized Territory and believed they should be treated as such. Radical House leader Thaddeus Stevens considered the Confederate states not as Territories but as conquered provinces and felt they should be treated that way. President Johnson refused to work with congressional moderates, insisting on having his own way. As a result, the Radicals gained control of both houses of Congress, and when Johnson opposed their harsh measures, they came within one vote of impeaching him.

General Grant was elected President in 1868, serving two scandal-ridden terms. He was an honest, upright person, but he greatly lacked political experience— and his greatest weakness was a blind loyalty to his friends. He absolutely refused to believe that his friends were not honest and stubbornly would not admit to their using him to further their own interests. One of the sad results of the war was the rapid growth of business and industry with large corporations controlled by unscrupulous men. However, after 1877, some degree of normalcy returned and there was time for rebuilding, expansion, and growth.

Plans for Reconstruction versus its actual implementation

Following the Civil War, the nation was faced with repairing the torn Union and readmitting the Confederate states. Reconstruction refers to this period between 1865 and 1877 when the federal and state governments debated and implemented plans to provide civil rights to freed slaves and to set the terms under which the former Confederate states might once again join the Union.

Planning for Reconstruction began early in the war, in 1861. Abraham Lincoln's Republican Party in Washington favored the extension of voting rights to black men but was divided as to how far to extend the right. Moderates, such as Lincoln, wanted only literate blacks and those who had fought for the Union to be allowed to vote. Radical Republicans wanted to extend the vote to all black men. Conservative Democrats did not want to give black men the vote at all. In the case of former Confederate soldiers, moderates wanted to allow all but former leaders to vote while the Radicals wanted to require an oath from all eligible voters that they had never borne arms against the U.S., which would have excluded all former rebels. On the issue of readmission into the Union, moderates favored a much lower standard, with the Radicals demanding nearly impossible conditions for rebel states to return.

Lincoln's moderate plan for Reconstruction was actually part of his effort to win the war. Lincoln and the moderates felt that if it remained easy for states to return to the Union and if moderate proposals on black suffrage were made, that Confederate states involved in the hostilities might be swayed to re-join the Union rather than continue fighting. The radical plan was to ensure that reconstruction did not actually start until after the war was over.

In 1863 Abraham Lincoln was assassinated leaving Vice President Andrew Johnson to oversee the beginning of the actual implementation of Reconstruction. Johnson struck a moderate pose, willing to allow former confederates to keep control of their state governments. These governments quickly enacted Black Codes that denied the vote to blacks and granted them only limited civil rights.

The radical Republicans in Congress responded to the Black Codes by continuing their hard line on allowing former rebel states back into the Union. In addition, they sought to override the Black Codes by granting U.S. citizenship to blacks by passing a civil rights bill. Johnson, supported by Democrats, vetoed the bill, but Congress had the necessary votes to override it, and the bill became law.

In 1866, the Radical Republicans won control of Congress and passed the Reconstruction Acts, which placed the governments of the southern states under the control of the federal military. With this backing, the Republicans began to implement their radical policies such as granting all black men the vote and denying the vote to former confederate soldiers. Congress had passed the Thirteenth, Fourteenth, and Fifteenth Amendments granting citizenship and civil rights to blacks, and made ratification of these amendments a condition of readmission into the Union by the rebel states. The Republicans found support in the South among former slaves, white southerners who had not supported the Confederacy, called Scalawags, and northerners who had moved to the South and were known as Carpetbaggers.

Military control continued throughout Grant's administration, despite growing conflict both inside and outside the Republican Party. Conservatives in Congress and in the states opposed the liberal policies of the Republicans. Some Republicans became concerned over corruption issues among Grant's appointees and dropped support for him.

Under President Rutherford B. Hayes, the federal troops were removed from the South. Without this support, the Republican governments were replaced by so-called "redeemer governments," who promised the restoration of the vote to those whites who had been denied it and limitations on civil rights for blacks.

The rise of the redeemer governments marked the beginning of the Jim Crow laws and official segregation. Blacks were still allowed to vote, but ways were found to make it difficult for them to do so, such as literacy tests and poll taxes. Reconstruction, which had set as its goal the reunification of the South with the North and the granting of civil rights to freed slaves was a limited success, at best, and in the eyes of many blacks was considered a failure. However, before being allowed to rejoin the Union, the Confederate states were required to agree to all federal laws.

Skill 5.8   **Evaluate the impact of agrarianism, industrialization, urbanization, and the reform movements on social, cultural, political, and economic development in the late 19th and early 20th centuries.**

There was a marked degree of industrialization before and during the Civil War, but at war's end, industry in America was small. After the war, dramatic changes took place: machines replacing hand labor, extensive nationwide railroad service making possible the wider distribution of goods, invention of new products made available in large quantities, large amounts of money from bankers and investors for expansion of business operations. American life was definitely affected by this phenomenal industrial growth. Cities became the centers of this new business activity resulting in mass population movements and tremendous growth. This new boom in business resulted in huge fortunes for some Americans and extreme poverty for many others. The discontent this caused resulted in a number of new reform movements from which came measures controlling the power and size of big business and helping the poor.

Of course, industry before, during, and after the Civil War was centered mainly in the North, especially the tremendous industrial growth after. The late 1800s and early 1900s saw the increasing buildup of military strength and the U.S. becoming a world power.

The use of machines in industry enabled workers to produce a large quantity of goods much faster than by hand. With the increase in business, hundreds of workers were hired, assigned to perform a certain job in the production process. This was a method of organization called "division of labor" and by its increasing the rate of production, businesses lowered prices for their products making the products affordable for more people. As a result, sales and businesses were increasingly successful and profitable.

A great variety of new products or inventions became available such as the typewriter, the telephone, barbed wire, the electric light, the phonograph, and the gasoline automobile. From this list, the one that had the greatest effect on America's economy was the automobile.

The increase in business and industry was greatly affected by the many rich natural resources that were found throughout the nation. The industrial machines were powered by the abundant water supply. The construction industry as well as products made from wood depended heavily on lumber from the forests. Coal and iron ore in abundance were needed for the steel industry, which profited and increased from the use of steel in skyscrapers, automobiles, bridges, railroad tracks, and machines. Minerals such as silver, copper, and petroleum played a large role in industrial growth—especially petroleum, from which gasoline was refined as fuel for the increasingly popular automobile.

Between 1870 and 1916, more than 25 million immigrants came into the United States, adding to the phenomenal population growth taking place. This tremendous growth aided business and industry in two ways: 1) the number of consumers increased creating a greater demand for products, thus enlarging the markets for the products. 2) With increased production and expanding business, more workers were available for newly created jobs. The completion of the nation's transcontinental railroad in 1869 contributed greatly to the nation's economic and industrial growth. Some examples of the benefits of using the railroads were raw materials being shipped quickly by the mining companies and finished products sent to all parts of the country. Many wealthy industrialists and railroad owners saw tremendous profits steadily increasing due to this improved method of transportation.

As business grew, methods of sales and promotion were developed. Salespersons went to all parts of the country, promoting the varied products, opening large department stores in the growing cities, and offering the varied products at reasonable affordable prices. People who lived too far from the cities and found it impossible to shop there had the advantage of using a mail order service, buying what they needed from catalogs furnished by the companies. The developments in communication, such as the telephone and telegraph, increased the efficiency and prosperity of big business.

Investments in corporate stocks and bonds resulted from business prosperity. As individuals began investing heavily, desiring to share in the profits, their investments made available the needed capital for companies to expand their operations. As a result, banks increased in number throughout the country, making loans to businesses and significant contributions to economic growth. At the same time, during the 1880s, government made little effort to regulate businesses. This gave rise to monopolies where larger businesses were rid of their smaller competitors and assumed complete control of their industries.

Some owners in the same business would join or merge to form one company. Others formed what were called "trusts," a type of monopoly in which rival businesses were controlled but not formally owned. Monopolies had some good effects on the economy. Out of them grew the large, efficient corporations, which made important contributions to the growth of the nation's economy. The monopolies enabled businesses to keep their sales steady and avoid sharp fluctuations in price and production. At the same time, the downside of monopolies was the unfair business practices of the business leaders. Some acquired so much power that they took unfair advantage of others. Those who had little or no competition would require their suppliers to supply goods at a low cost, sell the finished goods at high prices, and reduce the quality of the product to save money.

On the other hand, the late 1800s and early 1900s were a period of the efforts of many to make significant reforms and changes in the areas of politics, society, and the economy. There was a need to reduce the levels of poverty and to improve the living conditions of those affected by it.

Regulations of big business, ridding the government of corruption, and making it more responsive to the needs of the people were also on the list of reforms to be accomplished. Until 1890, there was very little success, but from 1890 on, the reformers gained increased public support and were able to achieve some influence in government. Since some of these individuals referred to themselves as "progressives," the period of 1890 to 1917 is referred to by historians as the progressive era.

Skilled laborers were organized into a labor union called the American Federation of Labor, in an effort to gain better working conditions and wages for its members. Farmers joined organizations such as the National Grange and Farmers Alliance. Farmers were producing more food than people could afford to buy. This was the result of new farmlands rapidly opening on the plains and prairies, and development and availability of new farm machinery along with newer and better methods of farming. Farmers tried selling their surplus abroad but faced stiff competition from other nations selling the same farm products. Other problems contributed significantly to their situation. Items they needed for daily life were priced exorbitantly high. Having to borrow money to carry on farming activities kept them constantly in debt. Higher interest rates, a shortage of money, falling farm prices, dealings with so-called middlemen, and the increasingly high charges by the railroads to haul farm products to large markets all contributed to the desperate need for reform to relieve the plight of American farmers.

A timeline of Women's Rights in the USA and the National Organization for Women can be found at www.now.org

American women began actively campaigning for the right to vote. Elizabeth Cady Stanton and Susan B. Anthony in 1869 founded the organization called National Women Suffrage Association, the same year the Wyoming Territory gave women the right to vote. Soon after, a few states followed, giving women the right to vote but limited to local elections only.

Governmental reform began with the passage of the Civil Service Act, also known as the Pendleton Act. It provided for the Civil Service Commission, a federal agency responsible for giving jobs based on merit rather than as political rewards or favors. Another successful reform was the adoption of the secret ballot in voting. Other reforms included such measures as the direct primary, referendum, recall, and direct election of U.S. senators by the people rather than by their state legislatures. Following the success of reforms made at the national level, the progressives were successful in gaining reforms in government at state and local levels.

After 1890, more and more attention was called to needs and problems through the efforts of social workers and clergy and the writings of Muckrakers such as Lincoln Steffans, Ida M. Tarbell, and Upton Sinclair.

Presidents Theodore Roosevelt, William Howard Taft, and Woodrow Wilson supported many of the reform laws after 1890, and in 1884, President Grover Cleveland did much to see that the Civil Service Act was enforced. After 1880, a number of political or "third" parties were formed, and although unsuccessful in getting their presidential candidates elected, significant reform legislation, including constitutional amendments, was passed by Congress and became law due to third party efforts.

Legislative acts included the Sherman Antitrust Act of 1890, the Clayton Antitrust Act of 1914, the Underwood Tariff of 1913, and the establishment of the Federal Trade Commission in 1914. By the late 1890s and early 1900s, the United States became a world power and began a leading role in international affairs. War loomed on the horizon again and the stage was set for increased activity in world affairs, which had been avoided since the end of the Civil War.

Skill 5.9   Evaluate the impact of immigration on social, cultural, political, and economic development in the late 19th and early 20th Centuries.

Immigration has played a crucial role in the growth and settlement of the United States from the start. With a large interior territory to fill and ample opportunity, the U.S. encouraged immigration throughout most of the nineteenth century, maintaining an almost completely open policy. Famine in Ireland and Germany in the 1840s resulted in over 3.5 million immigrants from these two countries alone between the years of 1830 and 1860.

Following the Civil War, rapid expansion in rail transportation brought the interior states within easy reach of new immigrants who still came primarily from Western Europe and entered the U.S. on the East Coast. As immigration increased, several states adopted individual immigration laws, and in 1875 the U.S. Supreme Court declared immigration a federal matter. Following a huge surge in immigration from Central and Eastern Europe into urban areas in the 1880s to fill needs of the new industrialization, the United States began to regulate immigration, first by passing a tax to new immigrants, then by instituting literacy requirements and barring those with mental or physical illness. A large influx of Chinese immigration to the western states resulted in the complete exclusion of immigrants from that country in 1882. In 1891, the Federal Bureau of Immigration was established. Even with these new limits in place, immigration remained relatively open in the U.S. to those from European countries.

With much of Europe left in ruins after World War I, immigration to the U.S. exploded in the years following the war. In 1920 and 1921, some 800,000 new immigrants arrived. Unlike previous immigrants who had come mainly from western European countries, the new wave of immigrants was from southern and eastern Europe. The U.S. responded to this sudden shift in the makeup of new immigrants with a quota system, first enacted by Congress in 1921. This system limited immigration in proportion to the ethnic groups that were already settled in the U.S. according to previous census records. This national-origins policy was extended and further defined by Congress in 1924.

This policy remained the official policy of the U.S. for the next 40 years. Occasional challenges to the law from non-white immigrants re-affirmed that the intention of the policy was to limit immigration primarily to white, western Europeans, whom the government felt were most likely to assimilate into American culture. Strict limitations on Chinese immigration were extended throughout the period and relaxed only in 1940. In 1965, Congress overhauled immigration policy, removing the quotas and replacing them with a preference-based system. Now, immigrants reuniting with family members, and those with special skills or education were given preference. As a result, immigration from Asian and African countries began to increase. The 40-year legacy of the immigration restrictions of the 1920s had a direct and dramatic impact on the makeup of modern American society. Had Congress not imposed what amounted to racial limits on new arrivals to the country, the U.S. would perhaps be a larger more diverse nation today.

Skill 5.10   Identify the causes, significant individuals, and effects of the events associated with the World War I era.

During the period of 1823 to the 1890s, the major interests and efforts of the American people were concentrated on expansion, settlement, and development of the continental United States. The Civil War, 1861-1865, preserved the Union and eliminated the system of slavery and from 1865 onward the focus was on taming the West and developing industry.

During this time, travel and trade between the United States and Europe were continuous. By the 1890s, American interests turned to areas outside the boundaries of the United States. The West was developing into a major industrial area, and people in the United States became very interested in selling their factory and farm surplus to overseas markets. In fact, some Americans desired getting and controlling land outside the U.S. boundaries. Before the 1890s, the U.S. had little, if anything, to do with foreign affairs. It was not a strong nation militarily and had inconsequential influence on international political affairs. In fact, the Europeans looked on the American diplomats as inept and bungling in their diplomatic efforts and activities. However, all of this changed, and the Spanish-American War of 1898 saw the entry of the United States as a world power.

During the 1890s, Spain controlled such overseas possessions as Puerto Rico, the Philippines, and Cuba. Cubans rebelled against Spanish rule and the U.S. government found itself besieged by demands from Americans to assist the Cubans in their revolt. When the battleship USS Maine blew up off the coast of Havana, Cuba, Americans blamed the Spaniards for it and demanded American action against Spain. Two months later, Congress declared war on Spain and the U.S. quickly defeated them. The peace treaty gave the U.S. possession of Puerto Rico, the Philippines, Guam—and Hawaii, which was annexed during the war.

This success enlarged and expanded the U.S. role in foreign affairs. Under the administration of Theodore Roosevelt, the U.S. armed forces were built up, greatly increasing strength. Roosevelt's foreign policy was summed up in the slogan of "Speak softly and carry a big stick," backing up the efforts in diplomacy with a strong military. During the years before the outbreak of World War I, evidence of U.S. emergence as a world power could be seen in a number of actions. Using the Monroe Doctrine of non-involvement of Europe in the affairs of the Western Hemisphere,

President Roosevelt forced Italy, Germany, and Great Britain to remove their blockade of Venezuela.

He gained the rights to construct the Panama Canal by threatening force and assumed the finances of the Dominican Republic to stabilize it and prevent any intervention by Europeans. In 1916 under President Woodrow Wilson, U.S. troops were sent to the Dominican Republic to keep order.

War broke out in 1914 and ended in 1918 in Europe. Eventually nearly 30 nations were involved. One of the major causes of the war was the tremendous surge of nationalism during the 1800s and early 1900s. People of the same nationality or ethnic group sharing a common history, language or culture began uniting or demanding the right of unification, especially in Central Europe. Getting stronger and more intense were the beliefs of these peoples in loyalty to common political, social, and economic goals considered to be before any loyalty to the controlling nation or empire.

Emotions ran high and minor disputes magnified into major ones and sometimes quickly led to threats of war. Especially sensitive to these conditions was the area of the states on the Balkan Peninsula. Along with the imperialistic colonization for industrial raw materials, military build-up (especially by Germany) and diplomatic and military alliances, the conditions for one tiny spark to set off the explosion were in place. In July 1914, a Serbian national assassinated the Austrian heir to the throne and his wife, and war began a few weeks later. There were a few attempts to keep war from starting, but these efforts were futile.

World War I saw the introduction of such warfare as tanks, airplanes, machine guns, submarines, poison gas, and flame throwers. Fighting on the Western front was characterized by a series of trenches that were used throughout the war until 1918. The U.S. did not join the war until 1916. When it began in 1914, President Woodrow Wilson declared that the U.S. was neutral, and most Americans were opposed to any involvement anyway. In 1916, Wilson was reelected to a second term based on the slogan proclaiming his efforts at keeping America out of the war. For a few months after, he put forth his efforts to stopping the war, but German submarines began unlimited warfare against American merchant shipping.

At the same time, Great Britain intercepted and decoded a secret message from Germany to Mexico urging Mexico to go to war against the U.S. The publishing of this information along with continued German destruction of American ships resulted in the eventual entry of the U.S. into the conflict, the first time the country prepared to fight in a conflict not on American soil. Though unprepared for war, governmental efforts and activities resulted in massive defense mobilization with America's economy directed to the war effort. Though America made important contributions of war materials, its greatest contribution to the war was manpower, soldiers desperately needed by the Allies.

Some ten months before the war ended, President Wilson had proposed a program called the Fourteen Points as a method of bringing the war to an end with an equitable peace settlement. In these Points he had five Points setting out general ideals; there were eight pertaining to immediately working to resolve territorial and political problems; and the fourteenth Point counseled establishing an organization of nations to help keep world peace.

When Germany agreed in 1918 to an armistice, it assumed that the peace settlement would be drawn up on the basis of these Fourteen Points. However, the peace conference in Paris ignored these points and Wilson had to be content with efforts at establishing the League of Nations. Italy, France, and Great Britain, having suffered and sacrificed far more in the war than America, wanted retribution. The treaties punished severely the Central Powers, taking away arms and territories and requiring payment of reparations. Germany was punished more than the others and, according to one clause in the treaty, was forced to assume the responsibility for causing the war.

Pre-war empires lost tremendous amounts of territories as well as the wealth of natural resources in them. New, independent nations were formed and some predominately ethnic areas came under control of nations of different cultural backgrounds. Some national boundary changes overlapped and created tensions and hard feelings as well as political and economic confusion. The wishes and desires of every national or cultural group could not possibly be realized and satisfied, resulting in disappointments for both—those who were victorious and those who were defeated. Germany received harsher terms than expected from the treaty. It weakened its post-war government, and along with the worldwide depression of the 1930s, set the stage for the rise of Adolf Hitler and his Nationalist Socialist Party and World War II.

President Wilson lost in his efforts to get the U.S. Senate to approve the peace treaty. The Senate at the time was a reflection of American public opinion and its rejection of the treaty was a rejection of Wilson. The approval of the treaty would have made the U.S. a member of the League of Nations but Americans had just come off a bloody war to ensure that democracy would exist throughout the world. Americans just did not want to accept any responsibility that resulted from its new position of power and were afraid that membership in the League of Nations would embroil the U.S. in future disputes in Europe.

Skill 5.11 Identify social, cultural, political, and economic developments (e.g., Roaring Twenties, Harlem Renaissance, Great Depression, New Deal) between World War I and World War II.

The end of World War I and the decade of the 1920s saw tremendous changes in the United States, signifying the beginning of its development into its modern society today. The shift from farm to city life was occurring in tremendous numbers. Social changes and problems were occurring at such a fast pace that it was extremely difficult and perplexing for many Americans to adjust to them.

Politically the Eighteenth Amendment to the Constitution, the so-called Prohibition Amendment, prohibited selling alcoholic beverages throughout the U.S. resulting in problems affecting all aspects of society. The passage of the Nineteenth Amendment gave to women the right to vote in all elections. The decade of the 1920s also showed a marked change in roles and opportunities for women with more and more of them seeking and finding careers outside the home. Woman began to assert themselves as the equal of men and not simply housewives and mothers. Racial attitudes began to shift slowly as a literary movement among African Americans gained steam in the 1920s. The Harlem Renaissance was to pave the way for the Civil Rights movement forty years later.

The influence of the automobile and the entertainment industry, and the rejection of the morals and values of pre-World War I life resulted in the fast-paced Roaring Twenties. There were significant effects on events leading to the Depression-era 1930s—and another world war. Many Americans greatly desired the pre-war life and supported political policies and candidates in favor of the return to what was considered normal. Many desired to end government's strong role and adopt a policy of isolating the country from world affairs.

Prohibition of the sale of alcohol caused the increased activities of bootlegging and the rise of underworld gangs and the illegal speakeasies, as well as the jazz music and dances they promoted. The customers of these clubs were considered "modern," reflected by extremes in clothing, hairstyles, and attitudes towards authority and life. Movies and, to a certain degree, other types of entertainment— along with increased interest in sports figures and the accomplishments of national heroes such as Lindbergh—influenced Americans to admire, emulate, and support individual accomplishments.

As African Americans left the rural South and migrated to the North in search of opportunity, many settled in Harlem in New York City. By the 1920s Harlem had become a center of life and activity for black Americans. The music, art, and literature of this community gave birth to a cultural movement known as the Harlem Renaissance. The artistic expressions that emerged from this community in the 1920s and 1930s celebrated black experience, black traditions, and the voices of black America. Major writers and works of this movement included: Langston Hughes (The Weary Blues), Nella Larsen (Passing), Zora Neale Hurston (Their Eyes Were Watching God), Claude McKay, Countee Cullen, and Jean Toomer.

As wild and uninhibited as modern behavior became, this decade witnessed an increase in a religious tradition known as "revivalism"—emotional preaching. Although law and order were demanded by many Americans, the administration of President Warren G. Harding was marked by widespread corruption and scandal, not unlike the administration of Ulysses S. Grant, except that Grant had been honest and innocent. The decade of the 1920s also saw the resurgence of such racist organizations as the Ku Klux Klan.

The U.S. economy experienced a tremendous period of boom. Restrictions on business because of war no longer existed and the conservatives in control adopted policies that helped and encouraged big business. To keep foreign goods from competing with American goods, tariffs were raised to the highest level. New products were developed by American manufacturers, and refrigerators, radios, washing machines, and, most importantly, the automobile became readily available to the people.

Americans in the 1920s heavily invested in corporation stocks, providing companies a large amount of capital for expanding their businesses. The more money investors put into the stock market, the more the value of the stocks increased. This, in turn, led to widespread speculation that increased stock value was justified by earnings and dividends.

Much of the stock speculation involved paying a small part of the cost and borrowing the rest. This led eventually to the stock market crash of 1929, financial ruin for many investors, a weakening of the nation's economy, and the Great Depression of the 1930s. The Depression hit the United States tremendously hard and resulted in bank failures, loss of jobs due to cut-backs in production, and a lack of money leading to a sharp decline in spending. This affected businesses, factories and stores, which resulted in higher unemployment. Farm products were not affordable, so the farmers suffered even more. Foreign trade sharply decreased, and in the early 1930s, the U.S. economy was effectively paralyzed.

Europe was affected even more so. The war had seriously damaged the economies of the European countries, leaving both the victors and the defeated, deeply in debt. There was difficulty on both sides paying off war debts and loans. It was hard to find jobs, and some countries, Japan and Italy, found themselves without enough resources and too many people. Solving these problems by expanding the territory merely set up conditions for war later. Germany suffered with runaway inflation ruining the value of its money and wiping out the savings of millions.

Even though the U.S. made loans to Germany, which helped the government to restore some order and provided a short existence of some economic stability in Europe, the Great Depression served to undo any good that had been done. Mass unemployment, poverty, and despair greatly weakened the democratic governments that had been formed and greatly strengthened the increasing power and influence of extreme political movements such as communism, fascism, and national-socialism. These movements promised to put an end to the economic problems.

Due to severe and prolonged drought in the Great Plains and previous reliance on inappropriate farming techniques, a series of devastating dust storms occurred in the 1930s that resulted in destruction, economic ruin for many, and dramatic ecological change. Plowing the plains for agriculture had removed the grass and exposed the soil. When the drought occurred, the soil dried out and became dust. Wind blew away the dust. Between 1934 and 1939 winds blew the soil to the east, all the way to the Atlantic Ocean. The dust storms, called "black blizzards," created huge clouds of dust that were visible all the way to Chicago. Topsoil was stripped from millions of acres. In Texas, Arkansas, Oklahoma, New Mexico, Kansas, and Colorado over half a million people were homeless. Many of these people journeyed west in the hope of making a new life in California.

Crops were ruined, the land was destroyed, and people either lost or abandoned homes and farms. Fifteen percent of Oklahoma's population left. Because so many of the migrants were from Oklahoma, the migrants came to be called "Okies" no matter where they came from. Estimates of the number of people displaced by this disaster range from 300,000 or 400,000 to 2.5 million.

The Great Depression and the New Deal

The 1929 Stock Market Crash was the powerful event that is generally interpreted as the beginning of the Great Depression in America. Although the crash of the Stock Market was unexpected, it was not without identifiable causes. The 1920s had been a decade of social and economic growth and hope. But the attitudes and actions of the 1920s regarding wealth, production, and investment created several trends that quietly set the stage for the 1929 disaster.

The other factor contributing to the Great Depression was the economic condition of Europe. The U.S. was lending money to European nations to rebuild. Many of these countries used this money to purchase U.S. food and manufactured goods. But they were not able to pay off their debts. While the U.S. was providing money, food, and goods to Europe, however, it was not willing to buy European goods. Trade barriers were enacted to maintain a favorable trade balance.

Several other factors are cited by some scholars as contributing to the Great Depression. First, in 1929, the Federal Reserve increased interest rates. Second, some believe that as interest rates rose and the stock market began to decline, people began to hoard money. This was certainly the case after the crash. There is a question that it was a cause of the crash.

In September 1929, stock prices began to slip somewhat, yet people remained optimistic. On Monday, October 21, prices began to fall quickly. The volume traded was so high that the tickers were unable to keep up. Investors were frightened, and they started selling very quickly. This caused further collapse. For the next two days prices stabilized somewhat. On Black Thursday, October 24, prices plummeted again. By this time investors had lost confidence. On Friday and Saturday an attempt to stop the crash was made by some leading bankers. But on Monday the 28th, prices began to fall again, declining by 13 percent in one day. The next day, Black Tuesday, October 29, saw 16.4 million shares traded. Stock prices fell so far, that at many times no one was willing to buy at any price.

Unemployment quickly reached 25 percent nationwide. People thrown out of their homes created makeshift domiciles of cardboard, scraps of wood, and tents. With unmasked reference to President Hoover, who was quite obviously overwhelmed by the situation and incompetent to deal with it, these communities were called Hoovervilles. Families stood in bread lines, rural workers left the Dust Bowl of the Plains to search for work in California, and banks failed. More than 100,000 businesses failed between 1929 and 1932. The despair that swept the nation left an indelible scar on all who endured the Depression.

When the stock market crashed, businesses collapsed. Without demand for products, other businesses and industries collapsed. This set in motion a domino effect, bringing down the businesses and industries that provided raw materials or components to these industries. Hundreds of thousands became jobless. Then the jobless often became homeless. Desperation prevailed. Little had been done to assess the toll. Hunger, inadequate nutrition, or starvation took on those who were children during this time. Indeed, food was cheap, relatively speaking, but there was little money to buy it.

Hoover's bid for re-election in 1932 failed. The new president, Franklin D. Roosevelt won the White House on his promise to the American people of a "new deal." Upon assuming the office, Roosevelt and his advisers immediately launched a massive program of innovation and experimentation to try to bring the Depression to an end and get the nation back on track.

Congress gave the President unprecedented power to act to save the nation. During the next eight years, the most extensive and broadly-based legislation in the nation's history was enacted. The legislation was intended to accomplish three goals: relief, recovery, and reform.

The first step in the New Deal was to relieve suffering. This was accomplished through a number of job-creation projects. The second step, the recovery aspect, was to stimulate the economy. The third step was to create social and economic change through innovative legislation.

The National Recovery Administration attempted to accomplish several goals:

- Restore employment
- Increase general purchasing power
- Provide character-building activity for unemployed youth
- Encourage decentralization of industry and thus divert population from crowded cities to rural or semi-rural communities
- To develop river resources in the interest of navigation and cheap power and light
- To complete flood control on a permanent basis
- To enlarge the national program of forest protection and to develop forest resources
- To control farm production and improve farm prices
- To assist home builders and home owners
- To restore public faith in banking and trust operations
- To recapture the value of physical assets, whether in real property, securities, or other investments

These objectives and their accomplishment implied a restoration of public confidence and courage.

Among the "alphabet organizations" set up to work out the details of the recovery plan, the most prominent were:

- Agricultural Adjustment Administration (AAA), designed to readjust agricultural production and prices thereby boosting farm income
- Civilian Conservation Corps (CCC), designed to give wholesome, useful activity in the forestry service to unemployed young men
- Civil Works Administration (CWA) and the Public Works Administration (PWA), designed to give employment in the construction and repair of public buildings, parks, and highways
- Works Progress Administration (WPA), whose task was to move individuals from relief rolls to work projects or private employment

The Tennessee Valley Authority (TVA) was of a more permanent nature, designed to improve the navigability of the Tennessee River and increase productivity of the timber and farmlands in its valley. The TVA built 16 dams to provide water control and hydroelectric generation.

The Public Works Administration (PWA) employed Americans on over 34,000 public works projects at a cost of more than $4 billion. Among these projects was the construction of a highway that linked the Florida Keys and Miami, the Boulder Dam (now the Hoover Dam), and numerous highway projects.

To provide economic stability and prevent another crash, Congress passed the Glass-Steagall Act, which separated banking and investing. The Securities and Exchange Commission was created to regulate dangerous speculative practices on Wall Street. The Wagner Act guaranteed a number of rights to workers and unions in an effort to improve worker-employer relations. The Social Security Act of 1935 established pensions for the aged and infirm as well as a system of unemployment insurance.

Much of the recovery program was an emergency response, but certain permanent national policies emerged. The intention of the public through its government was to supervise and, to an extent, regulate business operations, from corporate activities to labor problems. This included protecting bank depositors and the credit system of the country, employing gold resources and currency adjustments to aid permanent restoration of normal living, and, if possible, establishing a line of subsistence below which no useful citizen would be permitted to sink.

Many of the steps taken by the Roosevelt Administration have had far-reaching effects. They alleviated the economic disaster of the Great Depression, they enacted controls that would mitigate the risk of another stock market crash, and they provided greater security for workers. The nation's economy, however, did not fully recover until America entered World War II.

To be sure, there were negative reactions to some of the measures taken to pull the country out of the Depression. There was a major reaction to the deaths of the WWI veterans in the Labor Day Hurricane, ultimately resulting in a Congressional investigation into possible negligence. The Central Valley Project ruffled feathers of farmers who lost tillable land and some water supply to the construction of the aqueduct and the Hoover Dam. Tennesseans were initially unhappy with the changes in river flow and navigation when the Tennessee Valley Authority began its construction of dams and the directing of water to form reservoirs and to power hydroelectric plants. Some businesses and business leaders were not happy with the introduction of minimum wage laws and restrictions and controls on working conditions and limitations of work hours for laborers. The numerous import/export tariffs of the period were the subject of controversy.

In the long view, however, much that was accomplished under the New Deal had positive long-term effects on economic, ecological, social and political issues for the next several decades. The Tennessee Valley Authority and the Central Valley Project in California provided a reliable source and supply of water to major cities, as well as electrical power to meet the needs of an increasingly electricity-dependent society. For the middle class and the poor, the labor regulations, the establishment of the Social Security Administration, and the separation of investment and banking have served the nation admirably for more than six decades.

Skill 5.12   Identify the causes, significant individuals, and effects of the events associated with the World War I era.

The extreme form of patriotism called nationalism that had been the chief cause of World War I grew even stronger after the war ended in 1918. The political, social, and economic unrest fueled nationalism, and it became an effective tool enabling dictators to gain and maintain power from the 1930s to the end of World War II in 1945. In the Soviet Union, Joseph Stalin succeeded in gaining political control and establishing a strong harsh dictatorship. Benito Mussolini and the Fascist party, promising prosperity and order in Italy, gained national support and set up a strong government. In Japan, although the ruler was Emperor Hirohito, actual control and administration of government came under military officers.

In Germany, the results of war, harsh treaty terms, loss of territory, great economic chaos, and collapse all enabled Adolf Hitler and his Nazi party to gain complete power and control.

Germany, Italy, and Japan initiated a policy of aggressive territorial expansion with Japan being the first to conquer. In 1931, the Japanese forces seized control of Manchuria, a part of China containing rich natural resources, and in 1937 began an attack on China, occupying most of its eastern part by 1938. Italy invaded Ethiopia in Africa in 1935, having it totally under its control by 1936. The Soviet Union did not invade or take over any territory but along with Italy and Germany, actively participated in the Spanish Civil War, using it as a proving ground to test tactics and weapons setting the stage for World War II.

In Germany, almost immediately after taking power, in direct violation of the World War I peace treaty, Hitler began the buildup of the armed forces. He sent troops into the Rhineland in 1936, then invaded Austria in 1938 and united it with Germany. Then Germany seized control of the Sudetenland in 1938 (part of western Czechoslovakia that was populated by mostly Germans), the rest of Czechoslovakia in March 1939, and on September 1, 1939, began World War II in Europe by invading Poland. In 1940, Germany invaded and controlled Norway, Denmark, Belgium, Luxembourg, the Netherlands, and France.

After the war began in Europe, U.S. President Franklin D. Roosevelt announced that the United States was neutral. Most Americans, although hoping for an Allied victory, wanted the U.S. to stay out of the war. President Roosevelt and his supporters, called "interventionists," favored all aid except war to the Allied nations fighting Axis aggression. They were fearful that an Axis victory would seriously threaten and endanger all democracies. On the other hand, the "isolationists" were against any U.S. aid being given to the warring nations, accusing President Roosevelt of leading the U.S. into a war when very much unprepared to fight. Roosevelt's plan was to defeat the Axis nations by sending the Allied nations the equipment needed to fight: ships, aircraft, tanks, and other war materials.

In Asia, the U.S. had opposed Japan's invasion of Southeast Asia, an effort to gain Japanese control of that region's rich resources. Consequently, the U.S. stopped all important exports to Japan, whose industries depended heavily on petroleum, scrap metal, and other raw materials. Later Roosevelt refused the Japanese withdrawal of its funds from American banks. General Tojo became the Japanese premier in October 1941 and quickly realized that the U.S. Navy was powerful enough to block Japanese expansion into Asia. Deciding to cripple the Pacific Fleet, the Japanese aircraft, without warning, bombed the Fleet December 7, 1941, while at anchor in Pearl Harbor in Hawaii. Temporarily it was a success. It destroyed many aircraft and disabled much of the U.S. Pacific Fleet. In the end, it was a costly mistake as it quickly motivated the Americans to prepare for and wage war.

Military strategy in the European theater of war as developed by Roosevelt, Churchill, and Stalin was to concentrate on Germany's defeat first, then Japan's. The start was made in North Africa, pushing Germans and Italians off the continent, beginning in the summer of 1942 and ending successfully in May 1943. Before the war, Hitler and Stalin had signed a non-aggression pact in 1939, which Hitler violated in 1941 by invading the Soviet Union. The German defeat at Stalingrad, marked a turning point in the war, was brought about by a combination of entrapment by Soviet troops and death of German troops by starvation and freezing due to the horrendous winter conditions. This occurred at the same time that the Allies were driving them out of North Africa.

The liberation of Italy began in July 1943 and ended May 2, 1945. The third part of the strategy was D-Day, June 6, 1944, with the Allied invasion of France at Normandy. At the same time, starting in January 1943, the Soviets began pushing the German troops back into Europe, and they were greatly assisted by supplies from Britain and the United States. By April 1945, Allies occupied positions beyond the Rhine, and the Soviets moved on to Berlin, surrounding it by April 25. Germany surrendered May 7, and the war in Europe was finally over.

Meanwhile, in the Pacific, in the six months after the attack on Pearl Harbor, Japanese forces moved across Southeast Asia and the western Pacific Ocean. By August 1942, the Japanese Empire was at its largest size and stretched northeast to Alaska's Aleutian Islands, west to Burma, south to what is now Indonesia. Invaded and controlled areas included Hong Kong, Guam, Wake Island, Thailand, part of Malaysia, Singapore, the Philippines, and Darwin on the north coast of Australia.

The raid of General Doolittle's bombers on Japanese cities and the American naval victory at Midway along with the fighting in the Battle of the Coral Sea helped turn the tide against Japan. Island-hopping by U.S. Seabees and Marines and the grueling bloody battles fought resulted in gradually pushing the Japanese back towards Japan.

After victory was attained in Europe, concentrated efforts were made to secure Japan's surrender. Two atomic bombs were dropped on the Japanese cities of Hiroshima and Nagasaki to finally end the war in the Pacific. Japan formally surrendered on September 2, 1945, aboard the U.S. battleship Missouri, anchored in Tokyo Bay. The war was finally ended.

Before war in Europe had ended, the Allies had agreed on a military occupation of Germany. It was divided into four zones, with one to be occupied by Great Britain, another by France, another by the Soviet Union, and another by the United States with the four powers jointly administering Berlin. After the war, the Allies agreed that Germany's armed forces would be abolished, the Nazi Party outlawed, and the territory east of the Oder and Neisse Rivers taken away. Nazi leaders were accused of war crimes and brought to trial.

After Japan's defeat, the Allies began a military occupation directed by American General Douglas MacArthur, who introduced a number of reforms eventually ridding Japan of its military institutions transforming it into a democracy. A constitution was drawn up in 1947 transferring all political rights from the emperor to the people, granting women the right to vote, and denying Japan the right to declare war. War crimes trials of 25 war leaders and government officials were also conducted. The U.S. did not sign a peace treaty until 1951. The treaty permitted Japan to rearm but took away its overseas empire.

Again, after a major world war came efforts to prevent war from occurring again throughout the world. Preliminary work began in 1943 when the U.S., Great Britain, the Soviet Union, and China sent representatives to Moscow where they agreed to set up an international organization that would work to promote peace around the earth. In 1944, the four Allied powers met again and made the decision to name the organization the United Nations. In 1945, a charter for the U. N. was drawn up and signed, taking effect in October of that year.

Major consequences of the war included horrendous death and destruction, millions of displaced persons, the gaining of strength and spread of Communism and Cold War tensions as a result of the beginning of the nuclear age. World War II ended more lives and caused more devastation than any other war.

Besides the losses of millions of military personnel, the devastation and destruction directly affected civilians, reducing cities, houses, and factories to ruin and rubble and wrecking communication and transportation systems. Millions of civilian deaths, especially in China and the Soviet Union, were the result of famine.

More than twelve million people were uprooted by war's end, having no place to live. They were prisoners of war, those who survived Nazi concentration camps and slave labor camps, orphans, and people who escaped war-torn areas and invading armies. Changing national boundary lines also caused the mass movement of displaced persons.

Germany and Japan were completely defeated; Great Britain and France were seriously weakened; and the Soviet Union and the United States became the world's leading powers. Although allied during the war, the alliance fell apart as the Soviets pushed Communism in Europe and Asia. In spite of the tremendous destruction it suffered, the Soviet Union was stronger than ever. During the war, it took control of Lithuania, Estonia, and Latvia and by mid-1945 parts of Poland, Czechoslovakia, Finland, and Romania. It helped Communist governments gain power in Bulgaria, Romania, Hungary, Czechoslovakia, Poland, and North Korea. China fell to Mao Zedong's (Tse-Tung) Communist forces in 1949. Before the fall of the Berlin Wall in 1989 and the dissolution of Communist governments in Eastern Europe and the Soviet Union, the United States and the Soviet Union faced off in what was called a "Cold War."

Looming over both countries was the possibility of the terrifying destruction by nuclear weapons.

Skill 5.13   Identify the causes, significant individuals, and effects of the events associated with domestic and foreign affairs during the Cold War era.

The major thrust of U.S. foreign policy from the end of World War II to 1990 was the post-war struggle between non-Communist nations, led by the United States, and the Soviet Union and the Communist nations who were its allies. It was referred to as a "Cold War" because its conflicts did not lead to a major war of fighting, or a "hot war." Both the Soviet Union and the United States embarked on an arsenal buildup of atomic and hydrogen bombs as well as other nuclear weapons. Both nations had the capability of destroying each other, but because of the continuous threat of nuclear war and accidents, extreme caution was practiced on both sides. The efforts of both sides to serve and protect their political philosophies and to support and assist their allies resulted in a number of events during this 45-year period.

In 1946, Josef Stalin stated publicly that the presence of capitalism and its development of the world's economy made international peace impossible. This resulted in an American diplomat in Moscow named George F. Kennan to propose in response to Stalin, a statement of U.S. foreign policy. The idea and goal of the U.S. was to contain or limit the extension or expansion of Soviet Communist policies and activities. After Soviet efforts to make trouble in Iran, Greece, and Turkey, U.S. President Harry Truman stated what is known as the Truman Doctrine which committed the U.S. to a policy of intervention in order to contain or stop the spread of communism throughout the world.

After 1945, social and economic chaos continued in Western Europe, especially in Germany. Secretary of State George C. Marshall came to realize that the U.S. had greatly serious problems and to assist in the recovery, he proposed a program known as the European Recovery Program or the Marshall Plan.

Although the Soviet Union withdrew from any participation, the U.S. continued the work of assisting Europe in regaining economic stability. In Germany, the situation was critical with the American Army shouldering the staggering burden of relieving the serious problems of the German economy. In February 1948, Britain and the U.S. combined their two zones, with France joining in June.

The Soviets were opposed to German unification and in April 1948 took serious action to either stop it or to force the Allies to give up control of West Berlin to the Soviets. The Soviets blocked all road traffic access to West Berlin from West Germany. To avoid any armed conflict, it was decided to airlift into West Berlin the needed food and supplies. From June 1948 to mid-May 1949 Allied air forces flew in all that was needed for the West Berliners, forcing the Soviets to lift the blockade and permit vehicular traffic access to the city.

The first "hot war" in the post-World War II era was the Korean War, begun June 25, 1950, and ending July 27, 1953. Troops from Communist North Korea invaded democratic South Korea in an effort to unite both sections under Communist control. The United Nations organization asked its member nations to furnish troops to help restore peace. Many nations responded and President Truman sent American troops to help the South Koreans. The war dragged on for three years and ended with a truce, not a peace treaty. Like Germany then, Korea remained divided and does so to this day.

In 1954, the French were forced to give up their colonial claims in Indochina, the present-day countries of Vietnam, Laos, and Cambodia. Afterwards, the Communist northern part of Vietnam began battling with the democratic southern part over control of the entire country. In the late 1950s and early 1960s, U.S. Presidents Eisenhower and Kennedy sent to Vietnam a number of military advisers and military aid to assist and support South Vietnam's non-Communist government. During Lyndon Johnson's presidency, the war escalated with thousands of American troops being sent to participate in combat with the South Vietnamese. The war was extremely unpopular in America and caused such serious divisiveness among its citizens that Johnson decided not to seek reelection in 1968. It was in President Richard Nixon's second term in office that the U.S. signed an agreement ending war in Vietnam and restoring peace. This was done January 27, 1973, and by March 29, the last American combat troops and American prisoners of war left Vietnam for home. It was the longest war in U.S. history and to this day carries the perception that it was a "lost war."

In 1962, during the administration of President John F. Kennedy, Premier Khrushchev and the Soviets decided, as a protective measure for Cuba against an American invasion, to install nuclear missiles on the island. In October, American U-2 spy planes photographed over Cuba what were identified as missile bases under construction. The decision in the White House was how to handle the situation without starting a war. The only recourse was removal of the missile sites and preventing more being set up. Kennedy announced that the U.S. had set up a "quarantine" of Soviet ships heading to Cuba. It was in reality a blockade but the word itself could not be used publicly as a blockade was actually considered an act of war.

A week of incredible tension and anxiety gripped the entire world until Soviet ships carrying missiles for the Cuban bases turned back and the crisis eased. What precipitated the crisis was Khrushchev's underestimation of Kennedy. The President made no effort to prevent the erection of the Berlin Wall and was reluctant to commit American troops to invade Cuba and overthrow Fidel Castro. The Soviets assumed this was a weakness and decided they could install the missiles without any interference.

The Soviets were concerned about American missiles installed in Turkey aimed at the Soviet Union and about a possible invasion of Cuba. If successful, Khrushchev would demonstrate to the Russian and Chinese critics of his policy of peaceful coexistence that he was tough and not to be intimidated. At the same time, the Americans feared that if Russian missiles were put in place and launched from Cuba to the U.S., the short distance of 90 miles would not allow enough time for adequate warning. Furthermore, it would originate from a direction that radar systems could not detect. It was felt that if America gave in and allowed a Soviet presence practically at the back door that the effect on American security and morale would be devastating.

As tensions eased in the aftermath of the crisis, several agreements were made. The missiles in Turkey were removed, as they were obsolete. A telephone "hot line" was set up between Moscow and Washington to make it possible for the two heads of government to have instant contact with each other. The U.S. agreed to sell its surplus wheat to the Soviets.

After World War II and the Korean War, efforts had begun to relieve the problems of millions of African-Americans, including ending discrimination in education, housing, and jobs and the grinding widespread poverty. The efforts of civil rights leaders found success in a number of Supreme Court decisions, the best-known case, Brown vs. Board of Education of Topeka (1954) ending compulsory segregation in public schools. In the 1960s, the civil rights movement under the leadership of Dr. Martin Luther King, Jr. really gained momentum. Under President Lyndon B. Johnson the Civil Rights Acts of 1964 and 1968 prohibited discrimination in housing sales and rentals, employment, public accommodations, and voter registration.

Poverty remained a serious problem in the central sections of large cities resulting in riots and soaring crime rates, which ultimately found its way to the suburbs. The escalation of the war in Vietnam and the social conflict and upheaval of support versus opposition to U.S. involvement, led to antiwar demonstrations. The escalation of drug abuse, weakening of the family unit, homelessness, poverty, mental illness, along with increasing social, mental, and physical problems experienced by the Vietnam veterans returning to families, marriages, contributed to a country divided and torn apart.

Contemporary United States (1968 – present)

Probably the highlight of the foreign policy of President Richard Nixon, after the end of the Vietnam War and withdrawal of troops, was his 1972 trip to China. When the Communists gained control of China in 1949, the policy of the U.S. government was refusal to recognize the Communist government. It regarded as the legitimate government of China to be that of Chiang Kai-shek, exiled on the island of Taiwan. In 1971, Nixon sent Henry Kissinger on a secret trip to Peking to investigate whether or not it would be possible for America to give recognition to China. In February 1972, President and Mrs. Nixon spent a number of days in the country visiting well-known Chinese landmarks, dining with the two leaders, Mao Tse-tung and Chou En-lai. Agreements were made for cultural and scientific exchanges, eventual resumption of trade, and future unification of the mainland with Taiwan. In 1979, formal diplomatic recognition was achieved. With this one visit, the pattern of the Cold War was essentially shifted.

The Watergate scandal resulting in the first-ever resignation of a sitting American president was the most crucial domestic crisis of the 1970s, and it was due to President's Nixon's directions to invade Democratic headquarters in Washington, DC. The population of the U.S. had greatly increased and along with it the nation's industries and the resulting harmful pollution of the environment. Factory smoke, automobile exhaust, waste from factories and other sources all combined to create hazardous air, water, and ground pollution which, if not brought under control and significantly diminished, would severely endanger all life on earth. The Cold War continued to varying degrees from 1947 to 1991, when the Soviet Union collapsed. Other Eastern European countries had seen their communist governments overthrown by this time as well, marking the shredding of the "Iron Curtain."

Inflation increased in the late 1960s, and the 1970s witnessed a period of high unemployment, the result of a severe recession. The decision of the OPEC (Organization of Petroleum Exporting Countries) ministers to cut back on oil production thus raising the price of a barrel of oil created a fuel shortage. This made it clear that energy and fuel conservation was necessary in the

American economy, especially since fuel shortages created two energy crises during the decade of the 1970s. Americans experienced shortages of fuel oil for heating and gasoline for cars and other vehicles.

The 1980s saw the difficulties of rising inflation, recession, recovery, and the insecurity of long-term employment. Foreign competition and imports, the use of robots and other advanced technology in industries, the opening and operation of American companies and factories in other countries to lower labor costs all contributed to the economic and employment problems. The 1980s is the decade of the eleven-million gallon Exxon Valdez oil spill off the Alaskan coast and the nuclear accident and melt-down at the Ukrainian nuclear power plant at Chernobyl. The U.S. had a narrow escape with the near disaster at Three Mile Island Nuclear Plant in Pennsylvania.

Under the administration of President Jimmy Carter, Egyptian President Anwar el-Sadat and Israeli Prime Minister Menachem Begin met at presidential retreat Camp David and agreed, after a series of meetings, to sign a formal treaty of peace between the two countries. In 1979, the Soviet invasion of Afghanistan was perceived by Carter and his advisers as a threat to the rich oil fields in the Persian Gulf, but at the time U.S. military capability to prevent further Soviet aggression in the Middle East was weak. The last year of Carter's presidential term was involved in the 53 American hostages held in Iran. The shah had been deposed, and control of the government and the country was in the hands of Muslim leader, the Ayatollah Ruhollah Khomeini.

Khomeini's extreme hatred for the U.S. was the result of the 1953 overthrow of Iran's Mossadegh government, sponsored by the CIA. To make matters worse, the CIA proceeded to train the shah's ruthless secret police force. So when the terminally ill, exiled shah was allowed into the U.S. for medical treatment, a fanatical mob stormed into the American embassy taking the 53 Americans as prisoners, supported and encouraged by Khomeini.

President Carter froze all Iranian assets in the U.S., set up trade restrictions, and approved a risky rescue attempt, which failed. He appealed to the UN for aid in gaining release for the hostages and to European allies to join the trade embargo on Iran. Khomeini ignored UN requests for releasing the Americans, and Europeans refused to support the embargo so as not to risk losing access to Iran's oil. American prestige was damaged, and Carter's chances for reelection were doomed. The hostages were released on the day of Ronald Reagan's inauguration as President when Carter released Iranian assets as ransom.

The foreign policy of President Ronald Reagan was, in his first term, focused primarily on the Western Hemisphere, particularly in Central America and the West Indies. U.S. involvement in the domestic revolutions of El Salvador and Nicaragua continued into Reagan's second term when Congress held televised hearings on what came to be known as the Iran-Contra Affair. A cover-up was exposed showing that profits from secretly selling military hardware to Iran had been used to give support to rebels, called Contras, who were fighting in Nicaragua. In 1983 in Lebanon, 241 American Marines were killed when an Islamic suicide bomber drove an explosive-laden truck into U.S. Marines headquarters located at the airport in Beirut. This tragic event came as part of the unrest and violence between the Israelis and the Palestinian Liberation Organization (PLO) forces in southern Lebanon.

In the same month, 1,900 U.S. Marines landed on the island of Grenada to rescue a small group of American medical students at the medical school and depose the leftist government. Perhaps the most intriguing and far-reaching event towards the end of Reagan's second term was the arms-reduction agreement Reagan reached with Soviet General Secretary Mikhail Gorbachev. Gorbachev began easing East-West tensions by stressing the importance of cooperation with the West and easing the harsh and restrictive life of the people in the Soviet Union. In retrospect, it was clearly a prelude to the events occurring during the administration of President George Bush.

After Bush took office, it appeared for a brief period that democracy would gain a hold and influence in China, but the brief movement was quickly and decisively crushed. The biggest surprise was the fall of the Berlin Wall resulting in the unification of all of Germany. The loss of the Communists' power in other Eastern European countries, and the fall of Communism in the Soviet Union and the breakup of its republics into independent nations was no less surprising. The countries of Poland, Hungary, Romania, Czechoslovakia, Albania, and Bulgaria replaced Communist rule with democratic ones.

The former Yugoslavia broke apart into individual ethnic enclaves with the republics of Serbia, Croatia, and Bosnia-Herzegovina embarking on wars of ethnic cleansing among Catholics, Orthodox, and Muslims. In Russia, as in the other former republics and satellites, democratic governments were put into operation, and the difficult task of changing communist economies into ones of capitalistic free enterprise began. For all practical purposes, it appeared that the tensions and dangers of the post-World War II "Cold War" between the U.S. and Soviet-led Communism were over.

The nation's farmers experienced economic hardships, and October 1987 saw another one-day significant drop in the Dow Jones on the New York Stock Exchange. January 28, 1986, was the day of the loss of the seven crew members of the NASA space shuttle "Challenger." The reliability and soundness of numerous savings and loans institutions were in serious jeopardy when hundreds of these failed and others went into bankruptcy following deregulation of the industry and brokered deposits, costing U.S. taxpayers $124.6 billion, contributing to budget deficits of the early 1990s.

President Bush, in December of 1989, sent U.S. troops to invade Panama and arrest the Panamanian dictator Manuel Noriega. Although he had periodically assisted CIA operations with intelligence information, at the same time, Noriega laundered money from drug smuggling and gunrunning through Panama's banks. Though ignored for a short time, it became too embarrassing for the American intelligence community. When a political associate tried unsuccessfully to depose him and an off-duty U.S. Marine was shot and killed at a roadblock, Bush acted. Noriega was brought to the U.S. where he stood trial on charges of drug distribution and racketeering.

During the time of the American hostage crisis, Iraq and Iran were fighting a war in which the U.S. and most of Iraq's neighbors supported Iraq. In a five-year period, Saddam Hussein received from the U.S. $500 million worth of American technology, including lasers, advanced computers, and special machine tools used in missile development. The Iraq-Iran war was a bloody one resulting in a stalemate with a UN truce. Neighboring Kuwait, in direct opposition to OPEC agreements, increased oil production.

This caused oil prices to drop, which upset Hussein, who was deeply in debt from the war and totally dependent on oil revenues. After a short period, Saddam invaded and occupied Kuwait. The U.S. made extensive plans to put into operation strategy to successfully carry out Operation Desert Storm, the liberation of Kuwait. In four days, February 24-28, 1991, the war was over, and Iraq had been defeated, its troops driven back into their country. Saddam remained in power although Iraq's economy was seriously damaged.

President Bill Clinton sent U.S. troops to Haiti to protect the efforts of Jean-Bertrand Aristide to gain democratic power and to Bosnia to assist UN peacekeeping forces. He also inherited from the Bush administration the problem of Somalia in East Africa, where U.S. troops had been sent in December 1992 to support UN efforts to end the starvation of the Somalis and restore peace. The efforts were successful at first, but eventually failed due to the severity of the intricate political problems within the country. After U.S. soldiers were killed in an ambush along with 300 Somalis, American troops were withdrawn and returned home.

Skill 5.14   Identify the causes, significant individuals, and effects of the events associated with movements for equality, civil rights, and civil liberties in the 19th and 20th Centuries.

Civil Rights Movement

The phrase "the civil rights movement" generally refers to the nation-wide effort made by black people and those who supported them to gain equal rights to whites and to eliminate segregation. Discussion of this movement is generally understood in terms of the period of the 1950s and 1960s.

The key people in the civil rights movement are:

- Rosa Parks — A black seamstress from Montgomery Alabama who, in 1955, refused to give up her seat on the bus to a white man. This event is generally understood as the spark that lit the fire of the Civil Rights Movement. She has been generally regarded as the "mother of the Civil Rights Movement."

- Martin Luther King, Jr. — the most prominent member of the Civil Rights movement. King promoted nonviolent methods of opposition to segregation. The "Letter from Birmingham Jail" explained the purpose of nonviolent action as a way to make people notice injustice. He led the march on Washington in 1963, at which he delivered the "I Have a Dream" speech. He received the 1968 Nobel Prize for Peace.

- James Meredith – the first African American to enroll at the University of Mississippi.

- Emmett Till – a teenage boy who was murdered in Mississippi while visiting from Chicago. He was accused of the crime of "whistling at a white woman in a store." He was beaten and murdered, and his body was dumped in a river. His two white abductors were apprehended and tried. They were acquitted by an all-white jury. After the acquittal, they admitted their guilt, but remained free because of double jeopardy laws.

- Ralph Abernathy – A major figure in the Civil Rights Movement who succeeded Martin Luther King, Jr. as head of the Southern Christian Leadership Conference

- Malcolm X – A political leader and part of the Civil Rights Movement. He was a prominent Black Muslim.

- Stokely Carmichael – One of the leaders of the Black Power movement that called for independent development of political and social institutions for blacks. Carmichael called for black pride and maintenance of black culture. He was head of the Student Nonviolent Coordinating Committee.

- Jackie Robinson – The first black Major League baseball player of the modern era in 1947 and was inducted into the Baseball Hall of Fame in 1962. He was a member of six World Series teams. He actively campaigned for a number of politicians including Hubert Humphrey and Richard Nixon.

- Thurgood Marshall – The grandson of a slave and the first African American to serve on the Supreme Court of the United States. As a lawyer he was remembered for his high success rate in arguing before the Supreme Court and for his victory in the Brown v. Board of Education of Topeka case.

Key events of the Civil Rights Movement include:

- The murder of Emmett Till, 1955

- Rosa Parks and the Montgomery Bus Boycott, 1955-56 – After refusing to give up her seat on a bus in Montgomery, Alabama, Parks was arrested, tried, and convicted of disorderly conduct and violating a local ordinance. When word reached the black community, a bus boycott was organized to protest the segregation of blacks and whites on public buses. The boycott lasted 381 days, until the ordinance was lifted.

- Strategy shift to "direct action" – Nonviolent resistance and civil disobedience, 1955 – 1965. This action consisted mostly of bus boycotts, sit-ins, freedom rides.

- Formation of the Southern Christian Leadership Conference, 1957. This group, formed by Martin Luther King, Jr., John Duffy, Rev. C. D. Steele, Rev. T. J. Jemison, Rev. Fred Shuttlesworth, Ella Baker, A. Philip Randolph, Bayard Rustin and Stanley Levison. The group provided training and assistance to local efforts to fight segregation. Non-violence was its central doctrine and its major method of fighting segregation and racism.

- The Desegregation of Little Rock, 1957. Following the decision of the Supreme Court in Brown vs. Board of Education, the Little Rock, Arkansas school board voted to integrate the school system. The National Association for the Advancement of Colored People (NAACP) chose Arkansas as the place to push integration because it was considered a relatively progressive Southern state. However, the governor called up the National Guard to prevent nine black students from attending Little Rock's Central High School.

- Sit-ins – In 1960, students began to stage "sit-ins" at local lunch counters and stores as a means of protesting the refusal of those businesses to desegregate. The first was in Greensboro, NC. This led to a rash of similar campaigns throughout the South. Demonstrators began to protest parks, beaches, theaters, museums, and libraries. When arrested, the protesters made "jail-no-bail" pledges. This called attention to their cause and put the financial burden of providing jail space and food on the cities.

- Freedom Rides – Activists traveled by bus throughout the Deep South to desegregate bus terminals (required by federal law). These protesters undertook extremely dangerous protests. Many buses were firebombed, attacked by the KKK, and individuals beaten. They were crammed into small, airless jail cells and mistreated in many ways. Key figures in this effort included John Lewis, James Lawson, Diane Nash, Bob Moses, James Bevel, Charles McDew, Bernard Lafayette, Charles Jones, Lonnie King, Julian Bond, Hosea Williams, and Stokely Carmichael.

- The Birmingham Campaign, 1963-64. A campaign was planned to use sit-in, kneel-ins in churches, and a march to the county building to launch a voter registration campaign. Birmingham obtained an injunction forbidding all such protests. The protesters, including Martin Luther King, Jr., believed the injunction was unconstitutional and defied it. They were arrested. While in jail, King wrote his famous "Letter from Birmingham Jail." When the campaign began to falter, the "Children's Crusade" called students to leave school and join the protests. The events became news when more than 600 students were jailed. The next day more students joined the protest. The media was present, and broadcast to the nation, vivid pictures of fire hoses being used to knock down children and dogs attacking some of them. The resulting public outrage led the Kennedy administration to intervene. About a month later, a committee was formed to end hiring discrimination, arrange for the release of jailed protesters, and establish normative communication between blacks and whites. Four months later, the KKK bombed the Sixteenth Street Baptist Church, killing four girls.

- The March on Washington, 1963. This was a march on Washington, DC, for jobs and freedom. It was a combined effort of all major civil rights organizations. The goals of the march were meaningful civil rights laws, a massive federal works program, full and fair employment, decent housing, the right to vote, and adequate integrated education. It was at this march that Martin Luther King, Jr., made his famous "I Have a Dream" speech.

- Mississippi Freedom Summer, 1964. Students were brought from other states to Mississippi to assist local activists in registering voters, teaching in "Freedom schools" and forming the Mississippi Freedom Democratic Party. Three of the workers disappeared–murdered by the KKK. It took six weeks to find their bodies. The national uproar forced President Johnson to send in the FBI. Johnson was able to use public sentiment to effect passage in Congress of the Civil Rights Act of 1964.

- Selma to Montgomery Marches, 1965. Attempts to obtain voter registration in Selma, Alabama, had been largely unsuccessful due to opposition from the city's sheriff. The Rev. King came to the city to lead a series of marches. He and more than 200 demonstrators were arrested and jailed. Each successive march was met with violent resistance by police. In March, a group of over 600 intended to walk from Selma to Montgomery (54 miles). News media were on hand when six blocks into the march, state and local law enforcement officials attacked the marchers with billy clubs, tear gas, rubber tubes wrapped in barbed wire, and bullwhips. They were driven back to Selma. National broadcast of the footage provoked a nationwide response. President Johnson again used public sentiment to achieve passage of the Voting Rights Act of 1965. This law changed the political landscape of the South irrevocably.

- Brown v. Board of Education, 1954 – the Supreme Court declared that Plessy v. Ferguson was unconstitutional. This was the ruling that had established "Separate but Equal" as the basis for segregation. With the Brown decision, the Court ordered immediate desegregation.

- Civil Rights Act of 1964 – Bars discrimination in public accommodations, employment and education

- Voting Rights Act of 1965 – Suspends poll taxes, literacy tests, and other voter tests for voter registration.

The 1960 election was a contest between John F. Kennedy and Vice President Richard Nixon. The country was divided. The 1960 election was a close election, with President Kennedy winning by only 100,000 votes. President Kennedy faced Cold War challenges including Vietnam and the missile crisis in Cuba. Kennedy introduced economic reforms including a minimum wage increase. The civil rights movement led by Martin Luther King, Jr. was gaining steam and led the President to propose civil rights legislation. During a political trip to Dallas, Texas, on November 22, 1963, President Kennedy was assassinated by Lee Harvey Oswald, who was subsequently shot by Jack Ruby, a local nightclub owner. Vice President Lyndon Johnson became President.

Many conspiracy theories developed following the President's assassination. The Warren Commission, chaired by the Chief Justice of the Supreme Court was created to investigate the assassination. The Commission concluded that Oswald was the assassin and that he acted alone.

President Johnson continued President Kennedy's commitment to civil rights reform and elimination of poverty. Johnson led the passage of the Civil Rights Act of 1964 and proposed a series of policies around the Great Society program. Great Society proposed a war on poverty, Medicare, Medicaid, voting rights reforms, and other civil rights reforms.

President Johnson won reelection over Barry Goldwater. Goldwater, a conservative, is often credited with the building of the conservative movement in the United States although the Christian Right conflicted with his libertarian views. The Johnson campaign was able to paint Goldwater as an extremist who could lead to nuclear war.

The escalation of the Vietnam War led to a period of discontent in the United States. Increasing opposition to the war challenged the administration. President Johnson faced opposition during the 1968 Presidential campaign—first from Eugene McCarthy and then from Senator Robert F. Kennedy. President Johnson announced that he would not seek a second term. Increased civil disobedience followed the assassination of Dr. Martin Luther King, Jr., on April 4, 1968. James Earl Ray pleaded guilty to the murder. Rioting occurred in several major cities.

Senator Robert Kennedy was assassinated in June, 1968, following his victory in the California primary, by Sirhan Sirhan, who opposed the Senator's position on Israel. The summer of 1968 ended with riots at the Chicago Democratic convention in opposition to the Vietnam War. Hubert Humphrey won the Democratic nomination for President but lost the election to Richard Nixon.

The disability rights movement was a successful effort to guarantee access to public buildings and transportation, equal access to education and employment, and equal protection under the law in terms of access to insurance, and other basic rights of American citizens. As a result of these efforts, public buildings and public transportation must be accessible to persons with disabilities. Discrimination in hiring or housing on the basis of disability is also illegal. A "prisoners' rights" movement has been working for many years to ensure the basic human rights of persons incarcerated for crimes. Immigrant rights movements have provided for employment and housing rights, as well as preventing abuse of immigrants through hate crimes. In some states, immigrant rights movements have led to bi-lingual education and public information access.

Other group movements to obtain equal rights involved women, the lesbian, gay, bisexual and transgender social movement, and Hispanics. The groups seeking equal rights sought equal housing, freedom from social and employment discrimination, and equal recognition of relationships under the law.

The women's rights movement is concerned with the freedoms of women as differentiated from broader ideas of human rights. The rights the movement has sought to protect throughout history include:

- The right to vote
- The right to work
- The right to fair wages
- The right to bodily integrity and autonomy
- The right to own property

- The right to an education
- The right to hold public office
- Marital rights
- Parental rights
- Religious rights
- The right to serve in the military
- The right to enter into legal contracts

The movement for women's rights has resulted in many social and political changes. Many of the ideas that seemed very radical merely 100 years ago are now normative.
Some of the most famous leaders in the women's movement throughout American history are:

- Abigail Adams
- Susan B. Anthony
- Gloria E. Anzaldua
- Betty Friedan
- Olympe de Gouges
- Germaine Greer
- Gloria Steinem
- Harriet Tubman
- Mary Wollstonecraft
- Virginia Woolf

Many within the women's movement are primarily committed to justice and the natural rights of all people. This has led many members of the women's movement to be involved in the Black Civil Rights Movement, the gay rights movement, and the recent social movement to protect the rights of fathers.

Skill 5.15   Identify the causes, significant individuals, and effects of the events associated with contemporary domestic and foreign affairs.

Domestic Issues

The economy, national defense, health care, the Presidential Election of 2008, and energy are currently the most relevant domestic issues. The slowing economy has superseded a variety of other issues, as the impact of a slow economy spreads quickly.

The Economy and Housing

Investors have increasingly demanded large returns on principal; in order to achieve these aims Wall Street became more aggressive with its investments. The technology bubble of the late 1990's burst and many investors lost a great deal of money. This led to the search for the next "big thing" and the housing/credit bubble was created.

Low interest rates enticed current homeowners to refinance their existing mortgages. Many of these homeowners took the existing equity out of their homes and spent that money in a variety of ways. New vehicles, vacations, or another home became the most common new purchases. Another factor, rising home values, also enticed many homeowners to refinance. As a home became worth more, many people refinanced and took out the difference and used that money to buy other things.

More buyers meant more competition resulting in higher home prices. In order to get a bigger piece of action many mortgage companies began writing loans to people who wouldn't have qualified in the past, these homebuyers became known as "sub-prime" due to their lower credit scores. This group of people often got into boutique loans, which were far riskier. ARM or adjustable rate mortgages were especially volatile. A low-interest rate in 2007 and 2008 could spike to a high one within five years. A manageable monthly payment would turn into an unmanageable payment.

As home prices continued to rise, many speculators and "flippers" got involved in real estate. The goal was to buy a home, either sit on it or fix it up, then sell it for a handsome profit. Many of these investors bought these homes with short-term interest-only loans. They had no intention of ever living in the home.

Once home prices peaked the number of buyers began to stabilize and then decrease. At this point the speculators could no longer make as much money and they removed themselves from the market. This further decreased demand. As demand continued to decrease, prices dropped. Places most affected by this drop included Florida, the Southwest, and California. Many homes lost 40 percent of their value within 24 months.

Many homeowners are now left with a difficult decision. Those who cannot make the monthly payment are forced to walk away from the home. Even homeowners who made good choices are affected. As your neighbor's home drops in price, so does yours. Even if you have paid off your mortgage, the value of your home has likely significantly decreased.

Health Care

While most of Europe has government provided health care, the United States has remained as a private payer system. Despite having 47 million uninsured citizens, the United States spends a greater percentage of Gross Domestic Product on health care than such countries as France and Switzerland who provide health care to all citizens according to the National Coalition on Health Care (www.nchc.org).

Proponents of the current system argue that the best medical care in the world is provided in the United States. Opponents of the current system point to the high number of uninsured as well as the high cost of the system. The uninsured often end up costing more as they are unlikely to get preemptive doctor visits and most often access the system in the most costly way, emergency room visits.

As First Lady, Hillary Clinton attempted to overhaul the health care system in the United States. Though she failed to make a change, the discussion was brought to the forefront of policy discussion. Since her husband, Bill Clinton, left office in 2001 the cost of health care in the United States has increased at a level well above inflation.

At this point in time more Americans than ever are willing to consider a change in a system that is seen as too costly and leaves too many uninsured.

Energy

In order to guarantee a future where the United States has adequate access to energy, all stakeholders agree it is necessary to develop new forms of energy. The argument is about how best to achieve those aims. People on the right believe the government should give private companies incentives in the form of tax incentives to develop new technologies. Those on the left believe the government should take a more direct role in developing new technologies.

A great deal of momentum was built up by former Vice-President Al Gore and his documentary "An Inconvenient Truth." That got the United States talking about energy reduction and energy independence. However, it has become clear that the cost of many of these new technologies is currently high. In the current economic climate it is difficult to maintain the momentum of the "Green Movement" when moving in that direction is a significant financial hardship for many individuals and nations.

Presidential Election of 2008

After a contentious Democratic primary, Illinois Senator Barack Obama garnered the parties' Presidential nomination over early favorite New York Senator Hillary Clinton. Obama ran on a platform of change and captured the imagination of many young and minority voters early on. He used that momentum to significantly cut into Clinton's base. After a great deal of discussion Obama and his advisors settled on Delaware Senator Joe Biden as his running mate.

On the Republican side veteran Arizona Senator John McCain took the nomination after a primary race that included a large number of viable candidates including former Massachusetts Governor Mitt Romney, former Arkansas Governor Mike Huckabee, and former New York City mayor Rudy Giuliani. McCain ran into considerable opposition from Conservatives in his party who saw McCain as too moderate. In order to appease this group, McCain tabbed relatively unknown Alaskan Governor Sarah Palin as his running mate.

McCain's selection of Palin for the Republican ticket slightly narrowed the gap between the two tickets in national polls for several weeks, but Obama was always able to keep a narrow lead. On election night Obama ended up earning a decisive victory. The Democrats had consolidated power, controlling the Presidency, the House and the Senate. Republicans were seen as out of power and without a leader or a specific platform. As the Republicans scramble to get their house in order for the 2010 midterm election, the Democrats have begun a program of legislation to move the country to the left.

Foreign Policy

As technology improves the world is increasingly becoming a smaller place. Technology has given many citizens of poorer countries access to the global economy, but with that access has come a whole new set of foreign policy issues. In the last half of the 20th Century America's biggest adversaries were the Communist countries of China and the Soviet Union. Today the threats exist not only from other nations but also smaller groups within nations.

Historically the strongest allies the United States has had have come from Europe. That remains true today as Great Britain, France, and Germany continue to be strong American allies both militarily and economically. The rise of the European Union, a combination of 27 member countries, has strengthened the economies of many of its member nations. However, due to the current economic meltdown, the cooperation of many of these countries has waned. The United States has asked for significant government intervention in the global economy and many nations are reluctant to offer the help the United States has requested.

Instability in South America continues to be a concern for America. Venezuelan President Hugo Chavez was an outspoken critic of former President George W. Bush and U.S. foreign policy. Chavez was a former military officer and an advocate for socialism. Perhaps his most controversial move was nationalizing many of Venezuela's major corporations. He supported price controls on many food items which has led to temporary shortages and hoarding. He died in 2013.

South America's largest country, Brazil, was led by President Luiz Inacio Lula da Silva. He was often referred to simply as Lula. Before being elected President Lula was a strong advocate for deep social change; once elected he began governing from a more moderate position. He passed new labor and judicial laws, aimed mostly at reform. On foreign policy issues, Lula was seen as a pragmatist, usually negotiating with other leaders not maintaining his ideology. He was close with both George W. Bush and Hugo Chavez. Under his leadership, Brazil's influence increased and its trade deficits of the early 21st Century were replaced with surpluses. Dilma Vana Rousseff became the country's first female president when she was elected in 2011. Cristina Kirchner is the current President of Argentina and also wife of former President Nestor Kirchner. She dominated the October 27, 2007 election, winning office by 22 percent over her nearest rival. Her presidency got off to a difficult start as the result of allegations of campaign corruption by American officials. Kirchner and Hugo Chavez claimed the United States was trying to divide the countries of Latin America. The United States formally declared the allegations were not made by the U.S. government and relations improved. Many have accused her administration of being run by her husband and her current approval ratings are amongst the lowest in South America.

While the early part of the 21st Century saw rapid growth of the economies in Central America, the global financial meltdown has caused serious problems for the economies of Central America.

Mexican President Felipe Calderon is affiliated with the National Action Party, the most conservative party in that nation. Calderon won election in 2006 amid allegations of voter fraud.

As a staunch proponent of free markets Calderon was closely allied with Bush administration policies in that arena. Mexico is currently engaged in a large-scale war with drug cartels; this violence has been especially prevalent in the northern part of the country. Under Calderon the Mexican authorities have confiscated a large number of weapons, drugs, and cash. Despite these apparent gains, the cartels have stepped up their violence and public opinion is divided. As the cartels continue to escalate their violence, many Mexican citizens are wary of continued efforts by the government to crack down on the cartels.

Immigration continues to be a hot-button issue in Mexico as many migrants come from southern Latin America through Mexico en route to the United States. President Calderon has been a critic of the lack of immigration reform in the United States. With the slowing of the United States' economy many Mexican nationals have found work hard to get especially in the building sector and have returned to Mexico. This has led to increased unemployment in Mexico and a loss of the money those workers would have sent home from the United States.

The continent of Africa has seen a great deal of economic growth in the past decades, but continues to be hampered by disease and hunger. While the United States continues to increase aid to the continent, Africa continues to fight an uphill battle against AIDS and Malaria.

Instability on the continent continues to be a concern for the United States. Formerly stable countries such as Kenya have slowly destabilized. Allegations of election fraud have hurt a country that was considered a model for African Democracy.

Genocide in the Sudan has done much to paralyze that nation. Humanitarian efforts have focused on protecting Sudan's citizens in Darfur as the government is unable to do so. Sudan has a history of failing to provide even the most basic necessities to refugees from neighboring countries.

The United States has a long history with the nation of Somalia, but the current military problem there includes nations from all over the world. Piracy has become a huge problem, as Somalian natives have taken to the Red Sea and done much to disrupt commerce, including high jacking oil tankers.

Zimbabwe has also fallen into instability; its economy had been destroyed even before the global financial meltdown. Inflation in Zimbabwe had been amongst the worst in the modern history of the world, making the currency essentially worthless. President Robert Mugabe is seen internationally as promoting racist policies, including the confiscation of farms owned by whites, who are in the minority in Zimbabwe. Relations between Mugabe and the west continue to unravel and he is currently banned from traveling to the United States and the European Union.

China has about 20 percent of the world's population, a total of over 1.3 billion residents. The Chinese have used this population to fuel one of the fastest growing economies over the last 20 years. The worldwide economic recession has slowed demand for China's numerous exports; this has led to major problems in China's economy. The slowdown has come at a terrible time for China as the 2008 summer Olympics in Beijing served to showcase the country to the globe. Despite growth in the economy, job opportunities are limited for the nearly five million college graduates each year in the country. China's huge population was a great benefit in times of growth, but the strength has turned into a weakness during the slowdown.

India has made similar strides to China in the last several decades and has become a hub for technology and medicine. India maintains an arsenal of nuclear weapons and tensions between it and Pakistan are a cause for concern. Pakistan also has nuclear capabilities and developed its nuclear program in response to India. Tribal instability in Pakistan is cause for concern in the region.

After the fall of the Soviet Union, the new nation of Russia fell on hard times. The country struggled to make a clean transition between Communism and Democracy and many people looked back fondly on the time of Communism. From a United States perspective the Cold War had been won and though Russia was still a military power, the disorganization in the country meant that Russia was no longer a superpower.

Today led by Vladimir Putin who served as president before Dmitry Medvedev., Russia has again been asserting its power in global affairs. Many critics of Medvedev believe he was simply a figurehead and that the country was being run by Vladimir Putin who was serving as the Prime Minister during the Medvedev presidency. Putin had previously been President between 1999 and 2008.

Putin is seen as a somewhat sinister figure who has an intelligence background in the KGB. Putin and George W. Bush were at times very close, drawing a great deal of criticism from many in the United States. Russia flexed its muscle in Eastern Europe with an invasion of Georgia in 2008, and though this situation cooled quickly Eastern Europe remains a hot spot. The Russia takeover in the Crimea and the conflict between Russian-supported separatists in Ukraine and the Ukrainians can impact international relations and Putin's 2012 return to the Russian presidency.

After the fall of the Soviet Union a small group of businessmen gained a great deal of wealth and political influence by gaining control of certain businesses. They became known as oligarchs. Their political influence is somewhat overstated, but they did become astonishingly rich and are now often stereotyped as the enemies of communism. A large number of these oligarchs spend a significant amount of time in London, which is sometimes referred to as Moscow on the Thames. The most famous of the oligarchs in the western world is Roman Abramovich who owns the soccer team Chelsea F.C. and has spent a record amount on player salaries. Abramovich is also a large supporter of both women's and men's professional basketball in Russia. Many of the oligarchs have been hit particularly hard by the current recession as they had a big role in financing many banks in the country.

The conflict between Israel and the Palestinians continues to be one of the biggest global concerns. Israel continues to assert its right to defend itself against what it terms terrorism and the Palestinians continue to see the Israelis as an occupying government.

The United States continues to have a presence in the Middle East as it works to develop a Democratic government in Iraq. Iranian President Mahmoud Ahmadinejad is an outspoken critic of the United States and Israel. As Iran works to develop nuclear capability the U.S. has been working to stop the development of those weapons which would further destabilize the region.

Skill 5.16   Identify key individuals, events, and issues related to Florida history.

Florida's first human inhabitants were Indians, as shown by the burial mounds found in varying locations around the state. When Europeans eventually arrived, there were at least 10,000 Indians belonging to five major tribes. In southern Florida resided the Calusa and the Tequesta; the Ais were found on the Atlantic coast in the central part of the peninsula; the Timucuans lived in the central and northeast area of the state; and in the northwest part of Florida dwelt the Apalachee. Written records about life in Florida began with the arrival of the first European, Spanish explorer and adventurer Juan Ponce de León, in 1513, searching for the fabled fountain of youth. Sometime between April 2 and April 8, Ponce de León waded ashore on the northeast coast of Florida, possibly near present-day St. Augustine. He called the area la Florida, in honor of Pascua Florida ("feast of the flowers"), Spain's Easter celebration. Other Europeans may have reached Florida earlier, but no firm evidence of such achievement has been found.

The Spanish flag flew over Florida for the next 250 years. Other Spanish explorers who spent time in Florida included Panfilo de Narvaez and Hernando de Soto who became the first European to reach the Mississippi River. Pedro Menendez de Aviles who put an end to French attempts to settle in eastern Florida, founded the first permanent European settlement in the present-day United States, St. Augustine.

On another voyage in 1521, Ponce de León landed on the southwestern coast of the peninsula, accompanied by two hundred people, fifty horses, and numerous beasts of burden. His colonization attempt quickly failed because of attacks by native people. However, Ponce de León's activities served to identify Florida as a desirable place for explorers, missionaries, and treasure seekers.

In 1539, Hernando de Soto began another expedition in search of gold and silver which took him on a long trek through Florida and what is now the southeastern United States. For four years, de Soto's expedition wandered, in hopes of finding the fabled wealth of the Indian people. De Soto and his soldiers camped for five months in the area now known as Tallahassee. De Soto died near the Mississippi River in 1542. Survivors of his expedition eventually reached Mexico.

No great treasure troves awaited the Spanish conquistadores who explored Florida. However, their stories helped inform Europeans about Florida and its relationship to Cuba, Mexico, and Central and South America, from which Spain regularly shipped gold, silver, and other products. Groups of heavily-laden Spanish vessels, called plate fleets, usually sailed up the Gulf Stream through the straits that parallel Florida's Keys. Aware of this route, pirates preyed on the fleets. Hurricanes created additional hazards, sometimes wrecking the ships on the reefs and shoals along Florida's eastern coast.

In 1559, Tristán de Luna y Arellano led another attempt by Europeans to colonize Florida. He established a settlement at Pensacola Bay, but a series of misfortunes caused his efforts to be abandoned after two years.

Spain was not the only European nation that found Florida attractive. In 1562, the French Protestant Jean Ribault explored the area. Two years later, fellow Frenchman René Goulaine de Laudonnière established Fort Caroline at the mouth of the St. Johns River, near present-day Jacksonville.

These French adventurers prompted Spain to accelerate her plans for colonization. Pedro Menéndez de Avilés hastened across the Atlantic, his sights set on removing the French and creating a Spanish settlement. Menéndez arrived in 1565 at a place he called San Augustín (St. Augustine) and established the first permanent European settlement in what became the United States. He accomplished his goal of expelling the French, attacking and killing all settlers except for non-combatants and Frenchmen who professed belief in the Roman Catholic faith. Menéndez captured Fort Caroline and renamed it San Mateo.

French response came two years later, when Dominique de Gourgues recaptured San Mateo and made the Spanish soldiers stationed there pay with their lives. However, this incident did not halt the Spanish advance. Their pattern of constructing forts and Roman Catholic missions continued. Spanish missions established among native people soon extended across north Florida and as far north along the Atlantic coast as the area known now as South Carolina.

The English, also eager to exploit the wealth of the Americas, increasingly came into conflict with Spain's expanding empire. In 1586 the English captain Sir Francis Drake looted and burned the tiny village of St. Augustine. However, Spanish control of Florida was not diminished.

In fact, as late as 1600, Spain's power over what is now the southeastern United States was unquestioned. When English settlers came to America, they established their first colonies well to the North—at Jamestown (in the present state of Virginia) in 1607 and Plymouth (in the present state of Massachusetts) in 1620. English colonists wanted to take advantage of the continent's natural resources and gradually pushed the borders of Spanish power southward into present-day southern Georgia. At the same time, French explorers were moving down the Mississippi River valley and eastward along the Gulf Coast.

The English colonists in the Carolina colonies were particularly hostile toward Spain. Led by Colonel James Moore, the Carolinians and their Creek Indian allies attacked Spanish Florida in 1702 and destroyed the town of St. Augustine. However, they could not capture the fort named Castillo de San Marcos. Two years later, they destroyed the Spanish missions between Tallahassee and St. Augustine, killing many native people and enslaving many others. The French continued to harass Spanish Florida's western border and captured Pensacola in 1719, twenty-one years after the town had been established.

Spain's adversaries moved even closer when England founded Georgia in 1733, its southernmost continental colony. Georgians attacked Florida in 1740, assaulting the Castillo de San Marcos at St. Augustine for almost a month. While the attack was not successful, it did point out the growing weakness of Spanish Florida.

Britain gained control of Florida in 1763 in exchange for Havana, Cuba, which the British had captured from Spain during the Seven Years' War (1756–63). Spain evacuated Florida after the exchange, leaving the province virtually empty. At that time, St. Augustine was still a garrison community with fewer than five hundred houses, and Pensacola was a small military town.

The British had ambitious plans for Florida. First, it was split into two parts: East Florida, with its capital at St. Augustine; and West Florida, with its seat at Pensacola. British surveyors mapped much of the landscape and coastline and tried to develop relations with a group of Indian people who were moving into the area from the North. The British called these people of Creek Indian descent Seminolies or Seminoles. Britain attempted to attract white settlers by offering land on which to settle and help for those who produced products for export. Given enough time, this plan might have converted Florida into a flourishing colony, but British rule lasted only twenty years.

East and West Florida remained loyal to Great Britain throughout the War for American Independence (1776–83). However, Spain—participating indirectly in the war as an ally of France—captured Pensacola from the British in 1781. In 1784, it regained control of the rest of Florida as part of the peace treaty that ended the American Revolution. The second period of Spanish control lasted until 1821.

On one of those military operations in 1818, General Andrew Jackson made a foray into Florida. Jackson's battles with Florida's Indian people later would be called the First Seminole War. When the British evacuated Florida, Spanish colonists as well as settlers from the newly formed United States came pouring in. Many of the new residents were lured by favorable Spanish terms for acquiring property, called land grants. Others who came were escaped slaves, trying to reach a place where their U.S. masters had no authority and effectively could not reach them. Instead of becoming more Spanish, the two Floridas increasingly became more "American." Finally, after several official and unofficial U.S. military expeditions into the territory, Spain formally ceded Florida to the United States in 1821, according to terms of the Adams-Onís Treaty.

Andrew Jackson returned to Florida in 1821 to establish a new territorial government on behalf of the United States. What the U.S. inherited was a wilderness sparsely dotted with settlements of native Indian people, African Americans, and Spaniards.

As a territory of the United States, Florida was particularly attractive to people from the older Southern plantation areas of Virginia, the Carolinas, and Georgia, who arrived in considerable numbers. After territorial status was granted, East and West Florida were merged into one entity with a new capital city in Tallahassee. Established in 1824, Tallahassee was chosen because it was halfway between the existing governmental centers of St. Augustine and Pensacola.

As Florida's population increased through immigration, so did pressure on the federal government to remove the Indian people from their lands. The Indian population was made up of several groups—primarily, the Creek and the Miccosukee people; and many African American refugees lived with the Indians. Indian removal was popular with white settlers because the native people occupied lands that white people wanted and because their communities often provided a sanctuary for runaway slaves from northern states.

Among Florida's native population, the name of Osceola has remained familiar after more than a century and a half. Osceola was a Seminole war leader who refused to leave his homeland in Florida. Seminoles, already noted for their fighting abilities, won the respect of U.S. soldiers for their bravery, fortitude, and ability to adapt to changing circumstances during the Second Seminole War (1835–42). This war, the most significant of the three conflicts between Indian people and U.S. troops in Florida, began over the question of whether Seminoles should be moved westward across the Mississippi River into what is now Oklahoma.

Under President Andrew Jackson, the U.S. government spent $20 million and the lives of many U.S. soldiers, Indian people, and U.S. citizens to force the removal of the Seminoles. In the end, the outcome was not as the federal government had planned. Some Indians migrated "voluntarily." Some were captured and sent west under military guard; and others escaped into the Everglades, where they made a life for themselves away from contact with whites.

Today, reservations occupied by Florida's Indian people exist at Immokalee, Hollywood, Brighton (near the city of Okeechobee), and along the Big Cypress Swamp. In addition to the Seminole people, Florida also has a separate Miccosukee tribe.

By 1840 white Floridians were concentrating on developing the territory and gaining statehood. The population had reached 54,477 people, with African American slaves making up almost one-half of the population. Steamboat navigation was well established on the Apalachicola and St. Johns Rivers, and railroads were planned.

Florida now was divided informally into three areas: East Florida, from the Atlantic Ocean to the Suwannee River; Middle Florida, between the Suwannee and the Apalachicola Rivers; and West Florida, from the Apalachicola to the Perdido River. The southern area of the territory (south of present-day Gainesville) was sparsely settled by whites. The territory's economy was based on agriculture. Plantations were concentrated in Middle Florida, and their owners established the political tone for all of Florida until after the Civil War.

Florida became the twenty-seventh state in the United States on March 3, 1845. William D. Moseley was elected the new state's first governor, and David Levy Yulee, one of Florida's leading proponents for statehood, became a U.S. Senator. By 1850, the population had grown to 87,445, including about 39,000 African American slaves and 1,000 free blacks.

The slavery issue began to dominate the affairs of the new state. Most Florida voters—who were white males, ages twenty-one years or older—did not oppose slavery. However, they were concerned about the growing feeling against it in the North, and during the 1850s, they viewed the new anti-slavery Republican Party with suspicion. In the 1860 presidential election, no Floridians voted for Abraham Lincoln, although this Illinois Republican won at the national level. Shortly after his election, a special convention drew up an ordinance that allowed Florida to secede from the Union on January 10, 1861. Within several weeks, Florida joined other southern states to form the Confederate States of America.

During the Civil War Florida was not ravaged as several other southern states were. Indeed, no decisive battles were fought on Florida soil. While Union forces occupied many coastal towns and forts, the interior of the state remained in Confederate hands.

Florida provided an estimated 15,000 troops and significant amounts of supplies— including salt, beef, pork, and cotton—to the Confederacy, but more than 2,000 Floridians, both African American and white, joined the Union army. Confederate and foreign merchant ships slipped through the Union navy blockade along the coast, bringing in needed supplies from overseas ports. Tallahassee was the only southern capital east of the Mississippi River to avoid capture during the war, spared by southern victories at Olustee (1864) and Natural Bridge (1865). Ultimately, the South was defeated, and federal troops occupied Tallahassee on May 10, 1865.

Before the Civil War, Florida had been well on its way to becoming another of the southern cotton states. Afterward, the lives of many residents changed. The ports of Jacksonville and Pensacola again flourished due to the demand for lumber and forest products to rebuild the nation's cities. Those who had been slaves were declared free. Plantation owners tried to regain prewar levels of production by hiring former slaves to raise and pick cotton. However, such programs did not work well, and much of the land came under cultivation by tenant farmers and sharecroppers, both African American and white.

Beginning in 1868, the federal government instituted a congressional program of "reconstruction" in Florida and the other southern states. During this period, Republican officeholders tried to enact sweeping changes, many of which were aimed at improving conditions for African Americans.

At the time of the 1876 presidential election, federal troops still occupied Florida. The state's Republican government and recently enfranchised African American voters helped to put Rutherford B. Hayes in the White House. However, Democrats gained control of enough state offices to end the years of Republican rule and prompt the removal of federal troops the following year. A series of political battles in the state left African Americans with little voice in their government.

During the final quarter of the nineteenth century, large-scale commercial agriculture in Florida, especially cattle-raising, grew in importance. Industries such as cigar manufacturing took root in the immigrant communities of the state. Large phosphate deposits were discovered, citrus groves were planted and cultivated, swamplands were drained, and Henry Plant and Henry Flagler built railroad lines opening the state for further growth and development.

Potential investors became interested in enterprises that extracted resources from the water and land. These extractive operations were as widely diverse as sponge harvesting in Tarpon Springs and phosphate mining in the southwestern part of the state. The Florida citrus industry grew rapidly, despite occasional freezes and economic setbacks. The development of industries throughout the state prompted the construction of roads and railroads on a large scale. Jobs created by the state helped develop the natural resources; private industries' construction of paper mills resulted in conservation programs for the state's forests. To help preserve perishable fruits and vegetables, cooling plants were built. To aid farmers, cooperative markets and cooperative farm groups were established.

Beginning in the 1870s, residents from northern states visited Florida as tourists to enjoy the state's natural beauty and mild climate. Steamboat tours on Florida's winding rivers were a popular attraction for these visitors.

The growth of Florida's transportation industry had its origins in 1855, when the state legislature passed the Internal Improvement Act. Similar to legislation passed by several other states and the federal government, Florida's Act offered cheap or free public land to investors, particularly those interested in transportation. The Act, and other legislation like it, had its greatest effect in the years between the end of the Civil War and the beginning of World War I. During this period, many railroads were constructed throughout the state by companies owned by Henry Flagler and Henry B. Plant, who also built lavish hotels near their railroad lines. The Internal Improvement Act stimulated the initial efforts to drain the southern portion of the state in order to convert it to farmland.

These development projects had far-reaching effects on the agricultural, manufacturing, and extractive industries of late nineteenth century Florida. The citrus industry especially benefited, since it was now possible to pick oranges in south Florida; put them on a train heading north; and eat them in Baltimore, Philadelphia, or New York in less than a week.

In 1898, national attention focused on Florida, as the Spanish-American War began. The port city of Tampa served as the primary staging area for U.S. troops bound for the war in Cuba. Many Floridians supported the Cuban peoples' desire to be free of Spanish colonial rule.

By the turn of the century, Florida's population and per capita wealth were increasing rapidly; the potential of the "Sunshine State" appeared endless. By the end of World War I, land developers had descended on this virtual gold mine. With more Americans owning automobiles, it became commonplace to vacation in Florida. Many visitors stayed on, and exotic projects sprang up in southern Florida. Some people moved onto land made from drained swamps. Others bought canal-crossed tracts through what had been dry land. The real estate developments quickly attracted buyers, and land in Florida was sold and resold. Profits and prices for many developers reached inflated levels.

The early 1900s saw the settlement and economic development of south Florida, especially along the East Coast. A severe depression in 1926, the1926 and1928 hurricanes, and the Great Depression of the1930s burst the economic bubble.

During World War II, many military bases were constructed as part of the vital defense interests of the state and nation. After the war, prosperity and population grew resulting in tourism becoming the most important industry, and it remains so today. Continued agricultural development and industrial expansion also played an important role in the state's economy. Such industries as paper and paper products, chemicals, electronics, and ocean and space exploration gave a tremendous boost to the labor force. From the 1950s to the present day, the Kennedy

Space Center at Cape Canaveral has been a space and rocket center with the launching of orbiting satellites, manned space flights, and today's space shuttles.

There are serious problems to be faced. Many immigrants from places like Cuba and Haiti have entered the state by the thousands since the early 1960s, both legally and illegally. Increasing population growth puts a strain on public and social services, and pollution and overbuilding has threatened the environment.

Tremendous growth occurred during the 1970s with the opening of Walt Disney World. With other tourist attractions and the resulting need for hotels, restaurants, and a larger airport, Orlando leads Tampa, Miami, Jacksonville, Fort Lauderdale, and West Palm Beach as the fastest growing region of the state. Although the state's economy continues to rely mainly on tourism and the citrus industry, stable growth remains consistent due to the expanding trade, financial, and service industries.

For more information on the subject of Florida's history, consult the following:
http://www.floridahistory.org http://www.floridamemory.com

COMPETENCY 6.0   KNOWLEDGE OF SOCIAL SCIENCE AND ITS METHODOLOGY

Skill 6.1   Identify social science disciplines (e.g., anthropology, psychology, sociology).

The major disciplines within the social sciences are definitely intertwined and interrelated. Knowledge and expertise in one requires background that involves some or most of the others.

Anthropology is the field of study of human culture—how different groups of people live, how they have adapted to their physical environment, what they make or produce, and their relationship to other cultures, behavior, differences and similarities. To pursue the study of people, the anthropologist must know the history of the people being studied; their geography—physical environment; and their governmental structure, its organization and its impact on the people. Sociology is closely related to this field so knowledge and study in this area is helpful. Goods and produce and how they are used tie in with economics.

Archaeology is the study of human cultures in the past examining artifacts left behind to determine how certain people or groups lived their daily lives. Certainly, knowledge of history gives a background as a foundation of study. Geography makes its contribution by not only knowing where to look for remains but also how geographic conditions contributed to and affected the people or cultural groups being studied; and how physical factors contributed to artifacts left behind.

Civics deals with what is required and expected of a region's citizens, their rights and responsibilities to government and each other. Knowledge of history gives the background and foundation, and government or political science explains not only the organization and set-up of the government but also the impact of international relations on the country or area.

Economics is tied in mainly with history, geography, and political science. The different interrelationships include: history of economic theory and principles combined with historical background of areas; economic activities in the different countries, regions of the world and how international trade and relations are affected— which leads to political science or government— how political organization and government affect an area's economic activities.

Geography is the study of the earth, its people, and how people adapt to life on earth and how they use its resources. It is undeniably connected to history, economics, political science, sociology, anthropology, and even a bit of archaeology. Geography not only deals with people and the earth today but also asks these questions:

- How did it all begin?
- What is the background of the people of an area?
- What kind of government or political system do they have?
- How does that affect their ways of producing goods and the distribution of the goods?
- What kind of relationships do these people have with other groups?
- How is the way they live their lives affected by their physical environment?
- In what ways do they effect change in their way of living?

All of this is tied in with the physical environment, i.e., the earth and its people. History is without doubt an integral part of every other discipline in the social sciences. Knowing historical background on anything and anyone anywhere goes a long way towards explaining how what happened in the past leads up to and explains the present.

Political Science is the study of government, international relations, political thought and activity, and comparison of governments. It is tied in with history (historical background), anthropology (how government affects a group's culture and relationship with other groups), economics (governmental influence and regulation of producing and distributing goods and products), and sociology (insight into how social developments affect political life). Other disciplines are also affected, such as the study of political science which is crucial to understanding the political processes and the influence of government, civic duties, and responsibilities of people.

Psychology is defined as scientifically studying mental processes and behavior. It is related to anthropology and sociology, two social sciences that also study people in society. All three closely consider relationships and attitudes of humans within their social settings. Anthropology considers humans within their cultures, how they live, what they make or produce, and how different groups or cultures relate to each other. Sociology follows the angle of looking at behaviors, attitudes, conditions, and relationships in human society. Psychology focuses on individual behavior and how actions are influenced by feelings and beliefs.

Sociology studies human society with its attitudes, behaviors, conditions, and relationships with others. It is closely related to anthropology, especially applied to groups outside of one's region, nation, or hemisphere. History puts it in perspective with background. Political science is tied to sociology with the impact of political and governmental regulation of activities. Awareness of, influence of, and use of the physical environment as studied in geography also contributes to understanding. Economic activities are a part of human society. The field of psychology is also related.

Skill 6.2   Identify social science concepts (e.g., culture, class, technology, race, gender).

See Skills 6.1

Skill 6.3   Analyze the interrelationships between social science disciplines.

See Skill 6.1

Skill 6.4   Interpret tabular and graphic representations of information related to the social sciences.

We use illustrations of various sorts because it is often easier to demonstrate a given idea visually instead of orally. Sometimes it is even easier to do so with an illustration than a description. This is especially true in the areas of education and research because humans are visually stimulated. It is a fact that any idea presented visually in some manner is always easier to understand and to comprehend than simply getting an idea across verbally, by hearing it or reading it. Among the more common illustrations used are various types of maps, graphs and charts.

Photographs and globes are useful as well, but as they are limited in what kind of information that they can show, they are rarely used. Unless, as in the case of a photograph, it is of a particular political figure or a time that one wishes to visualize.

Although maps have advantages over globes and photographs, they do have a major disadvantage. This problem must be considered as well. The major problem of all maps comes about because most maps are flat and the Earth is a sphere. It is impossible to reproduce exactly on a flat surface an object shaped like a sphere. In order to put the earth's features onto a map they must be stretched in some way. This stretching is called distortion.

Distortion does not mean that maps are wrong. It simply means that they are not perfect representations of the Earth or its parts. Cartographers, or mapmakers, understand the problems of distortion. They try to design them so that there is as little distortion as possible in the maps.

Skill 6.5   Identify appropriate strategies, methods, tools, and technologies for the teaching of social science.

The interdisciplinary curriculum planning approach to student learning creates a meaningful balance inclusive of curriculum depth and breadth. Take for instance the following scenario: Mrs. Jackson presents her 9A Language Arts class with an assignment for collaborative group work. She provides them with the birth date and death of the infamous author Ernest Hemingway and asks them to figure how old he was when he died. She gives them five minutes as a group to work on the final answer. After five minutes, she asks each group for their answer and writes the answers on the board; each group gives a different answer. When Mrs. Jackson comes to the last group, a female student states, "Why do we have to do math in a Language Arts class?"

The application of knowledge learned from a basic math class would have problem-solved the Language Arts' question. Given the date of his birth and the date of his death, all students needed to do was subtract his birth from his death year to come up with a numerical answer = age when he died. Providing students with a constructivist modality of applying knowledge to problem-solve pertinent information for a language arts' class should be an integral part of instructional practice and learning in an interdisciplinary classroom.

Historically, previous centuries of educational research have shown a strong correlation between the need for interdisciplinary instruction and cognitive learning application. Understanding how students process information and create learning was the goal of earlier educators. Earlier researchers looked at how the brain connected information pieces into meaning and found that learning takes place along intricate neural pathways that formulate processing and meaning from data input into the brain. The implications for student learning are vast in that teachers can work with students to break down subject content area into bits of information that can be memorized and applied to a former learning experience and then processed into integral resources of information.

Technology

The Internet and other research resources provide a wealth of information on thousands of interesting topics for students preparing presentations or projects. Using search engines like Google, Microsoft and InfoTrac allow students to search multiple Internet resources or databases on one subject search. Students should have an outline of the purpose of a project or research presentation that includes:

- Purpose - identity the reason for the research information
- Objective - having a clear thesis for a project will allow the students opportunities to be specific on Internet searches
- Preparation - when using resources or collecting data, students should create folders for sorting through the information. Providing labels for the folders will create a system of organization that will make construction of the final project or presentation easier and less time consuming
- Procedure - organized folders and a procedural list of what the project or presentation needs to include will create A+ work for students and A+ grading for teachers
- Visuals or artifacts - choose data or visuals that are specific to the subject content or presentation. Make sure that poster boards or PowerPoint presentations can be visually seen from all areas of the classroom. Teachers can provide laptop computers for PowerPoint presentations.

Having the school's librarian or technology expert as a guest speaker in classrooms provides another method of sharing and modeling proper presentation preparation using technology. Teachers can also appoint technology experts from the students in a classroom to work with students on projects and presentations. In high schools, technology classes provide students with upper-class teacher assistants who fill the role of technology assistants.

Skill 6.6   Evaluate examples of primary (e.g., letters, photographs, political cartoons) and secondary (e.g., historical texts, encyclopedias) sources.

Primary Sources

Primary sources include interviews, focus groups, surveys, questionnaires, and experiments. Advantages of primary research are that the research is computer codable for rapid analysis. Coding enables multiple comparisons among all the variables in the research, and it can be generalized to a larger population. It is verifiable because it can be replicated. The respondents can be re-questioned. Of course, validity is dependent on the random sample and its size.

Primary sources also include original records created at the time, original records in the form of memoirs, diaries, journals, and oral histories. Primary sources may include letters, manuscripts, newspapers, speeches, interviews, documents produced by Congress or the Office of the President, photographs, audio recordings, moving pictures, video recordings, research data, and objects or artifacts such as works of art or ancient roads, buildings, tools, and weapons.

Secondary Sources

Secondary sources are generally easy to obtain, and they include the following kinds of materials:

- Books written on the basis of primary materials about the period of time
- Books written on the basis of primary materials about persons who played a major role in the events under consideration
- Books and articles written on the basis of primary materials about the culture, the social norms, the language, and the values of the period
- Quotations from primary sources
- Statistical data on the period
- Conclusions and inferences of other historians
- Multiple interpretations of the ethos of the time

Guidelines for the use of secondary sources:

- Do not rely upon only a single secondary source.
- Check facts and interpretations against primary sources whenever possible.
- Do not accept the conclusions of other historians uncritically.
- Place greatest reliance on secondary sources created by the best and most respected scholars.
- Do not use the inferences of other scholars as if they were facts.
- Ensure that you recognize any bias the writer brings to his/her interpretation of history.
- Understand the primary point of the book as a basis for evaluating the value of the material presented in it to your questions.

Literature and nonverbal materials, novels, stories, poetry and essays from the period, as well as coins, archaeological artifacts, and art produced during the period. Guidelines for the use of primary resources:

- Be certain that you understand how language was used at the time of writing and that you understand the context in which it was produced.
- Do not read history blindly; be certain that you understand both explicit and implicit referenced in the material.
- Read the entire text you are reviewing; do not simply extract a few sentences to read.
- Although anthologies of materials may help you identify primary source materials, the full original text should be consulted.

Secondary sources include the following kinds of materials:

- Books written on the basis of primary materials about the period of time
- Books written on the basis of primary materials about persons who played a major role in the events under consideration

- Books and articles written on the basis of primary materials about the culture, the social norms, the language, and the values of the period
- Quotations from primary sources
- Statistical data on the period
- The conclusions and inferences of other historians
- Multiple interpretations of the ethos of the time

Guidelines for the use of secondary sources:

- Do not rely upon only a single secondary source.
- Check facts and interpretations against primary sources whenever possible.
- Do not accept the conclusions of other historians uncritically.
- Place greatest reliance on secondary sources created by the best and most respected scholars.
- Do not use the inferences of other scholars as if they were facts.
- Ensure that you recognize any bias the writer brings to his/her interpretation of history.
- Understand the primary point of the book as a basis for evaluating the value of the material presented in it to your questions.

Resources

Adams, James Truslow. *March of Democracy*, Vol 1. "The Rise of the Union." (New York: Charles Scribner's Sons, 2006).

Annals of America: Selected Readings on Great Issues in American History 1620-1968. (United States of America: William Benton, 2006).

Barbini, John and Steven Warshaw. *The World Past and Present*. (New York: Harcourt, Brace, Jovanovich, 2006).

Berthon, Simon and Andrew Robinson. *The Shape of the World*. (Chicago: Rand McNally, 2006).

Bice, David A. *A Panorama of Florida II*. (2nd ed.). (Marceline, Missouri: Walsworth Publishing Co., Inc., 2006.)

Bram, Leon (Ed.). *Funk & Wagnalls New Encyclopedia*. (New York: Funk & Wagnalls. 2006).

Burns, Edward McNall and Philip Lee Ralph *World Civilizations: Their History and Culture* (5th Ed.). (New York: W.W. Norton & Company, Inc., 2006).

Dauben, Joseph W. (Ed.) *The World Book Encyclopedia*. Chicago: World Book Inc. A Scott Fetzer Company, 2006).

De Blij, H.J. and Peter O. Muller. *Geography Regions and Concepts* (6th ed.). (New York: John Wiley & Sons, Inc., 2006)

Encyclopedia Americana. (Danbury, Connecticut: Grolier Incorporated, 2006).

Heigh, Christopher (Ed.). *Cambridge Historical Encyclopedia of Great Britain and Ireland*. Cambridge: Cambridge University Press, 2006).

Hunkins, Francis P. and David G. Armstrong. *World Geography: People and Places*. Columbus, Ohio: Charles E. Merrill Publishing Co. A Bell & Howell Company, 2006).

Jarolimek, John; and J. Hubert Anderson and & Loyal Durand, Jr. *World Neighbors*. New York: Macmillan Publishing Company. London: Collier Macmillan, 2006).

McConnell, Campbell R. *Economics-Principles, Problems, and Policies* (10th ed). (New York: McGraw-Hill Book Company, 2006).

Millard, Dr. Anne & Vanags, Patricia. *Usborne Book of World History*. London: Usborne Publishing Ltd., 2006).

Novosad, Charles (Ed.). *Nystrom Desk Atlas*. Chicago: Nystrom Division of Herff Jones, Inc., 2006).

Patton, Clyde P.; Arlene C. Rengert; Robert N Saveland.; Kenneth S. Cooper and Patricia T. Cam (2006). *A World View*. (Morristown, N.J.: Silver Burdette Companion 2006).

Schwartz, Melvin and John R. O'Connor. *Exploring A Changing World*. (New York: Globe Book Company, 2006).

Tindall, George Brown and David E. Shi. *America-A Narrative History* (4th ed.). (New York: W.W. Norton & Company, 2006).

Todd, Lewis Paul and Merle Curti. *Rise of the American Nation* (3rd ed.). (New York: Harcourt, Brace, Jovanovich, Inc., 2006).

Tyler, Jenny; Lisa Watts; Carol Bowyer, Roma Trundle and Annabelle Warrender. *Usbome Book of World Geography*. London: Usbome Publishing Ltd., 2006).

Willson, David H. *A History of England*. Hinsdale, Illinois: The Dryder Press, Inc., 2006).

Sample Test

1. Studies in astronomy, skills in mapping, and other contributions to geographic knowledge came from: *(Skill 1.0)(Easy)*

    A. Galileo
    B. Columbus
    C. Eratosthenes
    D. Ptolemy

2. Which one of the following does not affect climate? *(Skill 1.2) (Rigorous)*

    A. Elevation or altitude
    B. Ocean currents
    C. Latitude
    D. Longitude

3. Soil erosion is most likely to occur in large amounts in: *(Skill 1.2) (Easy)*

    A. Mountain ranges
    B. Deserts
    C. Tropical rainforests
    D. River valleys

4. Which one of the following is not a use for a region's wetlands? *(Skill 1.2)(Average Rigor)*

    A. Produces fresh clean water
    B. Provides habitat for wildlife
    C. Provides water for hydroelectric power
    D. Controls floods

5. The geographical drought- stricken region of Africa south of the Sahara and extending east and west from Senegal to Somalia is: *(Skill 1.3) (Easy)*

    A. The Kalahari
    B. The Namib
    C. The Great Rift Valley
    D. The Sahel

6. Meridians, or lines of longitude, not only help in pinpointing locations but are also used for: *(Skill 1.4) (Average Rigor)*

    A. Measuring distance from the Poles
    B. Determining direction of ocean currents
    C. Determining the time around the world
    D. Measuring distance on the equator

7. The Yangtze River primarily flows in which direction? *(Skill 1.4) (Easy)*

    A. North
    B. South
    C. East
    D. West

8. The Nile River flows in which direction? *(Skill 1.4) (Easy)*

    A. North
    B. South
    C. East
    D. West

9. **The Ganges River empties into the:** *(Skill 1.4) (Easy)*

   A. Bay of Bengal
   B. Arabian Sea
   C. Red Sea
   D. Arafura Sea

10. **Maps as a rule are:** *(Skill 1.4) (Easy)*

    A. All subject to some sort of distortion
    B. Always entirely accurate
    C. Not very useful in political science studies
    D. Difficult usually to understand

11. **The name for those who make maps is:** *(Skill 1.4) (Easy)*

    A. Haberdasher
    B. Geographer
    C. Cartographer
    D. Demographer

12. **The "father" of modern economics is considered by most economists to be:** *(Skill 2.0) (Average Rigor)*

    A. Thomas Robert Malthus
    B. John Stuart Mill
    C. Adam Smith
    D. John Maynard Keynes

13. **Which political theorist says that capitalism could be maintained if there were sufficient checks on the economy?** *(Skill 2.0) (Average Rigor)*

    A. Marx
    B. Keynes
    C. Weber
    D. Locke

14. **The idea that continued population growth would, in future years, seriously affect a nation's productive capabilities was stated by:** *(Skill 2.1) (Rigorous)*

    A. Keynes
    B. Mill
    C. Malthus
    D. Friedman

15. **A boycott is:** *(Skill 2.1) (Average Rigor)*

    A. The refusal to buy goods or services
    B. An imbalance of trade
    C. The refusal to speak in court
    D. A Writ of Assistance

16. **The study of the ways in which different societies around the world deal with the problems of limited resources and unlimited needs and wants is in the area of:** *(Skill 2.2) (Average Rigor)*

    A. Economics
    B. Sociology
    C. Anthropology
    D. Political Science

17. **The idea or proposal for more equal division of profits among employers and workers was put forth by:** *(Skill 2.2) (Rigorous)*

    A. Karl Marx
    B. Thomas Malthus
    C. Adam Smith
    D. John Stuart Mill

18. The purchase of goods or services on one market for immediate resale on another market is: *(Skill 2.3) (Average Rigor)*

    A. Output
    B. Enterprise
    C. Arbitrage
    D. Mercantile

19. Potential customers for any product or service are not only called consumers but can also be called a: *(Skill 2.3) (Average Rigor)*

    A. Resource
    B. Base
    C. Commodity
    D. Market

20. The economic system promoting individual ownership of land, capital, and businesses with minimal governmental regulations is called: *(Skill 2.3) (Easy)*

    A. Macro-economy
    B. Micro-economy
    C. Laissez-faire
    D. Free enterprise

21. Government regulation of economic activities for favorable balance of trade was the first major economic theory. It was called: *(Skill 2.5) (Rigorous)*

    A. Laissez-faire
    B. Globalism
    C. Mercantilism
    D. Syndicalism

22. The economist who disagreed with the idea that free markets lead to full employment and prosperity and who suggested that increasing government spending would end depressions was: *(Skill 2.5) (Rigorous)*

    A. Keynes
    B. Malthus
    C. Smith
    D. Friedman

23. The belief that government should stay out of economic affairs is called: *(Skill 2.5) (Average Rigor)*

    A. Mercantilism
    B. Laissez-faire
    C. Democratic-Socialism
    D. Corporatism

24. A tariff is: *(Skill 2.5) (Easy)*

    A. A law passed by the Congress and vetoed by the President
    B. An appointed official mandated to preserve public order
    C. A tax a government places on internationally traded goods, usually goods entering a country
    D. A tax a government places on goods produced for domestic use, another name for it is a "sales tax"

25. George Washington's opinion of America trading with other nations was: *(Skill 2.5) (Average Rigor)*

    A. Approval in only some instances
    B. Disapproval
    C. Approval
    D. Unsure

26. **The process of the state taking over industries and businesses is called:** *(Skill 2.5) (Average Rigor)*

    A. Industrialization
    B. Nationalization
    C. Redistribution
    D. Amalgamation

27. **One method of trade restriction used by some nations is:** *(Skill 2.6) (Rigorous)*

    A. Limited treaties
    B. Floating exchange rate
    C. Bill of exchange
    D. Import quotas

28. **The "father of political science" is considered to be:** *(Skill 3.0) (Average Rigor)*

    A. Aristotle
    B. John Locke
    C. Plato
    D. Thomas Hobbes

29. **There is no doubt of the vast improvement of the U.S. Constitution over the weak Articles of Confederation. Which one of the four accurate statements below is a unique yet eloquent description of the document?** *(Skill 3.1) (Rigorous)*

    A. The establishment of a strong central government in no way lessened or weakened the individual states.
    B. Individual rights were protected and secured.
    C. The Constitution is the best representation of the results of the American genius for compromise.
    D. Its flexibility and adaptation to change gives it a sense of timelessness.

30. **In the U.S. government, the power of coining money is:** *(Skill 3.1) (Rigorous)*

    A. Implied or suggested
    B. Concurrent or shared
    C. Delegated or expressed
    D. Reserved

31. **In the United States government, the power of taxation and borrowing is:** *(Skill 3.1) (Rigorous)*

    A. Implied or suggested
    B. Concurrent or shared
    C. Delegated or expressed
    D. Reserved

32. **Marbury vs. Madison (1803)" was an important Supreme Court case which set the precedent for:** *(Skill 3.1) (Rigorous)*

    A. The elastic clause
    B. Judicial review
    C. The supreme law of the land
    D. Popular sovereignty in the territories

33. **What Supreme Court ruling established the principal of judicial review?** *(Skill 3.1) (Rigorous)*

    A. Jefferson vs. Madison
    B. Lincoln vs. Douglas
    C. Marbury vs. Madison
    D. Marbury vs. Jefferson

34. **To be eligible to be elected President one must:** *(Skill 3.1) (Rigorous)*

    A. Be a citizen for at least five years
    B. Be a citizen for seven years
    C. Have been born a citizen
    D. Be a naturalized citizen

35. **The first ten amendments to the Constitution are called the:** *(Skill 3.1) (Easy)*

    A. Bill of Petition
    B. Petition of Rights
    C. Rights of Man
    D. Bill of Rights

35. **The Congress can override a President's veto with a vote.** *(Skill 3.1) (Rigorous)*

    A. One-half
    B. Two-thirds
    C. Six-tenths
    D. Three-fourths

37. **To become a citizen, an individual must generally have lived in the United States for at least:** *(Skill 3.1) (Rigorous)*

    A. Six years
    B. Five years
    C. One year
    D. Ten years

38. **The ability of the President to veto an act of Congress is an example of:** *(Skill 3.1) (Rigorous)*

    A. Separation of Powers
    B. Checks and Balances
    C. Judicial Review
    D. Presidential Prerogative

39. **If a president neither signs nor vetoes a bill officially for ten days it is called:** *(Skill 3.1) (Average Rigor)*

    A. A pocket veto
    B. A refused law
    C. Unconstitutional
    D. A presidential veto

40. **The term that describes the division of government function is:** *(Skill 3.1) (Easy)*

    A. Free enterprise
    B. Constitutional Prerogative
    C. Checks and Balances
    D. Separation of Powers

41. **In the United States, the right to declare war is a power of:** *(Skill 3.1) (Rigorous)*

    A. The President
    B. Congress
    C. The Executive Branch
    D. The States

42. **In the U.S., checks and balances refers to:** *(Skill 3.1) (Average Rigor)*

    A. The ability of each branch of government to "check" or limit the actions of the theirs
    B. Balance of payments
    C. International law
    D. The federal deficit

43. **An amendment is:** *(Skill 3.1) (Easy)*

    A. A change or addition to the United States Constitution
    B. The right of a state to secede from the Union
    C. To add a state to the Union
    D. The right of the Supreme Court to check actions of Congress and the President

44. **The Bill of Rights was mostly written by:** *(Skill 3.1) (Average Rigor)*

    A. Thomas Jefferson
    B. James Madison
    C. George Washington
    D. Alexander Hamilton

45. **To be a *naturalized* citizen means:** *(Skill 3.1) (Easy)*

    A. To have been refused citizenship
    B. To have a dual-citizenship
    C. To be a "natural" or native born citizen
    D. To acquire citizenship

46. **In the United States government, power or control over public education, marriage, and divorce is:** *(Skill 3.1) (Rigorous)*

    A. Implied or suggested
    B. Concurrent or shared
    C. Delegated or expressed
    D. Reserved

47. **Under the brand new Constitution, the most urgent of the many problems facing the new federal government was that of:** *(Skill 3.1) (Rigorous)*

    A. Maintaining a strong army and navy
    B. Establishing a strong foreign policy
    C. Raising money to pay salaries and war debts
    D. Setting up courts, passing federal laws, and providing for law enforcement officers

48. **In the United States, federal investigations into business activities are handled by the:** *(Skill 3.2) (Rigorous)*

    A. Department of Treasury
    B. Security & Exchange Commission
    C. Government Accounting Office
    D. Federal Trade Commission

49. **The source of authority for national, state, and local governments in the U.S. is:** *(Skill 3.2) (Rigorous)*

    A. The will of the people
    B. The U.S. Constitution
    C. Written laws
    D. The Bill of Rights

50. **The programs such as unemployment insurance and health insurance for the elderly are the responsibility of:** *(Skill 3.2) (Rigorous)*

    A. Federal government
    B. Local government
    C. State government
    D. Communal government

51. **The term that best describes how the Supreme Court can block laws that may be unconstitutional from being enacted is:** *(Skill 3.2) (Rigorous)*

    A. Jurisprudence
    B. Judicial Review
    C. Exclusionary Rule
    D. Right of Petition

52. **The United States legislature is bicameral, this means:** *(Skill 3.2) (Easy)*

    A. It consists of several houses
    B. It consists of two houses
    C. The Vice President is in charge of the legislature when in session
    D. It has an upper and lower house

53. **Which of the three branches of government is responsible for taxation?** *(Skill 3.2) (Average Rigor)*

    A. Legislative
    B. Executive
    C. Judicial
    D. Congressional

54. **The U.S. government's federal system consists of:** *(Skill 3.2) (Average Rigor)*

    A. Three parts, the Executive, the Legislative, and the Judiciary
    B. Three parts, the Legislative, the Congress, and the Presidency
    C. Four parts, the Executive, the Judiciary, the courts, and the Legislative
    D. Two parts, the government and the governed

55. **To "impeach" a President means to:** *(Skill 3.2) (Average Rigor)*

    A. Bring charges against a President
    B. Remove a President from office
    C. Re-elect the President
    D. Override his veto

56. **The power to declare war, establish a postal system, and coin money rests with which branch of the government?** *(Skill 3.2) (Rigorous)*

    A. Presidential
    B. Judicial
    C. Legislative
    D. Executive

57. **Which of the following is an important idea expressed in the Declaration of Independence?** *(Skill 3.2) (Rigorous)*

    A. People have the right to change their government
    B. People should obey the government authority
    C. A monarch is a bad thing
    D. Indirect democracy is best

58. **The Judiciary Act of 1789 established the:** *(Skill 3.2) (Average Rigor)*

    A. Supreme Court
    B. Principle of Judicial Review
    C. State court system
    D. Federal and circuit court system

59. **The Executive branch refers to:** *(Skill 3.2) (Easy)*

    A. The Senate
    B. The Legislature
    C. Congress
    D. The President and Vice President

60. **An "Ex post facto law" is:** *(Skill 3.2) (Average Rigor)*

    A. A law made against an act after it has been committed
    B. A law proclaimed unconstitutional by the Supreme Court
    C. An Executive Act
    D. A law relating to the postal system

61. **The Judiciary refers to:** *(Skill 3.2) (Easy)*

    A. The President
    B. Congress
    C. The legal system
    D. The system of states' rights

62. **The highest appellate court in the United States is the:** *(Skill 3.2) (Rigorous)*

    A. National Appeals Court
    B. Circuit Court
    C. Supreme Court
    D. Court of Appeals

63. **Which one of the following is not a function or responsibility of the U.S. political parties?** *(Skill 3.3) (Rigorous)*

    A. Conducting elections or the voting process
    B. Obtaining funds needed for election campaigns
    C. Choosing candidates to run for public office
    D. Making voters aware of issues and other public affairs information

64. **On the spectrum of American politics, the label that most accurately describes voters to the "right of center" is:** *(Skill 3.3) (Average Rigor)*

    A. Moderates
    B. Liberals
    C. Conservatives
    D. Socialists

65. **What is the form of local government that acts as an intermediary between the state and the city?** *(Skill 3.4) (Average Rigor)*

    A. Metropolitan government
    B. Limited government
    C. The Mayor-Council system
    D. County Commission system

66. **The Bill of Rights says that any rights it does not mention are:** *(Skill 3.4) (Rigorous)*

    A. Reserved to the federal government
    B. Not important
    C. Judged by the Supreme Court
    D. Reserved to the states or to the people

67. **America's weak foreign policy and lack of adequate diplomacy during the 1870s and 1880s led to the comment that "a special Providence takes care of fools, drunkards, and the United States" is attributed to:** *(Skill 3.5) (Average Rigor)*

    A. Otto von Bismarck
    B. Benjamin Disraeli
    C. William Gladstone
    D. Paul von Hindenburg

68. **The doctrine that sought to keep Communism from spreading was:** *(Skill 3.5) (Average Rigor)*

    A. The Cold War
    B. Roll-back
    C. Containment
    D. Détente

69. **What was George Washington's advice to Americans about foreign policy?** *(Skill 3.5) (Rigorous)*

    A. America should have strong alliances
    B. America should avoid alliances
    C. Foreign policy should take precedence over domestic policy
    D. Domestic policy should take precedence over foreign policy

70. **"Walk softly and carry a big stick" is a statement associated with:** *(Skill 3.5) (Average Rigor)*

    A. Franklin Roosevelt
    B. Theodore Roosevelt
    C. George Washington
    D. Thomas Hobbes

71. **The foundation of modern constitutionalism is embodied in the idea that government is limited by law. This was stated by:** *(Skill 3.6) (Rigorous)*

    A. John Locke
    B. Rousseau
    C. St. Thomas Aquinas
    D. Montesquieu

72. **The idea of universal peace through world organization was a philosophy of:** *(Skill 3.6) (Rigorous)*

    A. Rousseau
    B. Immanuel Kant
    C. Montesquieu
    D. John Locke

73. **The principle that "men entrusted with power tend to abuse it" is attributed to:** *(Skill 3.6) (Average Rigor)*

    A. Locke
    B. Rousseau
    C. Aristotle
    D. Montesquieu

74. **A political system in which the laws and traditions put limits on the powers of government is:** *(Skill 3.6) (Average Rigor)*

    A. Federalism
    B. Constitutionalism
    C. Parliamentary system
    D. Presidential system

75. **A political philosophy favoring or supporting rapid social changes in order to correct social and economic inequalities is called:** *(Skill 3.6) (Rigorous)*

    A. Nationalism
    B. Liberalism
    C. Conservatism
    D. Federalism

76. **Marxism states which two groups are in continual conflict?** *(Skill 3.6) (Rigorous)*

    A. Farmers and landowners
    B. Kings and the nobility
    C. Workers and owners
    D. Structure and superstructure

77. **Which of the following is an example of a direct democracy?** *(Skill 3.6) (Rigorous)*

    A. Elected representatives
    B. Greek city-states
    C. The United States Senate
    D. The United States House of Representative

78. **The first organized city-states arose in:** *(Skill 3.6) (Average Rigor)*

    A. Egypt
    B. China
    C. Sumer
    D. Greece

79. **The founder of the first Communist party and the first leader of the Soviet Union was:** *(Skill 3.6) (Average Rigor)*

    A. Joseph Stalin
    B. Vladimir Lenin
    C. John Lennon
    D. Karl Marx

80. **Socialists believe that the government should have a role in the economy:** *(Skill 3.6) (Average Rigor)*

    A. Lesser
    B. Greater
    C. Equal with business
    D. Less than business

81. **One difference between totalitarianism and authoritarianism is that totalitarianism believes in:** *(Skill 3.6) (Average Rigor)*

    A. Total control over all aspects of society
    B. Minimum government control
    C. There is no difference
    D. The difference is unknown

82. **One difference between a presidential and a parliamentary system is in a parliamentary system:** *(Skill 3.6) (Rigorous)*

    A. The Prime Minister is head of government while a president or monarch is head of state
    B. The President is head of government and the Vice-President is head of state
    C. The President protempore of the Senate is head of state while the Prime Minister is head of government
    D. The President appoints the head of state

83. **In an indirect democracy:** *(Skill 3.6) (Rigorous)*

    A. All the people together decide on issues
    B. People elect representatives to act for them
    C. Democracy can never really work
    D. Government is less efficient than a direct democracy

84. **In a communist system, controls the means of production.** *(Skill 3.6) (Average Rigor)*

    A. A professional managerial class
    B. The owners of business and industry
    C. The workers
    D. The state

85. **Machiavelli was most concerned with describing:** *(Skill 3.6) (Average Rigor)*

    A. Modern warfare
    B. Ancient political philosophy
    C. Representative government
    D. Getting and keeping political power

86. **Oligarchy refers to:** *(Skill 3.6) (Easy)*

    A. Rule of a single leader
    B. The rule of a single political party
    C. Rule by a select few
    D. Rule by many

87. **Which statement closely resembles the political philosophy of Thomas Hobbes?** *(Skill 3.6) (Rigorous)*

    A. Citizens should give obedience to the state authority as a means of survival in a world where man's nature drives self-interest and makes man selfish and self-acting
    B. That citizens have a right to rise against the state whenever they choose
    C. All state authority is basically evil and should be eliminated
    D. People are generally good and cooperative if given a chance

88. **As a rule, the relationship between fascism and communism is:** *(Skill 3.6) (Average Rigor)*

    A. They are the same thing
    B. Unknown at present
    C. Antagonistic
    D. Cooperative

89. **In a parliamentary system, the person who becomes Prime Minister usually:** *(Skill 3.6) (Average Rigor)*

    A. Chosen by the cabinet
    B. Elected by a direct national vote
    C. Chosen by the president of the country
    D. Chosen by a majority or coalition of parties in the parliament

90. **The "cult of personality" is an idea most associated with:** *(Skill 3.6) (Average Rigor)*

    A. Democracy
    B. Anarchism
    C. Fascism
    D. Communism

91. **Which political economic system discourages private land ownership?** *(Skill 3.6) (Rigorous)*

    A. Capitalism
    B. Socialism
    C. Agriculturalism
    D. Welfare Capitalism

92. **The "history of all societies is one of class struggle" is a statement associated with:** *(Skill 3.6) (Average Rigor)*

    A. John Locke
    B. Thomas Jefferson
    C. Karl Marx
    D. Thomas Hobbes

93. **An obligation identified with citizenship is:** *(Skill 3.7) (Easy)*

    A. Belonging to a political party
    B. Educating oneself
    C. Running for political office
    D. Voting

94. **To plead "the Fifth Amendment" means to:** *(Skill 3.7) (Rigorous)*

    A. Refuse to speak so one does not incriminate oneself
    B. Plead "no contest" in court
    C. Ask for freedom of speech
    D. Ask to appear before a judge when charged with a crime

95. **A "tort" refers to:** *(Skill 3.7) (Average Rigor)*

    A. A private or civil action brought into court
    B. A type of confection
    C. A penal offense
    D. One who solicits

96. **The results of the Renaissance, Enlightenment, Commercial and Industrial Revolutions were more unfortunate for the people of:** *(Skill 4.0) (Rigorous)*

    A. Asia
    B. Latin America
    C. Africa
    D. Middle East

97. Which ancient civilization is credited with being the first to develop irrigation techniques through the use of canals, dikes, and devices for raising water? *(Skill 4.1) (Easy)*

    A. The Sumerians
    B. The Egyptians
    C. The Babylonians
    D. The Akkadians

98. An early cultural group was so skillful in navigating on the seas that they were able to sail at night guided by stars. They were the: *(Skill 4.1) (Average Rigor)*

    A. Greeks
    B. Persians
    C. Minoans
    D. Phoenicians

101. Bathtubs, hot and cold running water, and sewage systems with flush toilets were developed by the: *(Skill 4.1) (Average Rigor)*

    A. Minoans
    B. Mycenaeans
    C. Phoenicians
    D. Greeks

99. Development of a solar calendar, invention of the decimal system, and contributions to the development of geometry and astronomy are all the legacy of: *(Skill 4.1) (Average Rigor)*

    A. The Babylonians
    B. The Persians
    C. The Sumerians
    D. The Egyptians

100. The first ancient civilization to introduce and practice monotheism was the: *(Skill 4.1) (Average Rigor)*

    A. Sumerians
    B. Minoans
    C. Phoenicians
    D. Hebrews

102. The end to hunting, gathering, and fishing of prehistoric people was due to: *(Skill 4.1) (Average Rigor)*

    A. Domestication of animals
    B. Building crude huts and houses
    C. Development of agriculture
    D. Organized government in villages

103. The early ancient civilizations developed systems of government: *(Skill 4.1) (Rigorous)*

    A. To provide for defense against attack
    B. To regulate trade
    C. To regulate and direct the economic activities of the people as they worked together in groups
    D. To decide on the boundaries of the different fields during planting seasons

104. **Which one of the following is not an important legacy of the Byzantine Empire? (Skill 4.2) (Rigorous)**

    A. It protected Western Europe from various attacks from the East by such groups as the Persians, Ottoman Turks, and Barbarians
    B. It played a part in preserving the literature, philosophy, and language of ancient Greece
    C. Its military organization was the foundation for modern armies
    D. It kept the legal traditions of Roman government, collecting and organizing many ancient Roman laws

105. **The "father of anatomy" is considered to be: (Skill 4.2) (Easy)**

    A. Vesalius
    B. Servetus
    C. Galen
    D. Harvey

106. **"Poverty is the parent of revolution and crime" was from the writings of: (Skill 4.2) (Average Rigor)**

    A. Plato
    B. Aristotle
    C. Cicero
    D. Gaius

107. **The Roman Empire gave so much to the world, especially the Western world. Of the legacies below, the most influential, effective and lasting is: (Skill 4.2) (Rigorous)**

    A. The language of Latin
    B. Roman law, justice, and political system
    C. Engineering and building
    D. The writings of its poets and historians

108. **The circumference of the earth, which greatly contributed to geographic knowledge was calculated by: (Skill 4.2) (Easy)**

    A. Ptolemy
    B. Eratosthenes
    C. Galileo
    D. Strabo

109. **India's greatest ruler is considered to be: (Skill 4.3) (Rigorous)**

    A. Akbar
    B. Asoka
    C. Babur
    D. Jahan

110. **An extensive knowledge of surgery and medicine as well as principles of irrigation, fertilization and terrace farming was unique to: (Skill 4.3)(Easy)**

    A. The Mayans
    B. The Atacamas
    C. The Incas
    D. The Tarapacas

111. China's last imperial ruling dynasty was one of its most stable and successful and, under its rule, Chinese culture made an outstanding impression on Western nations. This dynasty was: *(Skill 4.3)* *(Rigorous)*

    A. Min
    B. Manchu
    C. Han
    D. Chou

112. The world religion which includes a caste system is: *(Skill 4.3) (Average Rigor)*

    A. Buddhism
    B. Hinduism
    C. Sikhism
    D. Jainism

113. The principle of zero in mathematics is the discovery of the ancient civilization found in: *(Skill 4.3) (Easy)*

    A. Egypt
    B. Persia
    C. India
    D. Babylon

114. In Western Europe, the achievements of the Renaissance were unsurpassed and made these countries outstanding cultural centers on the continent. All of the following were accomplishments except: *(Skill 4.4) (Rigorous)*

    A. Investment of the printing press
    B. A rekindling of interest in the learning of classical Greece and Rome
    C. Growth in literature, philosophy, and art
    D. Better military tactics

115. The changing focus during the Renaissance when artists and scholars were less concerned with religion but centered their efforts on a better understanding of people and the world was called: *(Skill 4.4) (Easy)*

    A. Realism
    B. Humanism
    C. Individualism
    D. Intellectualism

116. The ideas and innovations of the period of the Renaissance were spread throughout Europe mainly because of: *(Skill 4.4) (Rigorous)*

    A. Extensive exploration
    B. Craft workers and their guilds
    C. The invention of the printing press
    D. Increased travel and trade

117. **Which one of the following did not contribute to the early medieval European civilization?**
(Skill 4.4) (Rigorous)

   A. The heritage from the classical cultures
   B. The Christian religion
   C. The influence of the German Barbarians
   D. The spread of ideas through trade and commerce

118. **Charlemagne's most important influence on Western civilization is seen today in:**
(Skill 4.4) (Rigorous)

   A. Relationship of church and state
   B. Strong military for defense
   C. The criminal justice system
   D. Education of women

119. **Which French Renaissance writer wrote about the dangers of absolute powers and later examined himself in an effort to make inquiries into humankind and nature?**
(Skill 4.6) (Average Rigor)

   A. Francois Rabelais
   B. Desiderius Erasmus
   C. Michel de Montaigne
   D. Sir Francis Bacon

120. **Which one of the following is not a reason why Europeans came to the New World?** *(Skill 4.7) (Rigorous)*

   A. To find resources in order to increase wealth
   B. To establish trade
   C. To increase a ruler's power and importance
   D. To spread Christianity

Answer Key

1. D	41. B	81. A
2. D	42. A	82. A
3. C	43. A	83. B
4. C	44. B	84. D
5. D	45. D	85. D
6. C	46. D	86. C
7. C	47. C	87. A
8. A	48. D	88. C
9. A	49. A	89. D
10. A	50. C	90. C
11. C	51. B	91. B
12. C	52. B	92. C
13. B	53. A	93. D
14. C	54. A	94. A
15. A	55. A	95. A
16. A	56. C	96. C
17. D	57. A	97. A
18. C	58. D	98. D
19. D	59. D	99. D
20. D	60. A	100. D
21. C	61. C	101. A
22. A	62. C	102. C
23. B	63. A	103. C
24. C	64. C	104. C
25. C	65. A	105. A
26. B	66. D	106. B
27. D	67. A	107. B
28. A	68. C	108. B
29. C	69. B	109. A
30. C	70. B	110. C
31. B	71. C	111. B
32. B	72. B	112. B
33. C	73. D	113. C
34. C	74. B	114. D
35. D	75. B	115. B
36. B	76. C	116. C
37. B	77. B	117. D
38. B	78. C	118. A
39. A	79. B	119. C
40. D	80. B	120. B

Rigor Table

Easy 20%	Average 40%	Rigorous 40%
1,3,5,7,8,9,10,11,20,24,35,40,43,45,52,59,61,86,93,97,105,108,110,113,115	4,6,12,13,15,16,18,19,23,25,26,28,39,42,44,53,54,55,58,60,64,65,67,68,70,73,74,78,79,80,81,84,85,88,89,90,92,95,98,99,100,101,102,106,112,119	2,14,17,21,22,27,29,30,31,32,33,34,36,37,38,41,46,47,48,49,50,51,56,57,62,63,66,69,71,72,75,76,77,82,83,87,91,94,96,103,104,107,109,111,114,116,117,118,120

Rationales with Sample Questions

1. **Studies in astronomy, skills in mapping, and other contributions to geographic knowledge came from:** *(Skill 1.0) (Easy)*

    A. Galileo
    B. Columbus
    C. Eratosthenes
    D. Ptolemy

Answer: D. Ptolemy
Ptolemy (2ⁿᵈ century AD) was important in the fields of astronomy and geography. His theory stated that the earth was the center of the universe and all the other planets rotated around it, a theory that was later proven false. Ptolemy was important for his contributions to the fields of mapping, mathematics, and geography. Galileo (1564-1642) was also important in the field of astronomy but did not make the mapping and geographic contributions of Ptolemy. He invented and used the world's first telescope and advanced Copernicus' theory that the earth revolved around the sun, much to the dismay of the Church.

2. **Which one of the following does not affect climate?** *(Skill 1.2) (Rigorous)*

    A. Elevation and altitude
    B. Ocean currents
    C. Latitude
    D. Longitude

Answer: D. Longitude
Latitude is the primary influence of earth's climate as it determines the climatic region in which an area lies. Elevation or altitude and ocean currents are considered to be secondary influences on climate. Longitude is considered to have no important influence over climate.

3. **Soil erosion is most likely to occur in large amounts in:** *(Skill 1.2) (Easy)*

    A. Mountain ranges
    B. Deserts
    C. Tropical rainforests
    D. River valleys

Answer: C. Tropical rainforests
Soil erosion is most likely to occur in tropical rainforests as the large amount of constant rainfall moves the soil at a greater rate across a greater area. Mountain ranges and river valleys experience some soil erosion but don't have the levels of precipitation found in a tropical rainforest. Deserts have virtually no soil erosion due to their climate.

4. **Which one of the following is not a use for a region's wetlands?** *(Skill 1.2) (Average Rigor)*

   A. Produces fresh clean water
   B. Provides habitat for wildlife
   C. Provides water for hydroelectric power
   D. Controls floods

Answer: C. Provides water for hydroelectric power

5. **The geographical drought-stricken region of Africa south of the Sahara and extending east and west from Senegal to Somalia is:** *(Skill 1.3) (Easy)*

   A. The Kalahari
   B. The Namib
   C. The Great Rift Valley
   D. The Sahel

Answer: D. The Sahel
The (A) Kalahari is located between the Orange and Zambezi Rivers and has an annual rainfall of about 5 to 20 inches. The (B) Namib is a desert, rocky plateau along the coast of Namibia in Southwest Africa that receives less than .5 inches of rainfall annually. The (C) Great Rift Valley is a fault system that runs 3000 miles from Syria to Mozambique and has great variations in elevation. Therefore, it is the (D) Sahel, the region of Africa South of the Sahara and extending East and West from Senegal to Somalia. The Sahel experienced a serious drought in the 1960s and then again in the 1980s and 1990s. International relief efforts have been focused there in an effort to keep the region alive.

6. **Meridians, or lines of longitude, not only help in pinpointing locations, but are also used for:** *(Skill 1.4) (Average Rigor)*

   A. Measuring distance from the Poles
   B. Determining direction of ocean currents
   C. Determining the time around the world
   D. Measuring distance on the Equator

Answer: C. Determining the time around the world
Meridians, or lines of longitude, are the determining factor in separating time zones and determining time around the world.

7.   **The Yangtze River primarily flows in which direction?** *(Skill 1.4) (Easy)*

    A. North
    B. South
    C. East
    D. West

Answer: C. East
The Yangtze River runs from Tibet through China and flows eastward to the Pacific Ocean. The Yangtze River is an important travel and trade route through China and meets the Pacific at Shanghai.

8.   **The Nile River flows in which direction?** *(Skill 1.4) (Easy)*

    A. North
    B. South
    C. East
    D. West

Answer: A. North
The Nile River flows from Central Africa, north to the Mediterranean Sea. The Nile River Delta is in Egypt.

9.   **The Ganges River empties into the:** *(Skill 1.4) (Easy)*

    A. Bay of Bengal
    B. Arabian Sea
    C. Red Sea
    D. Arafura Sea

Answer: A. Bay of Bengal
The Ganges River runs 1,560 miles, northeast through India across the plains to the Bay of Bengal in Bangladesh. The Ganges is considered to be the most sacred river in India according to the Hindus.

10. **Maps as a rule are:** *(Skill 1.4) (Easy)*

    A. All subject to some sort of distortion
    B. Always entirely accurate
    C. Not very useful in political science studies
    D. Difficult usually to understand

Answer: A. All subject to some sort of distortion
Maps as a rule are all subject to some sort of distortion. Since they are representing a three-dimensional world in a two-dimensional representation, it will never be completely accurate. Even maps that are specifically designed to limit distortion still will lack total accuracy. Maps are still very helpful in most social science disciplines and generally designed to be understood easily using keys and symbols.

11. **The name for those who make maps is:** *(Skill 1.4) (Easy)*

    A. Haberdasher
    B. Geographer
    C. Cartographer
    D. Demographer

Answer: C. Cartographer
(A) Haberdasher is a "British dealer in men's furnishings" according to the dictionary. (B) Geographers study mostly locations, conditions, and spatial relations. (C) Cartographers are people who make maps. (D) Demographers would be most concerned with the study of human populations.

12. **The "father" of modern economics is considered by most economists today to be:** *(Skill 2.0) (Average Rigor)*

    A.   Thomas Robert Malthus
    B.   John Stuart Mill
    C.   Adam Smith
    D.   John Maynard Keynes

Answer: C. Adam Smith

Adam Smith (1723-1790) is considered by many to be the "father" of modern economics. In the *Wealth of Nations,* Smith advocated for little or no government interference in the economy. Smith claimed that individuals' self-interest would bring about the public's welfare. It is important to note that Smith was firmly against the free market systems of monopoly power and warned that the private sector, particularly large manufacturers, if left unregulated could potentially stand in opposition to the public welfare. John Maynard Keynes 1883-1946) was also an important economist. He advocated an economic system in which government regulations and spending on public works would stimulate the economy and lead to full employment. John Stuart Mill (1806-1873) was a progressive British philosopher and economist, whose ideas came closer to socialism than to the classical capitalist ideas of Adam Smith. Mill constantly advocated for political and social reforms, including emancipation for women, labor organizations, and farming cooperatives. Thomas Malthus (1766-1834) was a British economist who introduced the study of population and early on considered famine, war, and disease to be the primary checks on world population. He later modified his views and recognized his early theoretical shortcomings and shifted his focus to the causes of unemployment.

13. **Which political theorist says that capitalism could be maintained if there were sufficient checks on the economy?** *(Skill 2.0) (Average Rigor)*

   A. Marx
   B. Keynes
   C. Weber
   D. Locke

Answer: B. Keynes
The great German political and economic philosopher (A) Karl Marx (1818-1883), who is generally regarded as the founder of modern socialism and communism, believed that capitalism was not fixable and was the pretense for the rise of revolutionary socialism and communism. (B) John Maynard Keynes (1883-1946) advocated an economic system in which government regulations and spending on public works (checks and balances) would stimulate the economy and lead to full employment. This broke from the classical idea that free markets would lead to full employment and prosperity. He was still a firm believer in capitalism, but in a less classical sense. (C) Max Weber (1864-1920) was a German sociologist most concerned with examining social and environmental roles in the rise of capitalism, such as the ideals of religion (Calvinism) and its influence on economics (capitalism). (D) John Locke (1632-1704), whose book *Two Treatises of Government* has long been considered a founding document on the rights of people to rebel against an unjust government was an important figure in the founding of the U.S. Constitution and on general politics of the American colonies.

14. **The idea that continued population growth would, in future years, seriously affect a nation's productive capabilities was stated by:** *(Skill 2.1) (Rigorous)*

   A. Keynes
   B. Mill
   C. Malthus
   D. Friedman

Answer: C. Malthus
(C) John Maynard Keynes (1883-1946) advocated an economic system in which government regulations and spending on public works would stimulate the economy and lead to full employment. (C) Thomas Malthus (1766-1834) was the English economist who had the idea that population growth would seriously affect a nation's productive capabilities. Malthus' ideas also included predictions about running out of food and a natural selection-like process brought about by population that would maintain balance. (B) Mill (1806 -1973), an English economist and (D) Friedman (1912-) an American economist contrasted one another greatly. Mill was almost a Socialist and wrote the early work in political economy while Friedman was a financial advisor in the arch conservative government of President Ronald Reagan.

15. **A boycott is:**
    (Skill 2.1) (Average Rigor)

    A. The refusal to buy goods or services
    B. An imbalance of trade
    C. The refusal to speak in court
    D. A Writ of Assistance

Answer: A. The refusal to buy goods or services

A boycott is the refusal to buy goods or services. Boycotts were used as a powerful tool of nonviolent fighting during the 1950s and 1960s by civil rights activists. An example is the bus boycott in Montgomery, Alabama, in 1955 started when Mrs. Rosa Parks refused to obey the law forcing segregation on public buses. This boycott was successful in achieving the goal. In 1956 the Supreme Court outlawed segregation on public buses.

16. **The study of ways in which different societies around the world deal with the problems of limited resources and unlimited needs and wants is in the area of:**
    (Skill 2.2) (Average Rigor)

    A. Economics
    B. Sociology
    C. Anthropology
    D. Political Science

Answer: A. Economics

The study of the ways in which different societies around the world deal with the problems of limited resources and unlimited needs and wants is a study of Economics. Economists consider the law of supply and demand as fundamental to the study of the economy. However, Sociology and Political Science also consider the study of economics and its importance in understanding social and political systems.

17. **The idea or proposal for more equal division of profits among employers and workers was put forth by:** *(Skill 2.2) (Rigorous)*

    A. Karl Marx
    B. Thomas Malthus
    C. Adam Smith
    D. John Stuart Mill

Answer: D. John Stuart Mill
(A) Karl Marx (1818-1883) was the German social philosopher and economist who wrote *The Communist Manifesto* and numerous other landmark works in his goal to help the world understand the inability of capitalism to provide for the workers, the idea of class struggle, and the central role of economy. (B) Thomas Malthus (1766-1834) was a British economist who introduced the study of population and early on considered famine, war, and disease to be the primary checks on world population. He later modified his views and recognized his early theoretical shortcoming and shifted his focus to the causes of unemployment. (C) Adam Smith (1723-1790) is considered by many to be the "father" of modern capitalist economics. In the *Wealth of Nations*, Smith advocated for little or no government interference in the economy. Smith claimed that an individual's self-interest would bring about the public's welfare. It is important to note that Smith was firmly against the free market systems of monopoly power and warned that the private sector, particularly large manufacturers, if left unregulated could potentially stand in opposition to the public welfare. (D) John Stuart Mill (1806- 1873) was the progressive British philosopher and economist whose ideas came closer to socialism than to the classical capitalist ideas of Adam Smith. Mill constantly advocated for political and social reforms, including emancipation for women, labor organizations, farming cooperatives, and most importantly a more equal division of profits among employers and workers.

18. **The purchase of goods or services on one market for immediate resale on another market is:** *(Skill 2.3) (Average Rigor)*

    A. Output
    B. Enterprise
    C. Arbitrage
    D. Mercantile

Answer: C. Arbitrage
Output is an amount produced or manufactured by an industry. Enterprise is simply any business organization. Mercantile is one of the first systems of economics in which goods were exchanged. Therefore, arbitrage is an item or service that an industry produces. The dictionary definition of arbitrage is the purchase of securities on one market for immediate resale on another market in order to profit from a price discrepancy.

19. **Potential customers for any product or service are not only called consumers but can also be called a:** *(Skill 2.3) (Average Rigor)*

    A. Resource
    B. Base
    C. Commodity
    D. Market

Answer: D. Market
Potential customers for any product or service are not only customers but can also be called a market. A resource is a source of wealth; natural resources are the basis for manufacturing goods and services. A commodity is anything that is bought or sold, any product.

20. **The economic system promoting individual ownership of land, capital, and businesses with minimal governmental regulations is called:** *(Skill 2.3) (Easy)*

    A. Macro-economy
    B. Micro-economy
    C. Laissez-faire
    D. Free enterprise

Answer: D. Free Enterprise
(D) Free enterprise or capitalism is the economic system that promotes private ownership of land, capital, and business with minimal government interference. (C) Laissez-faire is the idea that an "invisible hand" will guide the free enterprise system to the maximum potential efficiency.

21. **Government regulation of economic activities for favorable balance of trade was the first major economic theory. It was called:** *(Skill 2.5) (Rigorous)*

    A. Laissez-faire
    B. Globalism
    C. Mercantilism
    D. Syndicalism

Answer: C. Mercantilism
(A) Laissez-faire is the doctrine that calls for no government interference in economic and political policy. (B) Globalism is not an economic or political theory, nor is it an actual word in the English language. Globalization is the idea that we are all increasingly connected in a worldwide system. (D) Syndicalism is similar to anarchism claiming that workers should control and govern economic policies and regulations as opposed to state control. Therefore, (C) mercantilism is the best regulation of economic activities for a favorable balance of trade.

22. **The economist who disagreed with the idea that free markets lead to full employment and prosperity and suggested that increasing government spending would end depressions was:** *(Skill 2.5) (Rigorous)*

    A. Keynes
    B. Malthus
    C. Smith
    D. Friedman

Answer: A. Keynes
John Maynard Keynes (1883-1946) advocated an economic system in which government regulations and spending on public works would stimulate the economy and lead to full employment. This broke from the classical idea that free markets would lead to full employment and prosperity. He was still a firm believer in capitalism, but in a less classical sense than Adam Smith (1723-1790), whose *Wealth of Nations* advocated for little or no government interference in the economy. Smith claimed that an individual's self-interest would bring about the public's welfare. It is important to note that Smith was firmly against the free market systems of monopoly power and warned that the private sector, particularly large manufacturers, if left unregulated could potentially stand in opposition to the public welfare.

23. **The belief that government should stay out of economic affairs is called:** *(Skill 2.5) (Average Rigor)*

    A. Mercantilism
    B. Laissez-faire
    C. Democratic-Socialism
    D. Corporatism

Answer: B. Laissez-faire
(A) Mercantilism was an economic system that dominated trade between the major nations of the 16th, 17th, and 18th centuries in which there was believed to be a fixed amount of wealth in the world and a country must attain the riches of another (usually in the form of precious metals in order to achieve economic growth. Mercantilism was characterized by intense government involvement in the economy. The belief that government should stay out of economic affairs, and thus the reactionary doctrine to mercantilism is called laissez-faire economics and follows a strict capitalist model of economics. (C) Democratic-Socialism showed up in European countries such as Sweden, Belgium, and the Netherlands following World War I. Democratic-Socialism called for democratic political parties to play an important role in shaping the economy in order to avoid the problems of free enterprise capitalism and exploitation in favor of more equality and nationalization.

24. A tariff is:
(Skill 2.5) (Easy)

A. A law passed by the Congress and vetoed by the President
B. An appointed official mandated to preserve public order
C. A tax a government places on internationally traded goods, usually goods entering a country
D. A tax a government places on goods produced for domestic use, another name for it is a "sales tax"

Answer: C. A tax a government places on internationally traded goods, usually goods entering a country
A tariff is a tax that a government places on goods imported and entering a country. A tariff is not a law, although it can be enforced by law. Tariffs are often in place as a protection to domestic producers. Tax on domestic goods that are sold to domestic consumers is a sales tax.

25. George Washington's opinion of America having trade with other nations was:
(Skill 2.5) (Average Rigor)

A. Approval in only some instances
B. Disapproval
C. Approval
D. Unsure

Answer: C. Approval
George Washington (1732-1799) approved of U.S. trade with other nations although he was firmly against creating permanent alliances with foreign countries as evidenced by his farewell address in 1796.

26. The process of the state taking over industries and businesses is called:
(Skill 2.5) (Average Rigor)

A. Industrialization
B. Nationalization
C. Redistribution
D. Amalgamation

Answer: B. Nationalization
The process by which the state takes over industries and businesses is called nationalization. This is characteristic of a socialist or communist system in which the state completely controls and regulates commerce. The opposite of nationalization, privatization, is the process by which business and industry previously controlled by the government comes under control of private enterprise.

27. One method of trade restriction used by some nations is: *(Skill 2.6) (Rigorous)*

A. Limited treaties
B. Floating exchange rate
C. Bill of exchange
D. Import quotas

Answer: D. Import quotas
One method of trade restriction used by some nations is import quotas. The amounts of goods imported are regulated in an effort to protect domestic enterprise and limit foreign competition. Both the United States and Japan, two of the world's most industrialized nations have import quotas to protect domestic industries.

28. The "father of political science" is considered to be: *(Skill 3.0) (Average Rigor)*

A. Aristotle
B. John Locke
C. Plato
D. Thomas Hobbes

Answer: A. Aristotle
(D) Thomas Hobbes (1588-1679) wrote the important work *Leviathan* in which he pointed out that people are by all means selfish, individualistic animals that will always look out for themselves; therefore, the state must combat this nature desire. (B) John Locke (1632-1704) whose book *Two Treatises of Government* has long been considered a founding document on the rights of people to rebel against an unjust government was an important figure in the founding of the U.S. Constitution and on general politics of the American colonies. (C) Plato (427-347 B.C.) and Aristotle (384-322 B.C.) both contributed to the field of political science.

Both believed that political order would result in the greatest stability. In fact, Aristotle studied under Plato. Both Plato and Aristotle studied the ideas of causality and the Prime Mover, but their conclusions were different. Aristotle, however, is considered to be "the father of political science" because of his development of systems of political order the true development, a scientific system to study justice and political order.

29. **There is no doubt of the vast improvement of the U.S. Constitution over the weak Articles of Confederation. Which one of the four statements below is not a description of the document?** *(Skill 3.1) (Rigorous)*

    A. The establishment of a strong central government in no way lessened or weakened the individual states
    B. Individual rights were protected and secured
    C. The Constitution demands unquestioned respect and subservience to the federal government by all states and citizens
    D. Its flexibility and adaptation to change gives it a sense of timelessness

Answer: C. The Constitution demands unquestioned respect and subservience to the federal government by all states and citizens.
The U.S. Constitution was indeed a vast improvement over the Articles of Confederation and the authors of the document took great care to assure longevity. It clearly stated that the establishment of a strong central government in no way lessened or weakened the individual states. In the Bill of Rights, citizens were assured that individual rights were protected and secured. Possibly the most important feature of the new Constitution was its flexibility and adaptation to change which assured longevity.
Therefore, the only statement made that doesn't describe some facet of the Constitution is "The Constitution demands unquestioned respect and subservience to the federal government by all states and citizens." On the contrary, the Constitution made sure that citizens could critique and make changes to their government and encourages such critiques and changes as necessary for the preservation of democracy.

30. **In the United States government, the power of coining money is:** *(Skill 3.1) (Rigorous)*

    A. Implied or suggested
    B. Concurrent or shared
    C. Delegated or expressed
    D. Reserved

Answer: C. Delegated or expressed
In the United States government, the power of coining money is delegated or expressed. Therefore, only the United States government may coin money, the states may not coin money for themselves.

31. **In the United States government, the power of taxation and borrowing is:** *(Skill 3.1)(Rigorous)*

    A. Implied or suggested
    B. Concurrent or shared
    C. Delegated or expressed
    D. Reserved

Answer: B. Concurrent or shared
In the United States government, the power of taxation is concurrent or shared with the states. An example of this is the separation of state and federal income tax and the separate filings of tax returns for each.

32. **Marbury vs Madison (1803) was an important Supreme Court case which set the precedent for:** *(Skill 3.1) (Rigorous)*

    A. The elastic clause
    B. Judicial review
    C. The supreme law of the land
    D. Popular sovereignty in the territories

Answer: B. Judicial review
Marbury vs. Madison (1803) was an important case for the Supreme Court as it established judicial review. In that case, the Supreme Court set precedence to declare laws passed by Congress as unconstitutional. Popular sovereignty in the territories was a failed plan pushed by Stephen Davis to allow states to decide the slavery question for themselves in his attempt to appeal to the masses in the pre-Civil War elections. The supreme law of the land is just that, the law that rules. The elastic clause is not a real term.

33. **What Supreme Court ruling established the principal of Judicial Review?** *(Skill 3.1) (Rigorous)*

    A. Jefferson vs Madison
    B. Lincoln vs Douglas
    C. Marbury vs Madison
    D. Marbury vs Jefferson

Answer: C. Marbury vs Madison
Marbury vs Madison established the principal of judicial review. The Supreme Court ruled that it held no authority in making the decision (regarding Marbury's commission as Justice of the Peace in District of Columbia) as the Supreme Court's jurisdiction (or lack thereof) in the case, was conflicted with Article III of the Constitution.

34. **To be eligible to be elected President one must:** *(Skill 3.1) (Rigorous)*

    A. Be a citizen for at least five years
    B. Be a citizen for seven years
    C. Have been born a citizen
    D. Be a naturalized citizen

Answer: C. Have been born a citizen

Article II, Section 1 of the United States Constitution clearly states, "No person except a natural-born citizen, or citizen of the United States at the time of the adoption of this Constitution, shall be eligible to the office of President, neither shall any person be eligible to that office who shall not have attained to the age of thirty-five years, and been fourteen years a resident within the United States."

35. **The first ten amendments to the Constitution are called the:** *(Skill 3.1) (Easy)*

    A. Bill of Petition
    B. Petition of Rights
    C. Rights of Man
    D. Bill of Rights

Answer: D. Bill of Rights

The Bill of Rights is the first ten Amendments to the Constitution. They were added to the Constitution within the first two years of ratification. *Rights of Man* was written by Thomas Paine.

36. **The Congress can override a President's veto with a vote.** *(Skill 3.1) (Rigorous)*

    A. One-half
    B. Two-thirds
    C. Six-tenths
    D. Three-fourths

Answer: B. Two-thirds

The Congress can override a President's veto with a two-thirds vote.

37. **To become a citizen, an individual must generally have lived in the United States for at least:** *(Skill 3.1)* *(Rigorous)*

    A. Six years
    B. Five years
    C. One year
    D. Ten years

Answer: B. Five years
To become a citizen, an individual must generally have lived in the United States for at least five years.

38. **The ability of the President to veto an act of Congress is an example of:** *(Skill 3.1)* *(Rigorous)*

    A. Separation of Powers
    B. Checks and Balances
    C. Judicial Review
    D. Presidential Prerogative

Answer: B. Checks and Balances
The ability of the President to veto an act of Congress is an example of checks and balances. Judicial review is the "checks and balances" exerted by the Judicial on the legislative Branch. The system of checks and balances helps to prevent any one branch of the United States government from becoming too powerful or corrupt.

39. **If a president neither signs nor vetoes a bill officially for ten days, it is called:** *(Skill 3.1)* *(Average Rigor)*

    A. A pocket veto
    B. A refused law
    C. Unconstitutional
    D. A presidential veto

Answer: A. A pocket veto
If the president neither signs nor vetoes a bill officially for ten days while the legislature is in session, there is an automatic veto called a "pocket veto." The legislature cannot override a pocket veto, however the bill may be reintroduced at a later time.

40. **The term that describes the division of government function is:** *(Skill 3.1) (Easy)*

    A. Free Enterprise
    B. Constitutional Prerogative
    C. Checks and Balances
    D. Separation of Powers

Answer: D. Separation of Powers
(A) Free enterprise is the system of capitalism in which there is little or no government involvement in the economy and private control over the means of production. (C) Checks and balances is the system in place to prevent over-concentration of power in any one branch of government. The term (D) "separation of powers" best describes the division of government.

41. **In the United States, the right to declare war is a power of:** *(Skill 3.1) (Rigorous)*

    A. The President
    B. Congress
    C. The Executive
    D. The States

Answer: B. Congress
In the United States, the right to declare war is a power of the Congress or legislative branch. After Congress declares war, the President is in control as the Commander-in-Chief of the military.

42. **In the United States, checks and balances refers to:** *(Skill 3.1) (Average Rigor)*

    A. The ability of each branch of government to "check" or limit the actions of the others
    B. Balance of payments
    C. International law
    D. The federal deficit

Answer: A. The ability of each branch of government to "check" or limit the actions of the others
In the United States, checks and balances refers to the ability of each branch of government (executive, legislative, and judicial) to "check" or limit the actions of the others. Examples of checks and balances are: The executive branch limits the legislature by power of veto over bills and appointments in the court system. The judicial branch limits the power of the legislature by judicial review and the ability to rule laws unconstitutional; it may also determine executive orders unconstitutional. The legislative branch checks the executive branch by power of impeachment.

43. **An amendment is:** *(Skill 3.1) (Easy)*

    A. A change or addition to the United States Constitution
    B. The right of a state to secede from the Union
    C. To add a state to the Union
    D. The right of the Supreme Court to check actions of Congress and the President

Answer: A. A change or addition to the United States Constitution
An amendment is a change or addition to the United States Constitution. No amendment refers to states' abilities to succeed or be annexed or the right of the Supreme Court to check actions of Congress and the President.

44. **The Bill of Rights was mostly written by:** *(Skill 3.1) (Average Rigor)*

    A. Thomas Jefferson
    B. James Madison
    C. George Washington
    D. Alexander Hamilton

Answer: B. James Madison
The Bill of Rights, along with the majority of the Constitution, was mostly written by James Madison. Thomas Jefferson wrote the Declaration of
Independence. Washington and Hamilton were present at the Constitutional Convention of 1787 in Philadelphia, and they were advocates of federalism or increasing the power of the federal government.

45. **To be a naturalized citizen means:** *(Skill 3.1) (Easy)*

    A. To have been refused citizenship
    B. To have dual-citizenship
    C. To be a "natural" or native born citizen
    D. To acquire citizenship

Answer: D. To acquire citizenship
To be a naturalized citizen in the United States is to acquire citizenship by meeting several requirements including a swearing to uphold the U.S. Constitution, a judgment of good character, and the ability to read and write English (often controversial as English is not the official language of the United States).

46. **In the United States government, power or control over public education, marriage, and divorce is:** *(Skill 3.1) (Rigorous)*

   A. Implied or suggested
   B. Concurrent or shared
   C. Delegated or expressed
   D. Reserved

   Answer: D. Reserved
   In the United States government, power or control over public education, marriage, and divorce is reserved. This is to say that these powers are reserved for the people of the states to decide for themselves.

47. **Under the brand new Constitution, the most urgent of the many problems facing the new federal government was that of:** *(Skill 3.1) (Rigorous)*

   A. Maintaining a strong army and navy
   B. Establishing a strong foreign policy
   C. Raising money to pay salaries and war debts
   D. Setting up courts, passing federal laws, and providing for law enforcement officers

   Answer: C. Raising money to pay salaries and war debts
   Maintaining strong military forces, establishment of a strong foreign policy, and setting up a justice system were important problems facing the United States under the newly ratified Constitution. However, the most important and pressing issue was how to raise money to pay salaries and war debts from the Revolutionary War. Alexander Hamilton (1755-1804) then Secretary of the Treasury proposed increased tariffs and taxes on products such as liquor. This money would be used to pay off war debts and to pay for internal programs. Hamilton also proposed the idea of a National Bank.

48. **In the United States, federal investigations into business activities are handled by the:** *(Skill 3.2) (Rigorous)*

   A. Department of Treasury
   B. Security and Exchange Commission
   C. Government Accounting Office
   D. Federal Trade Commission

   Answer: D. Federal Trade Commission
   The Department of Treasury (A) established in 1789, is an executive government agency that is responsible for advising the president on fiscal policy. There is no such thing as a Government Accounting Office. In the United States, Federal Trade Commission or FTC handles federal investigations into business activities. The establishment of the FTC in 1915 as an independent government agency was done so as to assure fair and free competition among businesses.

49. **The source of authority for national, state, and local governments in the United States is:** *(Skill 3.2) (Rigorous)*

    A. The will of the people
    B. The United States Constitution
    C. Written laws
    D. The Bill of Rights

Answer: A. The will of the people
The source of authority for national, state, and local governments in the United States is the will of the people. Although the United States Constitution, the Bill of Rights, and the other written laws of the land are important guidelines for authority, they may ultimately be altered or changed by the will of the people.

50. **The programs such as unemployment insurance and health insurance for the elderly are the responsibility of:** *(Skill 3.2) (Rigorous)*

    A. Federal Government
    B. Local Government
    C. State Government
    D. Communal Government

Answer: C. State Government
Assistance programs, such as unemployment insurance and free health insurance for the elderly is the responsibility of state governments.

51. **The term that best describes how the Supreme Court can block laws that may be unconstitutional from being enacted is:** *(Skill 3.2) (Rigorous)*

    A. Jurisprudence
    B. Judicial Review
    C. Exclusionary Rule
    D. Right of Petition

Answer: B. Judicial Review
(A) Jurisprudence is the study of the development and origin of law. (B) Judicial review is the term that best describes how the Supreme Court can block laws that they deem as unconstitutional as set forth in Marbury vs. Madison. The (C) "exclusionary rule" is a reference to the Fourth Amendment of the Constitution and says that evidence gathered in an illegal manner or search must be thrown out and excluded from evidence. There is nothing called the (D) "Right of Petition"; however, the Petition of Right is a reference to a statement of civil liberties sent by the English Parliament to Charles I in 1628.

52. The United States legislature is bicameral, which means: *(Skill 3.2) (Easy)*

   A. It consists of several houses
   B. It consists of two houses
   C. The Vice-President is in charge of the legislature when in session
   D. It has an upper house and a lower house

Answer: B. It consists of two houses
The bi-cameral nature of the United States legislature means that it has two houses, the Senate and the House of Representatives, which make up the Congress. The Vice President is part of the executive branch of government but presides over the Senate and may act as a tiebreaker. An upper and lower house would be parts of a parliamentary system of government such as the governments of Great Britain and Israel.

53. Which of the three branches of government is responsible for taxation? *(Skill 3.2) (Average Rigor)*

   A. Legislative
   B. Executive
   C. Judicial
   D. Congressional

Answer: A. Legislative
The legislative branch of government is responsible for taxation. The Congress is responsible for levying federal taxes while state legislatures determine the individual state's taxes. The executive branch is often thought by the public to be responsible for taxation since taxation is often a highly talked-about issue in presidential campaigns, but it is in fact Congress that is ultimately responsible.

54. The United States government's federal system consists of: *(Skill 3.2) (Average Rigor)*

   A. Three parts, the Executive, the Legislative, and the Judiciary
   B. Three parts, the Legislative, the Congress, and the Presidency
   C. Four parts, the Executive, the Judiciary, the courts and the Legislative
   D. Two parts, the government and the governed

Answer: A. Three parts, the Executive, the Legislative, and the Judiciary
The United States government's federal system consists of three parts: the Executive, the Legislative, and the Judiciary. The Executive branch consists of the President, Vice-President, and Cabinet. The Legislative branch consists of the Senate and the House of Representatives, also known as Congress, and the Judiciary is made up of the courts and the judiciary. All three branches keep each other in line through a system of checks and balances.

55. To "impeach" a President means to: *(Skill 3.2) (Average Rigor)*

A. Bring charges against a President
B. Remove a President from office
C. Re-elect the President
D. Override his veto

Answer: A. Bring charges against a President
It means to bring charges against a President. It is brought forth in the House of Representatives, and then the Senate makes the decision of the President's guilt in the matter. It does not mean to remove or re-elect the President. Andrew Jackson and William Jefferson Clinton are the only two United States Presidents to have been impeached. Jackson and Clinton were both acquitted during hearings and remained in office. Richard M. Nixon resigned from office as the House of Representatives prepared impeachment proceedings.

56. The power to declare war, establish a postal system, and coin money rests with which branch of the government: *(Skill 3.2) (Rigorous)*

A. Presidential
B. Judicial
C. Legislative
D. Executive

Answer: C. Legislative
The power to declare war, establish a postal system, and coin money rests with the legislative branch of the government. However, the President becomes the Commander-in-Chief and has strong influence over wartime activities. The President may veto Congress in its decision to go to war (although in our current political climate, more often it is the President who urges Congress to declare war).

57. Which of the following is an important idea expressed in the Declaration of Independence? *(Skill 3.2) (Rigorous)*

A. People have the right to change their government
B. People should obey the government authority
C. A monarchy is a bad thing
D. Indirect democracy is best

Answer: A. People have the right to change their government
Although "people should obey their government," "monarchy is a bad thing," and "indirect democracy is best" may have very well been sentiments held by the author of the Declaration of Independence. In the actual document the express statement is clearly that "people have the right to change their government," a sentiment that is still very important today.

58. The Judiciary Act of 1789 established the: *(Skill 3.2) (Average Rigor)*

    A. Supreme Court
    B. Principle of Judicial Review
    C. State court system
    D. Federal and circuit court system

Answer: D. Federal and circuit court system
The Supreme Court was established in 1789 by Article III of the United States Constitution. The principle of Judicial Review was established from Marbury vs. Madison in 1803. The state court system was established within the thirteen original colonies and since then the United States Constitution has existed side by side with the federal court system. The federal circuit system was established by the Judiciary Act of 1789.

59. The Executive branch refers to: *(Skill 3.2) (Easy)*

    A. The Senate
    B. The Legislature
    C. Congress
    D. The President and Vice-President

Answer: D. The President and Vice-President
The executive branch of government refers to the President and Vice President. The Senate, legislature, and Congress all refer to the legislative branch.

60. An "Ex Post facto Law" is: *(Skill 3.2) (Average Rigor)*

    A. A law made against an act after it has been committed
    B. A law proclaimed unconstitutional by the Supreme Court
    C. An Executive Act
    D. A law relating to the postal system

Answer: A. A law made against an act after it has been committed
An "ex post facto" law, is one in which a law makes illegal an act that when committed was legal, or it can change the penalty for a crime committed after the fact. Ex post facto laws are illegal under the United States Constitution and may not be carried out by any part of the justice system.

61. The Judiciary refers to: *(Skill 3.2) (Easy)*

    A. The President
    B. Congress
    C. The legal system
    D. The system of states' rights

Answer: C. The legal system
Judiciary refers to the legal system of courts, judges, and due process. The President is head of the executive branch, and Congress represents the legislative branch.

62. The highest appellate court in the United States is the: *(Skill 3.2) (Rigorous)*

    A. National Appeals Court
    B. Circuit Court
    C. Supreme Court
    D. Court of Appeals

Answer: C. Supreme Court
The highest appellate court in the United States is the Supreme Court. There is also a federal circuit court of appeals and a state system that includes appellate courts and state supreme courts, but they are not as high as the United States Supreme Court.

63. Which one of the following is not a function or responsibility of the U.S. political parties? *(Skill 3.3) (Rigorous)*

    A. Conducting elections or the voting process
    B. Obtaining funds needed for election campaigns
    C. Choosing candidates to run for public office
    D. Making voters aware of issues and other public affairs information

Answer: A. Conducting elections or the voting process
The U.S. political parties have numerous functions and responsibilities. Among them are obtaining funds needed for election campaigns, choosing the candidates to run for office, and making voters aware of the issues. The political parties, however, do not conduct elections or the voting process, as that would be an obvious conflict of interest.

64. **On the spectrum of American politics the label that most accurately describes voters to the "right of center" is:** *(Skill 3.3) (Average Rigor)*

   A. Moderates
   B. Liberals
   C. Conservatives
   D. Socialists

Answer: C. Conservatives
(A) Moderates are considered voters who teeter on the line of political centrality or drift slightly to the left or right. (B) Liberals are voters who stand to the left of center. (C) Conservative voters are those who are "right of center." (D) Socialists would land far to the left on the political spectrum of America.

65. **What is the form of local government that acts as an intermediary between the state and the city?** *(Skill 3.4)(Average Rigor)*

   A. Metropolitan Government
   B. Limited Government
   C. The Mayor-Council System
   D. County-Commission System

Answer: A. Metropolitan Government
Metropolitan Government was the form of local government that acts as an intermediary between the state and the city and comes from the idea of municipal home rule first enacted by Missouri in 1875. As suburbs grew and cities declined a bit, it became more important to have an intermediary between the city and state governments.

66. **The Bill of Rights says that any rights it does not mention are:** *(Skill 3.4) (Rigorous)*

   A. Reserved to the federal government
   B. Not important
   C. Judged by the Supreme Court
   D. Reserved to the states or to the people

Answer: D. Reserved to the states or to the people
The Bill of Rights says that any rights it does not mention are reserved to the states or to the people. This means that just because a right is not listed specifically in the Bill of Rights does not necessarily mean that that right does not exist or that it may not be violated.

67. **America's weak foreign policy and lack of adequate diplomacy during the 1870s and 1880s led to the comment that "a special Providence takes care of fools, drunkards, and the United States" is attributed to:** *(Skill 3.5) (Average Rigor)*

    A. Otto von Bismarck
    B. Benjamin Disraeli
    C. William Gladstone
    D. Paul von Hindenburg

Answer: A. Otto Von Bismarck
Benjamin Disraeli (1804-1881), a conservative, and William Gladstone (1809- 1898), a liberal, were political rivals in Great Britain. Gladstone was greatly disliked by both his rival Disraeli and his Queen for being such a staunch political and economic reformer. Paul von Hindenberg (1847-1934) was a German field marshal and president (1925-1934) who fought against the Americans in World War I.

However, it was Otto von Bismarck (1815-1898), the German statesman who came to be known as the Iron Chancellor, who once said "a special Providence takes care of fools, drunkards, and the United States." Bismarck was saying that despite the United States' shortcomings in foreign policy, leadership and military strength, they continued to grow and gained power in the face of much better run governments, armies and foreign policy makers.

68. **The doctrine that sought to keep communism from spreading was:** *(Skill 3.5) (Average Rigor)*

    A. The Cold War
    B. Roll-back
    C. Containment
    D. Détente

Answer: C. Containment
The doctrine that sought to keep communism from spreading was called (C) "Containment." Containment was the creation of the Truman Administration following World War II and spawned the creation of the North Atlantic Treaty Organization (NATO) in 1949. (A) The Cold War was the escalation of the threat of war between the United States and the Soviet Union following World War II up to the collapse of the Berlin Wall in 1989 and the full collapse of Communism in Eastern Europe in 1991. The Cold War was a nonviolent state of extreme tension in which fears ran high and threats were made but not carried out. The idea of (B) rollback is probably a reference to policy used at some point in the Vietnam War to scale back the intensity of fighting and pull U.S. troops out of Vietnam.

69. **What was George Washington's advice to Americans about foreign policy?** *(Skill 3.5) (Rigorous)*

   A. America should have strong alliances
   B. America should avoid alliances
   C. Foreign policy should take precedence over domestic policy
   D. Domestic policy should take precedence over foreign policy

Answer: B. America should avoid alliances
George Washington (1732-1799), the first President of the United States, after his refusal to run for a third term, did warn in his farewell speech in 1797 that the United States should avoid permanent foreign alliances. This sentiment could be seen throughout his presidency as he was very cautious and careful in his foreign policy by never getting in too deep.

70. **"Walk softly and carry a big stick" is a statement associated with:** *(Skill 3.5) (Average Rigor)*

   A. Franklin Roosevelt
   B. Theodore Roosevelt
   C. George Washington
   D. Thomas Hobbes

Answer: B. Theodore Roosevelt
"Walk softly and carry a big stick" is a statement made by Theodore Roosevelt (1858-1919) in reference to his foreign policy, which was just as aggressive as his domestic policy. Roosevelt advocated for a new extension of the Monroe Doctrine extending the idea all the way through South America. The statement also refers to Roosevelt's dealing with the Panama Canal situation, the open-door policy with China, and the formation of the Hague tribunal.

71. **The foundation of modern constitutionalism is embodied in the idea that government is limited by law. This law was stated by:** *(Skill 3.6) (Rigorous)*

    A. John Locke
    B. Rousseau
    C. St. Thomas Aquinas
    D. Montesquieu

Answer: C. St. Thomas Aquinas
(A) John Locke (1632-1704), whose book *Two Treatises of Government* has long been considered a founding document on the rights of people to rebel against an unjust government, was an important figure in the founding of the U.S. Constitution and on general politics of the American Colonies. (D) Montesquieu (1689-1755) and (B) Rousseau (1712-1778) were political philosophers who explored the idea of what has come to be known as liberalism. They pushed the idea that through understanding the interconnectedness of economics, geography, climate and psychology that changes could be made to improve life. Therefore, it was St. Thomas Aquinas (1225-1274) who merged Aristotelian ideas with Christianity, who helped lay the ideas of modern constitutionalism and the limiting of government by law.

72. **The idea of universal peace through world organization was a philosophy of:** *(Skill 3.6) (Rigorous)*

    A. Rousseau
    B. Immanuel Kant
    C. Montesquieu
    D. John Locke

Answer: B. Immanuel Kant
Immanuel Kant (1724-1804) was the German metaphysician and philosopher, who was a founding proponent of the idea that world organization was the means for achieving universal peace. Kant's ideas helped to found such world peace organizations as the League of Nations in the wake of World War I.

73. **The principle that "men entrusted with power tend to abuse it" is attributed to:** *(Skill 3.6) (Average Rigor)*

    A. Locke
    B. Rousseau
    C. Aristotle
    D. Montesquieu

Answer: D. Montesquieu
The principle that "men entrusted with power tend to abuse it" is attributed to Montesquieu (1689-1755), the great French philosopher whose ideas based much on Locke's ideas, along with Rousseau, had a strong influence on the French Revolution of 1789. Although it would be reasonable to assume that Locke, Rousseau, and Aristotle would probably agree with the statement, all four of these men had profound impacts on the ideas of the Enlightenment, from humanism to constitutionals.

74. **A political system in which the laws and traditions put limits on the powers of government is:** *(Skill 3.6) (Average Rigor)*

    A. Federalism
    B. Constitutionalism
    C. Parliamentary system
    D. Presidential system

Answer: B. Constitutionalism
Constitutionalism is a political system in which laws and traditions put limits on the powers of government. Federalism is the idea of a strong, centralized national government to hold together the nation. The parliamentary system, such as the governments of Great Britain and Israel, are systems in which a group of representatives are led by a prime minister contrasting with a presidential system which is run by a head of state, the elected (or sometimes self-appointed) president.

75. **A political philosophy favoring or supporting rapid social changes in order to correct social and economic inequalities is called:** *(Skill 3.6) (Rigorous)*

    A. Nationalism
    B. Liberalism
    C. Conservatism
    D. Federalism

Answer: B. Liberalism
A political philosophy favoring rapid social changes in order to correct social and economic inequalities are called Liberalism. Liberalism was a theory that could be said to have started with the great French philosophers Montesquieu (1689- 1755) and Rousseau (1712-1778). It is important to understand the difference between political, economic, and social liberalism, as they are different and how they sometimes contrast one another in the modern world.

76. **Marxism believes which two groups are in continual conflict:** *(Skill 3.6) (Rigorous)*

    A. Farmers and landowners
    B. Kings and the nobility
    C. Workers and owners
    D. Structure and superstructure

Answer: C. Workers and owners

Marxism believes that the workers and owners are in continual conflict. Marxists refer to these two groups as the proletariat and the bourgeoisie. The proletariat is exploited by the bourgeoisie and will, according to Marxism, rise up over the bourgeoisie in class warfare in an effort to end private control over the means of production.

77. **Which of the following is an example of a direct democracy?** *(Skill 3.6) (Rigorous)*

    A. Elected representatives
    B. Greek city-states
    C. The Constitution
    D. The Confederate States

Answer: B. Greek city-states

The Greek city-states are an example of a direct democracy as their leaders were elected directly by the citizens and the citizens themselves were given voice in government. (A) Elected representatives in the United States as in the case of the presidential elections are actually elected by an electoral college that is supposed to be representative of the citizens. As we have learned from the elections of 2000, this is a flawed system. The United States Congress, the Senate, and the House of Representatives are also examples of indirect democracy as they represent the citizens in the legislature as opposed to having citizens represent themselves.

78. **The first organized city-states arose in:** *(Skill 3.6) (Average Rigor)*

    A. Egypt
    B. China
    C. Sumer
    D. Greece

Answer: C. Sumer

Although Greece is well known for their advance organization of city-states, it was the Sumerians in Southern Mesopotamia around the fourth millennium B.C. who first established organized city-states.

79. **The founder of the first Communist Party and the first leader of the Soviet Union was:** *(Skill 3.6) (Average Rigor)*

   A. Joseph Stalin
   B. Vladimir Lenin
   C. John Lennon
   D. Karl Marx

Answer: B. Vladimir Lenin
Vladimir Lenin (1870-1924) was the founder of the first Communist Party and led the Soviets to victory in the October Revolution of 1917. The Bolshevik based his ideas for revolution and socialism on the works of the great German political and philosopher Karl Marx (1818-1883), who is generally regarded as the founder of modern socialism and communism. Joseph Stalin (1879-1953) took over the USSR after Lenin's death and fought off Trotsky for power in the party. Stalin was well known for his intensely repressive tactics against dissent in the party.

80. **Socialists believe that the government should have a role in the economy.** *(Skill 3.6) (Average Rigor)*

   A. Lesser
   B. Greater
   C. Equal with business
   D. Less than business

Answer: B. Greater
Socialists believe that the government should have a greater role in the economy, including state control of the means of production, in order to assure that there is an equal distribution of wealth and resources to all of the people. Capitalists by contrast believe that government should have little or no involvement with the economy and that free enterprise and private ownership over the means of production will regulate itself in the best interest of the people.

81. **One difference between *totalitarianism* and *authoritarianism* is that totalitarianism believes in:** *(Skill 3.6) (Average Rigor)*

   A. Total control over all aspects of society
   B. Minimum government control
   C. There is no difference
   D. The difference is unknown

Answer: A. Total control over all aspects of society
One difference between totalitarianism and authoritarianism is that totalitarianism believes in total control over all aspects of society. Totalitarian governments seek to control all aspects of society; political, economic, and social. An authoritarian regime is the forerunner of totalitarianism.

82. **One difference between a presidential and a parliamentary system is a parliamentary system:** *(Skill 3.6) (Rigorous)*

    A. The Prime Minister is head of government, while a president or monarch is head of state
    B. The President is head of government and the Vice-President is head of state
    C. The President, pro-tempore of the Senate is head of state while the prime minister is head of government
    D. The President appoints the head of state

Answer: A. The Prime Minister is head of government, while a president or monarch is head of state.
In a parliamentary system, the Prime Minister is the head of the government and the president or monarch is the head of state. In a presidential system, the President is the head of government and the head of state.

83. **In an <u>indirect</u> democracy** *(Skill 3.6) (Rigorous)*

    A. All the people together decide on issues
    B. People elect representatives to act for them
    C. Democracy can never really work
    D. Government is less efficient than a direct democracy

Answer: B. People elect representatives to act for them
In an indirect democracy, people elect representatives to act for them. An example of an indirect democracy would be the United States government in which the people elect a president, vice-president, senators, and representatives to make decisions and run the government. An example of a direct democracy would be the government of the Greeks in Athens during the Classical Period, in which citizens represented themselves in their own government.

84. **In a communist system, controls the means of production.** *(Skill 3.6) (Average Rigor)*

    A. A professional managerial class
    B. The owners of business and industry
    C. The workers
    D. The state

Answer: D. The state
In a communist system, the state controls the means of production as opposed to a capitalist system in which the owners of business and industry control the means of production or an anarchist system in which workers themselves would control the means of production.

85. Machiavelli was most concerned with describing: *(Skill 3.6) (Average Rigor)*

    A. Modern warfare
    B. Ancient political philosophy
    C. Representative government
    D. Getting and keeping political power

Answer: D. Getting and keeping political power

Niccolo Machiavelli (1469-1527) was an Italian Renaissance writer who, in his 1532 principle work *The Prince*, describes the way a young prince must gain and hold power. Contrary to ideas of representative government, *The Prince* claims that through tyranny and repression a unified Italian State may be achieved. Debates still exist over whether or not *The Prince* was in fact a satire of the Medici regime under which Machiavelli was a statesman.

86. Oligarchy refers to: *(Skill 3.6) (Easy)*

    A. Rule of a single leader
    B. The rule of a single political party
    C. Rule by a select few
    D. Rule by many

Answer: C. Rule by a select few

Monarchy is the (A) rule of a single leader. The (B) rule of a single political party has no clear definition but can range from fascism or national-socialism like that of Hitler's Germany to the socialism of Castro's Cuba. (C) Rule by a select few is an oligarchy. Oligarchy was described by Aristotle as rule by a few economic elite in efforts to advance their interests and often involves notions of aristocracy and limited democracy of Classical Athens to the indirect democracy of the United States.

87. **Which statement closely resembles the political philosophy of Thomas Hobbes?** *(Skill 3.6) (Rigorous)*

    A. Citizens should give obedience to the state authority as a means of survival in a world where man's nature drives self-interest and makes man selfish and self-acting
    B. That citizens have a right to rise against the state whenever they choose
    C. All state authority is basically evil and should be eliminated
    D. People are generally good and cooperative if given a chance

Answer: A. Citizens should give obedience to the state authority as a means of survival in a world where man's nature drives self-interest and makes man selfish and self-acting
Thomas Hobbes (1588-1679), the English philosopher, mathematician, and rationalist believed that men were basically self-serving and would destroy one another in their personal quest for power; therefore, he said that the state must be created (he favored a monarch) to ensure the safety of man against himself and his neighbors.

88. **As a rule, the relationship between fascism and communism is:** *(Skill 3.6) (Average Rigor)*

    A. They are the same thing
    B. Unknown at present
    C. Antagonistic
    D. Cooperative

Answer: C. Antagonistic
Fascism and communism are more or less polar opposites. While fascism sits to the extreme right of the political spectrum, communism sits at the extreme left. Therefore, they are by nature antagonistic of one another.

89. **In a parliamentary system, the person who becomes Prime Minister is usually:** *(Skill 3.6) (Average Rigor)*

    A. Chosen by the cabinet
    B. Elected by a direct national vote
    C. Chosen by the president of the country
    D. Chosen by a majority or coalition of parties in the parliament

Answer: D. Chosen by a majority or coalition of parties in the parliament
The Prime Minister is not chosen by the cabinet. He, in fact, chooses the cabinet from the majority party in parliament. The Prime Minister is not elected by a direct national vote like the president of a constitutionalist government such as the United States. The Prime Minister is in fact chosen by a majority or coalition in power in the parliament.

90. The "cult of personality" is an idea most associated with: *(Skill 3.6) (Average Rigor)*

A. Democracy
B. Anarchism
C. Fascism
D. Communism

Answer: C. Fascism
The "cult of personality" is an idea most associated with fascism. Democracy, anarchism, and communism all place the importance of the citizens and their collective welfare over the needs or egos of the leaders. Fascism is quite the contrast as it depends on the power and obedience of a totalitarian leader such as Germany's Hitler or Italy's Mussolini in the rise to state power. This utilization of a "cult of personality" is usually through a one-party system and a repression of dissidents. Some communist regimes such as Mao in China or Stalin in Russia have been accused of capitalizing on the cult of personality as well, but it is a tool most associated with fascism.

91. Which political economic system discourages private land ownership? *(Skill 3.6)(Rigorous)*

A. Capitalism
B. Socialism
C. Agriculturalism
D. Welfare Capitalism

Answer: B. Socialism
Capitalism and welfare capitalism both encourage the private ownership of land. Socialism encourages the nationalization and redistribution of land in which the government owns the land and allocates its usage in the best interests of the people.

92. **The "history of all societies is one of class struggle" is a statement associated with:** *(Skill 3.6) (Average Rigor)*

  A. John Locke
  B. Thomas Jefferson
  C. Karl Marx
  D. Thomas Hobbes

Answer: C. Karl Marx
(A) John Locke (1632-1704) was the English enlightenment philosopher who believed in the middle class' right to property and prosperity. (B) Thomas Jefferson (1743-1826) was the third President of the United States, and his Jeffersonian democracy was concerned with preserving individual and states' rights from the federal government. (C) Karl Marx (1818-1883), who is generally regarded as the founder of modern socialism and communism, claimed that the "History of all societies is one of class struggle". This illustrates his placement of class struggle as the central struggle within a society. (D) Thomas Hobbes (1588-1679) the English philosopher, mathematician, and rationalist believed that men were basically self-serving and would destroy one another in their personal quest for power. Therefore, he said that the state must be created (he favored a monarchy) to ensure the safety of man against himself and his neighbors.

93. **An obligation identified with citizenship is:** *(Skill 3.7) (Easy)*

  A. Belonging to a political party
  B. Educating oneself
  C. Running political office
  D. Voting

Answer: D. Voting
(A) Although belonging to a political party and (B) educating oneself are often done in preparation for voting, and (C) running for political office is the right of citizens who feel that they could serve their constituency well, only (D) voting is considered to be an obligation identified with citizenship.

94. **To plead "the Fifth Amendment" means to:** *(Skill 3.7) (Rigorous)*

  A. Refuse to speak so one does not incriminate oneself
  B. Plead "no contest" in court
  C. Ask for freedom of speech
  D. Ask to appear before a judge when charged with a crime

Answer: A. Refuse to speak so one does not incriminate oneself
To plead the Fifth Amendment means to refuse to speak so one does not incriminate oneself. Pleading "no contest" is a term of the judiciary in which a defendant admits to having committed a crime in return for a favorable plea bargain. Freedom of speech is assured in the First Amendment.

95. **A "tort" refers to:** *(Skill 3.7) (Average Rigor)*

   A. A private or civil action brought into court
   B. A type of confection
   C. A penal offense
   D. One who solicits

Answer: A. A private or civil action brought into court
A tort refers to a private or civil action brought into court. An example of a tort could be a breach of contract in which the injured party may sue for compensatory damages. The earliest tort law was created as a protection from property and personal trespass.

96. **The results of the Renaissance, Enlightenment, Commercial and the Industrial Revolutions were more unfortunate for the people of:** *(Skill 4.0) (Rigorous)*

   A. Asia
   B. Latin America
   C. Africa
   D. Middle East

Answer: C. Africa
The results of the Renaissance, Enlightenment, Commercial, and Industrial Revolutions were quite beneficial for many people in much of the world. New ideas of humanism, religious tolerance, and secularism were spreading. Increased trade and manufacturing were surging economies in much of the world. The people of Africa, however, suffered during these times. Largely left out of the developments, the people of Africa were stolen, traded, and sold into slavery to provide a cheap labor force for the growing industries of Europe and the New World.

97. **Which ancient civilization is credited with being the first to develop irrigation techniques through the use of canals, dikes, and devices for raising water?** *(Skill 4.1)(Easy)*

   A. The Sumerians
   B. The Egyptians
   C. The Babylonians
   D. The Akkadians

Answer: A. The Sumerians
The ancient (A) Sumerians of the Fertile Crescent of Mesopotamia are credited with being the first to develop irrigation techniques through the use of canals, dikes, and devices for raising water. The (B) Egyptians also practiced controlled irrigation but that was primarily through the use of the Nile's predictable flooding schedule. The (C) Babylonians were more noted for their revolutionary systems of law than their irrigation systems.

98. **An early cultural group was so skillful in na0vigating on the sea that they were able to sail at night guided by stars. They were the:** *(Skill 4.1) (Average Rigor)*

   A. Greeks
   B. Persians
   C. Minoans
   D. Phoenicians

Answer: D. Phoenicians
Although the Greeks were quite able sailors and developed a strong navy in their defeat of the Persians at sea in the Battle of Marathon, it was the Eastern Mediterranean culture of the Phoenicians that had first developed the astronomical skill of sailing at night with the stars as their guide. The Minoans were an advanced early civilization off the Greek coast on Crete more noted for their innovations in terms of sewage systems, toilets, and running water.

99. **Development of a solar calendar, invention of the decimal system, and contributions to the development of geometry and astronomy are all the legacy of:** *(Skill 4.1) (Average Rigor)*

   A. The Babylonians
   B. The Persians
   C. The Sumerians
   D. The Egyptians

Answer: D. The Egyptians
The (A) Babylonians of ancient Mesopotamia flourished for a time under their great contribution of organized law and code, called Hammurabi's Code (1750 B.C.), after the ruler Hammurabi. The fall of the Babylonians to the Persians in 539 B.C. made way for the warrior-driver Persian Empire that expanded from Pakistan to the Mediterranean Sea until the conquest of Alexander the Great in 331 B.C. The Sumerians of ancient Mesopotamia were most noted for their early advancements as one of the first civilizations and their contributions towards written language known as cuneiform. It was the (D) Egyptians who were the first true developers of a solar calendar, the decimal system, and made significant contributions to the development of geometry and astronomy.

100. The first ancient civilization to introduce and practice monotheism was the: *(Skill 4.1) (Average Rigor)*

    A. Sumerians
    B. Minoans
    C. Phoenicians
    D. Hebrews

Answer: D. Hebrews

The (A) Sumerians and (C) Phoenicians both practiced religions in which many gods and goddesses were worshipped. Often these gods/goddesses were based on a feature of nature such as a sun, moon, weather, rocks, water, etc. The (B) Minoan culture shared many religious practices with the Ancient Egyptians. It seems that the king was somewhat of a god figure and the queen, a goddess. Much of the Minoan art point to worship of multiple gods. Therefore, only the (D) Hebrews introduced and fully practiced monotheism, or the belief in one God.

101. Bathtubs, hot and cold running water, and sewage systems with flush toilets were developed by the: *(Skill 4.1) (Average Rigor)*

    A. Minoans
    B. Mycenaeans
    C. Phoenicians
    D. Greeks

Answer: A. Minoans

The (A) Minoans were one of the earliest Greek cultures and existed on the island of Crete and flourished from about 1600 B.C. to about 1400 B.C. During this time, the (B) Mycenaean were flourishing on the mainland of what is now Greece. However, it was the Minoans on Crete that are best known for their advanced ancient civilization in which such advances as bathtubs, hot and cold running water, sewage systems and flush toilets were developed. The (C) Phoenicians also flourished around 1250 B.C.; however, their primary development was in language and arts. The Phoenicians created an alphabet that has still considerable influence in the world today. The great developments of the (D) Greeks were primarily in the fields of philosophy, political science, and early ideas of democracy.

102. The end to hunting, gathering, and fishing of prehistoric people was due to: *(Skill 4.1) (Average Rigor)*

    A. Domestication of animals
    B. Building crude huts and houses
    C. Development of agriculture
    D. Organized government in villages

Answer: C. Development of agriculture
Although the domestication of animals, the building of huts and houses and the first organized governments were all very important steps made by early civilizations, it was the development of agriculture that ended the once dominant practices of hunting, gathering, and fishing among prehistoric people. The development of agriculture provided a more efficient use of time and a surplus of food. This greatly improved the quality of life and contributed to early population growth.

103. The early ancient civilizations developed systems of government: *(Skill 4.1) (Rigorous)*

    A. To provide for defense against attack
    B. To regulate trade
    C. To regulate and direct the economic activities of the people as they worked together in groups
    D. To decide on the boundaries of the different fields during planting seasons

Answer: C. To regulate and direct the economic activities of the people as they worked together in groups
Although ancient civilizations were concerned with defense, trade regulation and the maintenance of boundaries in their fields, they could not have done any of them without first regulating and directing the economic activities of the people as they worked in groups. This provided for a stable economic base from which they could trade and actually had something worth providing defense for.

104. Which one of the following is not an important legacy of the Byzantine Empire? *(Skill 4.2) (Rigorous)*

A. It protected Western Europe from various attacks from the East by such groups as the Persians, Ottoman Turks, and Barbarians
B. It played a part in preserving the literature, philosophy, and language of ancient Greece
C. Its military organization was the foundation for modern armies
D. It kept the legal traditions of Roman government, collecting and organizing many ancient Roman laws.

Answer: C. Its military organization was the foundation for modern armies
The Byzantine Empire (1353-1453) was the successor to the Roman Empire in the East and protected Western Europe from invaders such as the Persians and Ottomans. The Byzantine Empire was a Christian incorporation of Greek philosophy, language, and literature along with Roman government and law. Therefore, although regarded as having a strong infantry, cavalry, and engineering corps along with excellent morale amongst its soldiers, the Byzantine Empire is not particularly considered a foundation for modern armies.

105. The "father of anatomy" is considered to be: *(Skill 4.2) (Easy)*

A. Vesalius
B. Servetus
C. Galen
D. Harvey

Answer: A. Vesalius
Andreas Vesalius (1514-1564) is considered to be the "father of anatomy" as a result of his revolutionary work on the human anatomy based on dissections of human cadavers. Prior to Vesalius, men such as Galen, (130-200) had done work in the field of anatomy, but they had based the majority of their work on animal studies.

106. "Poverty is the parent of revolution and crime" was from the writings of: *(Skill 4.2) (Average Rigor)*

A. Plato
B. Aristotle
C. Cicero
D. Gaius

Answer: B. Aristotle
Aristotle once wrote "Poverty is the parent of revolution and crime", a comment that is probably as relevant today as it was in Aristotle's day. It showed his true insight as one of the great political and social commentators and philosophers of all time.

107. The Roman Empire gave so much to the world, especially the Western world. Of the legacies below, the most influential, effective and lasting is: *(Skill 4.2) (Rigorous)*

A. The language of Latin
B. Roman law, justice, and political system
C. Engineering and building
D. The writings of its poets and historians

Answer: B. Roman law, justice, and political system
Of the lasting legacies of the Roman Empire, it is the law, justice, and political system that has been most influential on our Western world today. The idea of a Senate and different houses is still maintained by our United States government and their legal justice system is also the foundation of our own. We still use many Latin words in our justice system, terms such as *habeas corpus* and *voir dire*. English, Spanish, Italian, French, and others are all based on Latin. The Roman language, Latin, has died out. Roman engineering and building and their writings and poetry have also been influential but not nearly to the degree that their governmental and justice systems have been.

108. The circumference of the earth, which greatly contributed to geographic knowledge, was calculated by: *(Skill 4.2) (Easy)*

A. Ptolemy
B. Eratosthenes
C. Galileo
D. Strabo

Answer: B. Eratosthenes
There is no doubt to Ptolemy and Galileo's influence as astronomers. (A) Ptolemy as an earlier theorist and (C) Galileo as a founder of modern scientific knowledge of astronomy and our place in the galaxy. However, it was (B) Eratosthenes (275 B.C. – 195 B.C.), the Greek writer, philosopher, and astronomer, who is credited with measuring the earth's circumference as well as the distances between Earth, sun, and moon. (D) Strabo was more concerned with geography and history than astronomy.

109. India's greatest ruler is considered to be: *(Skill 4.3) (Rigorous)*

    A. Akbar
    B. Asoka
    C. Babur
    D. Jahan

Answer: A. Akbar
Akbar (1556-1605) is considered to be India's greatest ruler. He combined a drive for conquest with a magnetic personality and went so far as to invent his own religion, Dinillahi, a combination of Islam, Christianity, Zoroastrianism, and Hinduism. Asoka (273 B.C.-232 B.C.) was also an important ruler as he was the first to bring together a fully united India. Babur (1483-1540) was both considered to be a failure as he struggled to maintain any power early in his reign, but later to be somewhat successful in his quest to reunite Northern India. Jahan's (1592- 1666) rule of India is considered to be the golden age of art and literature in the region.

110. An extensive knowledge of surgery and medicine as well as principles of irrigation, fertilization and terrace farming was unique to: *(Skill 4.3) (Easy)*

    A. The Mayans
    B. The Atacamas
    C. The Incas
    D. The Tarapacas

Answer: C. The Incas
The Incas of Peru had an extensive knowledge of surgery and medicine as well as principles of irrigation, fertilization, and terrace farming. These were unique achievements for an ancient civilization.

111. **China's last imperial ruling dynasty was one of its most stable and successful and under its rule, Chinese culture made an outstanding impression on Western nations. This dynasty was:** *(Skill 4.3) (Rigorous)*

    A. Ming
    B. Manchu
    C. Han
    D. Chou

Answer: B. Manchu
The (A) Ming Dynasty lasted from 1368-1644 and was among the more successful dynasties but focused attention towards foreign trade and encouraged growth in the arts. Therefore, it was the (B) Manchu Dynasty, the last imperial ruling dynasty, which came to power in the 1600s and expanded China's power in Asia greatly that was and still is considered to be among the most important, most stable, and most successful of the Chinese dynasties. The (C) Han and (D) Chou Dynasties were part of the "ancient" dynasties of China and while important in Chinese History, their influence did not hold impression on Western nations as the Manchu.

112. **The world religion, which includes a caste system, is:** *(Skill 4.3) (Average Rigor)*

    A. Buddhism
    B. Hinduism
    C. Sikhism
    D. Jainism

Answer: B. Hinduism
Buddhism, Sikhism, and Jainism all rose out of protest against Hinduism and its practices of sacrifice and the caste system. The caste system, in which people were born into castes, would determine their class for life including who they could marry, what jobs they could perform, and their overall quality of life.

113. **The principle of zero in mathematics is the discovery of the ancient civilization found in:** *(Skill 4.3) (Easy)*

    A. Egypt
    B. Persia
    C. India
    D. Babylon

Answer: C. India
Although the Egyptians practiced algebra and geometry, the Persians developed an alphabet, and the Babylonians developed Hammurabi's Code, which would come to be considered among the most important contributions of the Mesopotamian civilization, it was the Indians that created the idea of zero in mathematics changing drastically our ideas about numbers.

114. **In Western Europe, the achievements of the Renaissance were unsurpassed and made these countries outstanding cultural centers on the continent. All of the following were accomplishments except:** *(Skill 4.4) (Rigorous)*

    A. Invention of the printing press
    B. A rekindling of interest in the learning of classical Greece & Rome
    C. Growth in literature, philosophy, and art
    D. Better military tactics

Answer: D. Better military tactics
The Renaissance in Western Europe produced many important achievements that helped push immense progress among European civilization. Some of the most important developments during the Renaissance were Gutenberg's invention of the printing press in Germany and a reexamination of the ideas and philosophies of classical Greece and Rome that eventually helped Renaissance thinkers to approach more modern ideas. Also important during the Renaissance was the growth in literature (Petrarch, Boccaccio, Erasmus), philosophy (Machiavelli, More, Bacon) and art (Van Eyck, Giotto, da Vinci). Therefore, improved military tactics is the only possible answer as it was clearly not a characteristic of the Renaissance in Western Europe.

115. **The changing focus during the Renaissance when artists and scholars were less concerned with religion but centered their efforts on a better understanding of people and the world was called:** *(Skill 4.4) (Easy)*

    A. Realism
    B. Humanism
    C. Individualism
    D. Intellectualism

Answer: B. Humanism
Realism is a medieval philosophy that contemplated independence of existence of the body, the mind, and God. The idea of individualism is usually either a reference to an economic or political theory. Intellectualism is the placing of great importance and devotion to the exploring of the intellect. Therefore, the changing focus during the Renaissance when artists and scholars were less concerned with religion but centered their efforts on a better understanding of people and the world was called humanism.

116. The ideas and innovations of the period of the Renaissance were spread throughout Europe mainly because of: *(Skill 4.4) (Rigorous)*

    A. Extensive exploration
    B. Craft workers and their guilds
    C. The invention of the printing press
    D. Increased travel and trade

Answer: C. The invention of the printing press
The ideas and innovations of the Renaissance were spread throughout Europe for a number of reasons. While exploration, increased travel, and spread of craft may have aided the spread of the Renaissance to small degrees, nothing was as important to the spread of ideas as Gutenberg's invention of the printing press in Germany.

117. Which one of the following did not contribute to the early medieval European civilization? *(Skill 4.4) (Rigorous)*

    A. The heritage from the classical cultures
    B. The Christian religion
    C. The influence of the German Barbarians
    D. The spread of ideas through trade and commerce

Answer: D. The spread of ideas through trade and commerce
The heritage of the classical cultures such as Greece, the Christian religion which became dominant, and the influence of the Germanic Barbarians (Visigoths, Saxons, Ostrogoths, Vandals and Franks) were all contributions to early medieval Europe and its plunge into feudalism. During this period, lives were often difficult and lived out on one single manor, with very little travel or spread of ideas through trade or commerce. Civilization seems to have halted progress during these years.

118. Charlemagne's most important influence on Western civilization is seen today in: *(Skill 4.4) (Rigorous)*

    A. Relationship of church and state
    B. Strong military for defense
    C. The criminal justice system
    D. Education of women

Answer: A. Relationship of church and state
Charlemagne was the leader of the Germanic Franks responsible for the promotion of the Holy Roman Empire across Europe. Although he unified governments and aided the Pope, he re-crowned himself in 802 A.D. to demonstrate that his power and right to rule was not a grant from the Pope, but rather a secular achievement. Therefore, although he used much of the Church's power in his rise to power, the Pope in turn used Charlemagne to ascend the Church to new heights. Thus, Charlemagne had an influence on the issues between Church and state.

119. Which French Renaissance writer wrote about the dangers of absolute powers and later examined himself in an effort to make inquiries into humankind and nature? *(Skill 4.6) (Average Rigor)*

    A. Francois Rabelais
    B. Desiderius Erasmus
    C. Michel de Montaigne
    D. Sir Francis Bacon

Answer: C. Michel de Montaigne
(A) Francois Rabelais (1490-1553) was a French writer and physician who was both a practicing monk (first Franciscan then later Benedictine) and a respected humanist thinker of the Renaissance. (B) Desiderius Erasmus (1466-1536) was a Dutch humanist who was very critical of the Catholic Church but was equally conflicted with Luther's Protestant Reformation. Although Luther had once considered him an ally, Erasmus opposed Luther's break from the church and favored a more internal reform to corruption, he never left the Catholic Church. (D) Sir Francis Bacon (1561-1626) was an English philosopher and writer who pushed the idea that knowledge must come from thorough scientific knowledge and experiment, and insufficient data must not be used in reaching conclusions. (C) Michel de Montaigne (1533-1592), a French essayist from a mixed background, half-Catholic and half-Jewish, did write some about the dangers of absolute powers, primarily monarchs but also of the Church. His attitude changed as his examination of his own life developed into a study of mankind and nature.

120. Which one of the following is not a reason why Europeans came to the New World? *(Skill 4.7) (Rigorous)*

    A. To find resources in order to increase wealth
    B. To establish trade
    C. To increase a ruler's power and importance
    D. To spread Christianity

Answer: B. To establish trade
The Europeans came to the New World for a number of reasons; often they came to find new natural resources to extract for manufacturing. The Portuguese, Spanish and English were sent over to increase the monarch's power and spread influences such as religion (Christianity) and culture. Therefore, the only reason given that Europeans didn't come to the New World was to establish trade.

CPSIA information can be obtained at www.ICGtesting.com
Printed in the USA
BVOW10s1213041114

373600BV00016B/53/P

9 781607 873815